PEARL JAM

PEARL JAM

MICK WALL

Music Book Service Corporation

A Music Book Services paperback exclusively distributed in the USA by
MBS Corporation, 16295 N. W. 13th Avenue, Suite B, Miami, Florida 33169.

ISBN 1 886894 33 7

First published 1994 in Great Britain by Sidgwick & Jackson Limited.

This book is dedicated to Annie and Arnie,
for always wagging their tails, not their tongues.

ACKNOWLEDGEMENTS

The author wishes to say that this book simply could not have been written without the enormous help, insight, and patience of the following people.

First and foremost, the most diligent researchers in the world, Linda Laban and Laura Wurzal. You know what you did and so do I. I will not forget. Peter Doggett for the keys to his files. Richard Boote for the 2+2. Helen Gummer for stopping the clock. Marianne for the visions. Peter Datyner for always being in the hat. Peter N. Lewis for Justine Daf. Ross Halfin for being a friend indeed. And last, but definitely not least, Arnold Amberwell Laban Wall for that big old arm.

Special thanx also to Charles R. Cross and all the good people at *The Rocket*, Jon Hotten at *RAW*, Geoff Barton at *Kerrang!*, Gene Stout at the *Seattle Times*, the staff of *Record Collector*, and Karen Sutton of *WHY?*. You were the light in a very dark tunnel.

Mick Wall, London, March 1994

CONTENTS

Such were the notes,
thy once-beloved Poet sung
Till Death untimely stopp'd
his tuneful tongue . . .

Alexander Pope

CHAPTER ONE

THE VIRTUOUS CITY

'Green River helped set off a revolution. Stone Gossard and Jeff Ament (Pearl Jam) and Mark Arm (Mudhoney) spent the '80s raging out at the Metropolis, the legendary all-ages hardcore club in Seattle. Growing tired of the dogma of punk and finding a common interest in '70s trash-rock like the Stooges, Alice Cooper and the New York Dolls, Green River formed, and (along with The Melvins and Soundgarden) started playing a heavier sound. One part metal, one part punk, one part sleaze. If you've ever wondered what Pearl Jam would look like in mascara look no further . . . These are the twisted roots of the Seattle explosion . . .'

—entry from the Sub Pop catalogue, Seattle, 1993

1

Like truck-drivin' Elvis in Fifties Memphis, or the pre-suited Beatles in Sixties Liverpool, the twisted roots of the Pearl Jam legend are inextricably bound to the time and place that birthed them. In this instance, Seattle, Washington State, in the mid- to late-Eighties.

A small town destined to make the biggest noise of the first half of the caring, staring Nineties, Seattle, which has long been the capital of the Pacific Northwest states of Washington, Oregon and Idaho, has a strangely cyclical history in capturing the imagination of America before fading again from the national consciousness as quickly as it had first gathered there, a dream shooed away by morning.

Ever since the earliest nineteenth-century settlers, dead-ended in California, decided the only way to continue was to escape west and then up, Northwesterners have had to deal with a steady stream of wall-eyed incomers looking for something more from life than what they had left behind. The first visitors to the Klondike were the usual no-shit frontiersmen: gold-prospectors and Indian traders. By the time the settlement had grown big enough to be given its own name – after an American Indian, Chief Seattle, in 1853 – Seattle had evolved into a small logging port. The original Skid Row was located here along one of the steep, narrow alleyways that wind down to the harbour.

The closest major American city to Asia, circled by tall mountains and creeping glaciers, silvery mirrored lakes and vast unsilent forests, Seattle is actually nearer to Siberia than it is to Washington, DC. This is the wolf-clawed, near-Arctic lumberland of Jack London's *Call of the Wild* and *White Fang*; the lateral-moving world David Lynch's *Twin Peaks* was inspired to emulate.

Hugely expanded by government spending on the aircraft industry during World War II, by the start of the Fifties Seattle was still a small, easy to get to know city about to embark on a slow but steady urban renewal. With regular Defense Department orders ensuring that the locally situated Boeing Company became the biggest builder of airships in the world, Seattle became known for a time as Jet City. Then, in the early Seventies, an enigmatic new 'software' company called Microsoft also set its virtual-roots down in Northwestern soil, and over the next twenty years Seattle gradually became known for a quality of life quite different to that experienced in the ghetto-ized urban sprawls of better known, more 'glamorous' US hearthstones like Los Angeles, San Francisco, Miami or New York.

The lowest crime rate of any city in the US, with an average of less than 1.5 murders a week, compared with more than one a day, for example, in Washington, DC, this once sleepy Northern outpost had, by the mid-1980s, been transformed into a hotbed of consumer culture; a favourite homing-zone for twentysomething yuppie *émigrés*, newly with brat, looking for somewhere decent to grow old and complicated together. Seattle had become the emblematic right-on American town; the virtuous city where everyone recycled, where street crimes were fewer and generally less violent, and where people cared about the size of the hole in the ozone layer as much as they did about how the Washington Cougars were going to fare in the current football season. 'It's a very good place to live from a standpoint of reality,' reflected Geoff Tate, vocalist with Seattle's most successful arch-metallists, Queensryche. 'There is a blue-collar element, and it's a very moody place due to the weather. It has the same sort of atmosphere as Birmingham, England.'[1]

It rains a lot, of course – locals like to tell visitors that the rainy season starts on November 1st and ends on October 31st – but for the last few swaggering years of the Eighties, Seattle boom-boomed like no other American city. A port which had come to dominate US trade with the Pacific Rim, between them Boeing and Microsoft – now the world's most successful computer company – had filled the city with half a million Filofaxing young professionals. Mountain-bike shops proliferated; kayacking became popular, backpacking the norm. A beautiful new museum of art was commissioned and designed by Robert Venturi.

And drugs weren't a problem the way they were in Harlem or East LA (coke and smack were always available, of course, the same as anywhere, but crack was virtually unheard of until the Nineties, and still remains a social taboo, most Seattle-ites being too damn *smart* for that sort of thing) and the most popular non-alcoholic high of choice was, and remains, the good cheap weed, grown under glass locally. Most Seattle-ites seemed to spend their leisure time sipping espresso and gassing in quaint, friendly little corner cafés, or quaffing beer from one of the city's several excellent micro-breweries. Everybody knew everybody. And of course, occasionally the younger ones would get riled up and want to make some noise . . .

2

Good living and clean air aside though, up to the Sixties, the most glamorous thing you could say about Seattle was that it had one hundred and sixty-one bridges and the Space Needle. Oh, and Elvis was seen on the Seattle Center grounds in *It Happened At The World's Fair*.

Nevertheless, long before the Northwest became known for the nose-first sound of bands like Pearl Jam and their *alter ego*, Nirvana, Seattle had a tradition for producing obscure musical heavyweights. Most people remember that Jimi Hendrix was born and now rests in peace there. Some may happen to know that Quincy Jones came from there, or that Duff McKagen of Guns N' Roses, another former Seattle-ite, played in, by his own count, 'at least thirty of those new wave type bands there'.

But the Eighties also marked a breakthrough for Seattle music on every level, with sudden stardom for such conspicuously ungrungy local artists as jazz singer Diane Schuur, ex-Seattle Symphony saxophonist Kenny G, new wave bluesman Robert Cray, heavy metal sophisticates Queensryche and the post-modern classical composer David Harrington and his timeless Kronos Quartet.

Arguably, it was that most famous Seattle rock denizen of all, James Marshall Hendrix, who first defined the grunge ethos when he used to pour lighter-fluid over his guitar, set fire to it, turn his amp up to eleven, then stalk off stage, leaving his dying Strat to finish the song for him. Flannel-shirted purists might insist, however, that the origins of the modern Seattle scene reach all the way back to Paul Revere and The Raiders ('Like Long Hair' was their progressively titled first hit), The Ventures ('Perfidia') and The Kingsmen, all of whom came from the Northwest, where The Kingsmen's nerve-jangling reworking of Richard Berry's 'Louie, Louie' – surely the original grunge classic – first became a hit in 1964, and, incredibly, was just a few votes short of becoming the official Washington State song, in 1985.

'I don't know how much you want to get into the pre-grunge Seattle history but that whole Northwest sound goes right back to the early Sixties,' says Peter Doggett, editor of *Record Collector* and acclaimed Lou Reed biographer. 'There's definitely a sonic link between that and the fact that Seattle became the capital of grunge twenty years later. The Fugs, for example, were definitely ahead of their time . . .'

Two of the first musicians in the world to know how to spell 'psychedelic', Ed Sanders and Tuli Kupferberg – assisted by a revolving cast of mostly unsung personages that included such contributors as the Beat poets Allen Ginsberg and Gregory Corso and known collectively as The Fugs – were into layering Blakean poetry over such rock and roll-your-owns as 'Kill For Peace' and 'I Feel Like Homemade Shit'.

Significantly, neither Sanders nor Kupferberg saw themselves prim-
arily as would-be rock stars but as post-modern poets taking things
that one back-lit stage further. Based in New York, Sanders even had
his own small press for a while. His first publication, *Fuck You (A
Magazine For The Arts)*, set the tone for everything The Fugs would
do later.

Typically, The Fugs peaked early with *Virgin Forest*, their jaw-
grinding second album, released in 1968 on the infamous ESP-Disk,
an Esperanto-oriented label that also gave much-needed oxygen to the
high-altitude likes of Sun Ra, Albert Ayler, The Godz and Patty
Waters (whose hanky-clutching fifteen-minute screams that passed for
'Black Is The Colour Of My True Love's Hair' make Yoko Ono's
run-over rabbit squeal sound nice). After that, The Fugs were signed
to a major record company, Reprise – then the home of Frank Sinatra
– and as the late critic and early grunge historian Lester Bangs wrote
at the time, 'their albums just got worse and worse, until we'd lost
another great musical yeti for ever'.[2]

3

The Fugs left an oddly shaped hole no one else was likely to want to
follow them down in a hurry. While Jimi Hendrix enthralled with his
between-the-teeth guitar-schtick, to the rest of the world he was a
black American first and a former citizen of Seattle last. It wasn't until
the early Seventies, when Seattle produced proto-punks like the
Sonics, the Walters and the Galaxies that the Northwest began to
re-establish itself as a viable regional scene worth mentioning. The
Sonics, inspired by the extraterrestrial wail and haunted looks of
vocalist Gerry Roslie, were particularly influential. Originally from
Tacoma, they quickly made a name for themselves, gleefully breaking
the rules in staid teen-grottos like Parkers Ballroom in Seattle, or
nearby Lake Hills Arena on the outskirts of Bellevue. Three of their
most memorable titles from a well of gothic nomenclatures included
'Strychnine', 'Psycho' and 'The Witch'. As Peter Doggett says: 'You
only have to listen to Mudhoney's 'Touch Me, I'm Sick' to realize the

extent to which the Sonics were, and to some extent still are, revered. Play that next to 'Psycho' and you immediately begin to get the picture . . .'

The next landmark in the history of the Seattle scene was the appearance in the late Seventies by The Ramones at the city's trad-elegant Olympic Hotel Ballroom (there hasn't been a rock band allowed in there since). Overnight a new breed of spiky-breathed punkoids emerged from the Northwest, most prevalent being Sonic Youth – ancestral grunge-punk – and The Vainz, featuring a school-age Duff McKagen, who later joined the tastefully named Fartz, which in turn evolved into seminal Seattle no-wavers, Ten Minute Warning (which also featured future Mother Love Bone drummer Greg Gilmour). With the honourable exception of Sonic Youth – who continue to release speciously relevant albums today and enjoy something of a 'godfather of grunge' mantle amongst the Nirvana and Pearl Jam fans too young to really remember them – few of these bands lived long enough to record. Instead, they belonged in the pure punk tradition of getting up anywhere any time and blasting out just the same: instant disintegration was all part of the deal.

'There was no recording scene at this time. It was more or less a live thing. At the time, everyone was talking about going to New York or LA, to be geniuses there,'[3] remembered Conrad Uno of PopLlama Records, recalling Seattle in the late Seventies, when he played with Uncle Cookie, an early new wave band. By contrast, the Seattle club scene of the early and mid-Eighties was almost non-existent. With the Reagan years came ever-stricter surveillance of the over-twenty-one drinking laws, which very soon meant a complete dearth of all-ages shows in the established clubs. Occasional gigs and parties in specially rented halls or one-off haunts like the Metropolis, the Showbox and the Rainbow, which would allow live music only occasionally, became the norm.

In the year-end 'Best Of . . .' polls for 1983 printed in *The Rocket*, a local bi-weekly free-sheet and Seattle's most credible music paper, under the heading for 'Best All-Ages Club' was the Metropolis, and under the heading for 'Best Venue' was the Moore Theater. By the end of 1984, 'Best Venue' was sardonically though not entirely inac-curately proclaimed 'Your Living-Room'. The only available model for success seemed to involve relocating. The Blackouts, a brilliantly self-styled art-punk band, moved to Chicago, mixed their drugs up and somehow mutated into Ministry ... Duff McKagan left Ten Minute Warning for Los Angeles and a garage band with attitude called Guns N' Roses ... by 1984, even The Melvins had fled Aberdeen for San Francisco.

As Jonathan Kay, vocalist in the early Eighties with one of Seattle's then up-and-coming heavy metal outfits, Q5, said, it was 'a crying shame because the scene [was] becoming huge ... [But] the clubs in Seattle and the surrounding area did not accept original music at all.'[4] Or as Room 9's Ron Rudzitis prophesied in *The Rocket* at the time: 'I think for a lot of bands it's going to be back to the basement.'[5] Which is exactly what happened, but instead of killing the scene off once and for all as had been feared, it proved to be, paradoxically, the chief factor in the genesis of a new, intensely individualistic form of heavy rock music unencumbered by the need to write a big opener, a stirring middle section or a stormin' end bit. This was to be rock music let loose to do things other than merely pleasing the crowd.

And yet the phenomenon that quickly became labelled the 'Seattle Sound' wouldn't have been possible without the network of college radio, fanzines and independent-minded distributors that had sprung up in the wake of punk rock. Sonic Youth's Thurston Moore and Kim Gordon were particularly active in the vital US underground of the time, where an independent network of like-minded bands from all over America – Husker Du in Minneapolis, REM in Atlanta, and the disaffected anti-sceners of New York, San Francisco and LA – helped each other put on gigs and release records ... Ironically, in that context, it was an unknown heavy metal band from nearby Redmond called Queensryche that, picking up on the lessons already learnt by the knowledgeable Seattle indie crowd, took the next unprecedented step, in 1982, of releasing their own independently produced four-song EP – *Queen Of The Reich*, a clear and powerful, even slightly pompous, version of a new age Judas Priest – without even playing a show. A move bold enough to capture the attention of EMI America, who duly wrapped Queensryche up in a long-term major contract in 1983.

It showed other locally-based bands that with just a little financing (Queensryche's initial pressing of five thousand 12-inch discs was co-financed by the owners of a local Seattle record store), a record could be produced and released not just without leaving town, but without begging for gigs first. The knock-on effect was immediate, inspiring other earnest Seattle-based headbangers like TKO, Metal Church, Q5 and Rail to begin putting together their own basement-made recordings and hawking around for deals.

'I think a lot of times people forget that Nirvana, and the alternative aspect of the music scene, is almost a second thought. This really came out of a very strong heavy metal scene,' says Charles Cross, founding editor and publisher of *The Rocket*, who has lived in Seattle since 1975. 'Seattle for years has a history for supporting loud heavy groups. AC/DC were bigger here than anywhere else in America. The Scorpions were giant here. Metallica was supported here before many other markets. Led Zeppelin were, of course, huge here . . .' (It was at the Edgewater Inn in Seattle that the infamous red snapper incident supposedly took place, in which a young redheaded groupie was tied naked to a bed in the hotel while various members of Led Zeppelin and their entourage proceeded to insert the nose of a red snapper fish, caught fresh that morning, into her vagina and rectum.)

'This area . . . was always a very blue-collar, poor white trash area of America,' Cross points out: 'It wasn't a town with a lot of old money. It was a town with a lot of machinists and machinists' kids and consequently heavy metal music was their [thing]. As recently as three years ago, the biggest group in Seattle was Queensryche, by far . . . for years it seemed that we only had heavy metal groups that would be big. Groups like TKO and Metal Church – they were considered a very big and very successful local group. Nowadays it's like they are totally forgotten, it's like they're not even in the history books . . . I think people forget how glam it was, too. It was very Kiss-inspired.'

4

Remembered more for their make-up than their music, Kiss are the missing link between Seattle punk and generic Northwest metal. Formed by New Yorkers Gene Simmons (bass/vocals) and Paul Stanley (vocals/guitar) in 1972, they immediately started gigging in heavy 'futuristic' greasepaint that also served to preserve their facial anonymity, a side-kink which became their main marketing gimmick. In their late-Seventies heyday, Kiss were probably the biggest rock band in America: Marvel created a comic around them; Disney made a film starring them; millions bought their records. They inspired Queensryche and Metal Church, and they inspired Pearl Jam and Nirvana; nobody was immune to their desultory cartoonish charms. 'In America, the thirtysomethings of today all fell in love with Kiss at some point in the Seventies, it seems,' muses Peter Doggett. 'Garth Brooks, the country hero, is a big Kiss fan. If you ask him who were his influences it's, "Oh, Kiss!" Ask what the best show was he'd ever seen and he says, "Queen!"'

The first Seattle band to usher in the modern grunge era, The Melvins, formed in 1980, were the most Kiss-inspired Northwesterners of all. 'Kiss [are] our big spiritual influence – real Kiss only, though. Nothing after '79 and that's pushing it,' claimed Melvins vocalist Buzz Osbourne. 'Our sound comes, in part, from years of listening only to Kiss and living in Grays Harbour.'6 A three-piece from Aberdeen, Washington State, originally featuring bassist Matt Lukin and drummer Dale Crover, the real Melvin was a man of around fifty who got caught in a Monesano Thriftway stealing trees.

Melvins music was punk-metal at its most bones-into-dust irreverent. Young fellow Aberdonian Kurt Cobain, for one, worshipped The Melvins, hanging out at, by his own estimation, over two hundred of their early rehearsals. He even drove their tour van for a while, hauling their equipment around just for the privilege of getting in to see the band play one of their occasional gigs for free. It was Buzz Osbourne who took the sixteen-year-old Cobain to his first rock show in Seattle – Black Flag. It was about this time that the left-handed Cobain first picked up a guitar and began playing it upside-down . . . Northwest musicians of every stripe, whether they were conspicuously influenced by them or not, have been paying The Melvins lip service on MTV ever since.

Other like-minded young snots also taking their first lily-livered steps in rehearsal rooms and occasional bottom-of-the-bill stages in the early thrifty-gig Eighties included the U-Men, Green River, Soundgarden and Malfunkshun. All these bands attempted music that sounded like a collision, to a greater or lesser cacophony, between punk, funk and heavy metal. Then there was Shadow, very well thought of locally and featuring a tasty lead guitarist from the local Roosevelt High School called Mike McCready. 'They used to have like a twelve-year old drummer,' remembers a close friend who is a well-known local scene-maker from those days. 'There were two brothers in the band, one was the drummer, they were really good. I guess [McCready] was real bummed when they broke up . . . He was a real guitar prodigy.'

'A couple of bands in New York were successful with the noise thing,' recalled Soundgarden's Chris Cornell. 'So everyone else started doing it. Us and Green River and The Melvins were doing well with the heavy thing and a few bands saw that and started doing it too.'[7] Or as Mudhoney's Mark Arm, then of Green River, put it: 'There was this one corner of the map that was busy being really inbred and ripping off each other's ideas.'[8] Eventually, The Melvins went from being the fastest underground band in town to being the slowest. Some put this down to the isolation caused by the demise of the all-ages clubs (reasoning that it was only the teenhooders that wanted things kept fast so they could stage dive). According to others, it was more probably due to the arrival in Seattle in the mid-Eighties of the first serious batches of Ecstasy.

Never was a drug more perfectly named than Ecstasy. The *Chambers 20th Century Dictionary* defines the word 'ecstasy' as, 'a state of temporary mental alienation and altered or diminished consciousness: excessive joy . . . or any exalted feeling', which is as accurate a description of the peculiar effects of the drug Ecstasy as you will find, not least from the people who regularly take it. 'X made the sounds heavier but *slower*,' recalled a regular face from those days who requested that her name not be used here. 'It was like, overnight the music just changed. People started working on long way out riffs that like went on for ever. It was hypnotic and spacy and but totally like hard, too. And X was what did it. Soundgarden, Green River . . . all those guys were into it.'

A chest-thumping amalgam of punk, glam, quasi-funk and metal, the emerging 'Sound of Seattle' laboured initially under many flags of inconvenience – 'noise-art', 'pain-rock', 'thrash-punk' – until finally it got pinned down to that carelessly apt one-syllable bowel-sound headline writers the world over would soon make their own: g-r-u-n-g-e. And the purest, earliest definition of what constituted Seattle grunge was what Sub Pop house-producer Jack Endino called 'Seventies-influenced, slowed-down punk music'.[9] 'When we first started out the crowd used to scream for us to play faster,' said Mark Arm. 'Not any more.'[10]

5

The four main tributaries that flowed together to form Green River began as a trickle of Seattle bands back in 1982: The Limp Richards, Deranged Diction, The Ducky Boys and Mr Epp. All trawled the same dark pools of glam-punk-metal for their inspiration; line-ups tended to vacillate. Essentially, The Limp Richards were a play-dead off-night vehicle for lead guitarist Steve Turner and drummer Mark Arm; Arm's serious interest was in Mr Epp, which he played guitar and sang in, while Turner also traded stump-fingered guitar-licks with one Stone Gossard in The Ducky Boys, an off-shoot of Gossard's earlier basement outfit, March of Crimes.

Jeff Ament, twenty years old and fresh from Missoula, Montana, played bass in Deranged Diction, which also included guitarist Bruce Fairweather. Born on March 10, 1963, the son of a small-town barber, Jeff had attended Big Sandy High School in Montana, where he was good enough to become a regular all-conference basketball player. 'There was a long period in my life where it revolved around basketball,' he once reminisced. 'All of those old cats . . . Lew Alcindor, Nate Archibald, Connie Hawkins, Spencer Haywood, they were my first idols.'[11]

Drawn to music at the age of four, when he began listening to an uncle's Beatles and Santana records, the young Ament was soon spending his pocket-money on Motown singles, 'three for eighty-nine cents'.[12] He taught himself to play bass by thumbing along to all the records he could lay his big hands on. These days, of course, the more worldly Ament professes to a fondness for the riffs of John Coltrane, the groove of old Free or the satire of The Dead Boys. But early on, Iron Maiden ruled his heart; as a teenager Jeff was smitten by the frenetic, machine-gun technique of Maiden bassist Steve Harris. It was what made him want to get serious about the bass; to want to be in a band.

'A couple of us are from that heavy metal background – I grew up listening to the usual metal stuff: Aerosmith, Iron Maiden, Judas Priest, but . . . heavy metal is a bit sterile and we do tend to try and get away from all that,' Jeff says now. 'I'm an artist. I get inspired even musically, by artists, painters, books or whatever.'[13] 'I remember the first time I ever met him he started telling me how he used to cut out all my pictures of Maiden and pin them on his bedroom wall,' says the photographer Ross Halfin, who worked for Iron Maiden for many years. 'But then you have to remember that in those days Maiden were big in America and Steve was being voted Best Bass Player in the world by *Guitar* magazine . . .'

For a time, Jeff studied art at high school. But, in his own words, he 'had a problem with [the] teachers because they weren't wild enough for me. Art was supposed to be this expressive medium where you could do anything, and there were all these barriers and confines within the school . . . So I quit.'[14] At first, his friends thought he was crazy. His parents knew he was. 'My parents had their concerns. I was the first kid, so they always wanted what was best for me, and they naturally assumed college was the best thing.'[15]

Instead, Jeff moved to Seattle in 1982 just in time to watch the clubs close and the local scene go underground. For the next five years he 'pulled espresso in a café full of transsexuals and artists',[16] spending his evenings either rehearsing with Deranged Diction or checking out the rooms where The Duckys or the Epps did the same. None of these bands recorded; all of them fragmented pretty quickly. The Limp Richards were the first to go, Steve Turner and Mark Arm deciding to do the logical thing and join forces in Mr Epp. Steve, however, not wanting to burn too many of his bridges, also formed another side band, Spluii Numa, with guitarist Charlie Guain from the Richards, and Alex Vincent on drums. Twelve months or so of crab-like basement-only deliberations ensued.

Finally, in 1984, getting absolutely nowhere on their own, Mr Epp and Spluii Numa folded and Green River was formed. Named after an area near Seattle where a serial killer claimed many lives during the mid-Eighties, police suspect that the Green River Murderer, as he became known, has killed up to thirty people, and, eerily, remains at large to this day. Steve came up with the idea for the name; Mark adored it. It was camp and fey and darkly humorous with just a tinge of uncertainty about it, like The Stooges or the New York Dolls.

The original Green River consisted, then, of Mark Arm on guitar and vocals, Steve Turner on lead guitar, Deranged Diction's Jeff Ament on bass and Spluii Numa's Alex Vincent on drums. This was the line-up first unveiled on *Deep Six*, the multi-artist compilation issued in the summer of 1985 by C/Z Records. The same enterprising indie that later released the *Teriyaki Asthma Vol. 1* set that first featured Nirvana, C/Z was the brainchild of Daniel House, the bass player in another local Seattle bandoid called Skin Yard. 'One morning [he] awoke with the realization that something had happened in Seattle,' Arm later recalled. 'He decided that, along with his 8-track recording studio, he would start a record label and release a compilation of Seattle rock 'n' roll acts. So he rounded up The Melvins, Malfunkshun, the U-Men, Soundgarden, Skin Yard and Green River, and stuck us all in a studio … Then all the bands got together and played two nights in a stinky rented hall.'[17]

Deep Six featured the first – and in some cases only – recordings of such original Northwest grunge-peregrines as Malfunkshun, Green River, U-Men, Soundgarden, The Melvins and Skin Yard. The two Green River tracks – '10,000 Things' and 'Your Own Best Friend' – showcased the band at its most acned and fraught, Turner and Arm trying just that bit too hard to come across as the no-generation's bully-boys from hell. But it was a start.

Initially, House regarded the project as a hobby. Even though he later took a full-time job at Sub Pop, soon to be Seattle's premier independent label, it wasn't until he was laid off in 1990 that he turned his attention to C/Z full time. These days, C/Z rivals Sub Pop as an independent of international acclaim, their biggest successes so far including two 'guest-star' tribute anthologies (one to The Buzzcocks, one to Kiss), and putting out regular product from such buzznames as Hammerbox, Tree People and Seven Year Bitch. Very difficult to find copies of these days, House has sworn that *Deep Six* will never be reissued because, he claimed, 'most of the bands would be pissed off and embarrassed'.[18]

6

By the beginning of 1985, The Ducky Boys had long taken their last forlorn dive and Stone Gossard – an old high-school pal of Steve Turner's – was immediately recruited to the Green River line-up. With another full-time guitarist in tow, it allowed Mark Arm to switch from second guitar to full-time vocals, something he had been longing to do since the beginning.

Born in Seattle, on July 20, 1965, Stone (his real name – he has a sister called Star) Gossard's whole background – his father is a lawyer, his mother an artist – is comfortable, upwardly gold top middle America. It may be why, of all the members of Pearl Jam, Gossard has always remained the calmest amidst the blizzard of attention that's surrounded their every move; cool, confident, relaxed, into it – the polar opposite, in fact, to the man who would one day write the words to all his best tunes.

Three-fifths of the future Green River – Stone Gossard, Steve Turner and Alex Vincent – all went to the Northwest High School, in Seattle: an expensive private school situated on leafy Capitol Hill where, according to the official brochure, 'all students participate in International Studies, the Arts, Athletics and a hands-on Environmental program . . .' Housed in a 1905 building that is listed as a National Historical Landmark, its ample spaces, rooted in tradition, help engender 'a calm sense of purpose' in the life of the school, according to Ellen Taussig, Head of School.

'I liked school,' Gossard would shrug unapologetically when asked about those days. 'There are great things about school, and I had some really great professors . . . They'd be honest with you, and let you know you're doing a good job, or that you could be doing a better job. But for the most part . . . It's a conditioning system. You get up early, you go to your classes. If you take these required classes then you'll get this job and you'll have to wear these clothes.'[19]

A keen student of the arts division (which included music, ensembles, chorus and theory classes plus a jazz class, dance, theatre and visual arts studies) Stone has always insisted that his unique 'alternative tuning' guitar style developed more from listening to and being influenced by a guitarist named Paul Solger, who played with Seattle bands Metaphysical and Ten Minute Warning, than it did from anything he ever learnt at school. 'He used Egyptian modes a lot,'[20] explained Gossard obliquely. Or 'Arabic madams', if you want to get technical, though it's worth remembering that Stone, like every other aspiring young gunslinger in North America growing up in the late Seventies, was first and last a Led Zeppelin man, and nobody in the rock spectrum has ever put 'alternative tunings' to such mystically Western use as Zeppelin guitarist Jimmy Page . . .

14

According to another of his teachers at Northwest High, as a teenager Stone was 'a crazy kind of guy who set himself apart from the others. The Northwest school caters for children that do that ... Grunge started in these corridors.' She smiled, referring to the fact that Stone, Alex, Steve and their friends all played together in the huge corridors during recreation periods; the Head of School always kept an acoustic guitar in her office, which anyone could use. Stone still keeps in contact with the school and sent Ellen Taussig one gold and two platinum discs when *Ten* went through the roof in 1992, in recognition of the excellent education he had received there. Mrs Taussig keeps one on the wall of her office. The school auctioned the other two for charity but Mrs Taussig says they did not get a lot of money for them.

'I went to school with Stoney for like fourth, fifth and sixth grade,' recalls a close friend. 'He was always a wise-ass kid . . . Then he went off to private school. This kind of hippy art school, kind of expensive . . . the principal had like a mohawk and stuff. Green River were like art kids. I think Stone played guitar and dulcimer in their bands, it was kind of embarrassing . . .'

7

It was with the Arm/Turner/Ament/Vincent/Gossard line-up that Green River released their first 12-inch record in their own right. Entitled 'Come On Down', the release was a largely mail-order affair, available through the New York-based Homestead Records indie, but was nevertheless released into a few like-minded New York and Seattle stores late in the summer of 1985, in the same batch of Homestead releases as *Dinosaur*, the début album by the future Dinosaur Jnr.

As founding members, Mark Arm and Steve Turner took responsibility for most of the original material back then and as a result. 'Come On Down' shows the band at its most punk-drunk and uncompromising. Mark doesn't sing, he shouts; Steve doesn't riff, he roars; Stone and Jeff and Alex seem to be lost in their own just as over-eager world ... Clearly, this was a band steeped in the mainstream rock tradition, but aware of something most mainstream rock bands aren't –

that technical finesse is *never* an end in itself. Beneath Mark's Iggyonics, once Stone had plugged his guitar in, Green River enjoyed a very layered sound; surprisingly disciplined, though not so showy as to detract from the music's ability to work on noise level alone. 'Come On Down' was toothsomely described by the otherwise scant Homestead press release at the time as sounding 'like the Flesheaters jamming with Aerosmith', while *The Rocket* said it sounded like 'a mixture of Metallica and Lynyrd Skynyrd with Henry Rollins as singer',[21] either of which is as good a definition of the fabled early grunge sound as you will find and more accurate than most of the florid subsequent descriptions.

Soundgarden, which took their name from the huge pipe sculpture in Seattle's sand-point, were Green River's most prominent rivals in the mid-Eighties. Where Queensryche were traditionalists attempting subtle, intellectually infused readjustments within the established heavy metal conventions, Soundgarden – fronted by charismatic corkscrew-haired singer-songwriter Chris Cornell and brutal-looking guitarist Kim Thayil – were always outsiders, whose apparent aim was to recast metal wholesale. Not least of the methods available to them was the enviable ability to poke fun at themselves and what they saw as the creeping conservatism of most heavy metal – a good example being the track '665–667', from their début 1988 SST album, *Ultramega OK*, a thinly veiled reference to the numerals 666, so long a fixture of heavy metal folklore as the number of the – ahem – beast.

Green River also liked to send themselves up, though it was less clear where the joke ended and the out-and-out flaunting of the glam side of their nature began. A friend who saw both Green River and Soundgarden says there was always 'a lot of rock posturing' going on at both their sporadic performances, citing Jeff Ament with his frequent application of tongue to fingertips in classic Whitesnake too-hot-to-touch mode – 'he'd lick his finger and do that . . . like, check it out!' – as the worst offender of an over-the-top bunch. 'Those guys were more like a punk rock band, but Stoney and Jeff were into getting all dressed up . . . Jeff would do his hair like the guy in Poison.'

One person who definitely did not get the joke was Steve Turner, who increasingly isolated himself from Green River's more overt rock mannerisms. 'Steve ended up quitting the band cos he just couldn't stand all the rock star stuff. He would just sit on a stool at the side of the stage playing his guitar while the others were hopping around.' Steve finally quit in disgust with the direction he felt the band was heading in not long after 'Come On Down' was released, leaving right before Green River's first proper tour – a two-week swing through the clubs and one-stops of New York at the beginning of 1986 – claiming that the band's sound had 'changed drastically'[22] from the simple junk riffs they had started with to long, overblown songs more reminiscent of Jeff's beloved Iron Maiden.

Mark was a little more circumspect in his own explanation of his former partner's abrupt departure. 'At the time of "Come On Down", all the bass-lines consisted of Steve Harris triplets – "here come the horses over the hill". Steve [Turner] hated that stuff. [He] left right at the peak of that. Then we concentrated on writing simpler songs and things got a lot better and people started liking us.'[23]

Steve's replacement was guitarist Bruce Fairweather – from Jeff's former band, Deranged Diction. It was with the new Arm/Ament/Vincent/Gossard/Fairweather line-up that Green River set about recording the five-track EP that followed, *Dry As A Bone*. Produced for them by Jack Endino at Reciprocal Recording Studios in June 1986, it was to be their début on the newly formed Seattle-based Sub Pop label, but the release kept being pushed back and back. Concerned that the delay was interrupting their fragile momentum, the band recorded and released a quicky self-financed single, issued on the independent ICP label, towards the end of 1986, called 'Together We'll Never' (a song that later resurfaced on *Rehab Doll*) coupled with their frazzled version of 'Ain't Nothing To Do' (an old piece of Dead Boys schlock).

Neither number was Green River at its most prickly but the record served its purpose as the band looked forward to the new year and their first go at some club dates out on the West Coast, with a couple of nights in Texas thrown in along the way, hoping that someone with the right size cheque-book would pick them up. They didn't. Back home, though, as Green River lurched blithely into 1987, the story was being told more promisingly. One of the few local bands to swing a tour further than Portland, Green River were accorded all due respect by supportive Washington college radio stations like KCMU and KJET, while their hard-to-find records and occasional clutches of gigs were always given lavish space in local taste-making tabloids like *The Rocket* and the now defunct *Backlash*.

By the end of 1986, though, with clubs like the Showbox, the Metropolis and the Gorilla Gardens all long gone, Green River were still playing only occasional gigs in Seattle; either at the Central, where they tried to get a gig as often as possible, or on all-ages bills at the Lincoln Arts Center. More often than not, they were marooned in their rehearsal rooms, writing songs they still didn't have a regular outlet for. They thought they had found one in Sub Pop, but it had been six months since the *Dry As A Bone* sessions and it still hadn't come out yet. Elsewhere, things looked bleakly similar. Room 9, another Seattle outfit from those days competing for amp-space, released a homemade cassette in 1986, received a few dinners and polite talk from a clutch of reps from the major labels, sniffily turned down a contract with Enigma and ended up with nothing at all released. The Walkabouts did land a contract for their album, *Weights And Rivers*, with the well-meaning Echo Records indie, but it was a largely self-financed project and Green River had already been that route with Homestead and IPC.

It wasn't until two outsiders to Seattle by the name of Bruce Pavitt and Jonathan Poneman got together to turn Sub Pop from Pavitt's good idea into a viable on-going mothership that the jigsaw, so long a frustrating mess of ill-fitting pieces, began to resemble a proper picture; one that would some day hang with pride of place upon the mantle of many, not least those of Stone Gossard and Jeff Ament. 'Seattle was once an undeveloped area as far as the music business goes ... everything could develop at a slow pace. There wasn't a rush to get signed,' Stone reflected. 'Soundgarden and [Green River] became great bands because they had a chance to develop naturally. They weren't thinking about major tours, they just wanted to put a record out on this little label called Sub Pop, cos that was the coolest thing that could happen.'[24]

8

The origins of the Sub Pop story go back to the childhood friendship of Sub Pop founder Bruce Pavitt, and Kim Thayil and Hiro Yamamoto – guitarist and bassist, respectively, of Soundgarden. All three grew up in the Chicago suburb of Park Forest and graduated together from an 'alternative learning program' at Rich East High School, a less expensive though not dissimilar establishment to the one Gossard and Turner had attended. Wishing to further their education in a similarly progressive manner, the trio enrolled in Evergreen State College in Olympia, Washington State, in 1979. Pavitt worked part time for *OP* (now *Options*) magazine and began writing feverish pieces about the flickering American independent scene in his own *Subterranean Pop* fanzine (issue No. 1 had a print run of approximately two hundred copies). Eight editions appeared between 1979 and 1983, but from issue No. 3 its title was abbreviated to *Sub Pop*; issues No. 5, No. 7 and No. 9 were special 'cassette-zine' releases, featuring the fanzine plus a cassette of rough homemade recordings of unknown treasured Pavitt ragbags like All Night Movies, Cool Rays and Steve Fisk.

After graduating in 1981, Thayil and Yamamoto moved to Seattle. Pavitt followed two years later, paying his way by working briefly at Yesco – now Musak – the programmers of bland music tapes designed to produce soothing background noise for shopping malls, elevators and airport lounges. 'I thoroughly enjoyed the irony of that!'[25] Pavitt cawed merrily. Sidelining the fanzine-cassette business in 1983, he had kept the Sub Pop title alive by hosting his own *Sub Pop* show on KCMU at the University of Washington. He also began writing a regular column which ran for another five years in *The Rocket*, called – what else? – 'Sub Pop'.

By now, though, Pavitt's magpie-like interest had evolved into wanting his own record label, under the Sub Pop banner naturally, but this time focusing specifically on the nascent alternative music scene of the Northwest. 'When I first moved to Seattle, it seemed that every band wanted to be Joy Division,' he said. 'Some of them even went so far as to affect British accents . . . they're always reading about bands from England, New York and LA, [and so] they think those bands are better . . . Then there are some people who say, "Fuck New York. Fuck LA. We don't care what's happening there, we want to make something happen here." And that's what Seattle is about right now.'[26]

Pavitt's idea was to create an environment not unlike that which existed at ground-breaking American independent labels in the Fifties and Sixties like Berry Gordy Jr.'s Tamla Motown or Jim Stewart and Estelle Axton's Stax Records, but with the added post-punk street-suss of California's SST indie, or, better still, in England, (producer) Martin Hannett and Factory Records; innovative hands-on labels that had their own studios, staff producers and consistent album art. Sub Pop would have the same pop-auteur philosophy. 'I wanted it to be a

Northwest record label the same as Motown was a Detroit label,' said Pavitt. 'I wanted to establish an *identity*.'[27]

From the start, Sub Pop had been a constant gamble. The immensely modest by major-label standards budget for Green River's *Dry As A Bone* EP, and the first Soundgarden single, 'Hunted Down', issued at the same time, almost bankrupted the company before it even got off the ground. 'A lot of people don't know this but we almost went out of business after sixty days,' Pavitt confessed years later. 'It was only through a fluke, only because the jacket manufacturer in Canada decided to let the Green River jacket leave before we paid – that's the only way we stayed in business.'[28]

Sub Pop's first vinyl release, in July 1986, was *Sub Pop 100*: a compilation of more Pavitt parvenus, in a numbered limited edition of five thousand, spotlighting alternative talents from all over America such as Skinny Puppy and Big Black's Steve Albini, as well as featuring contributions from Northwestern artists like Sonic Youth, Steve Fisk and the U-Men.

Destined to become a highly collectable label, the launching of the Sub Pop empire on vinyl played a vital role in crystallizing what was soon to become the most famous regional scene in the world, its reputation strengthened by the fact that so many of its artists would go on to much greater fame with major labels – Nirvana to Geffen Records' street-suss off-shoot DGC, Soundgarden to A&M; Mudhoney are with Warner Brothers' subsidiary, Reprise. Other acclaimed acts that would get their first breaks on the label include the Walkabouts, the Reverend Horton Heat, Tad, the late street poet Jesse Bernstein, and the Smashing Pumpkins. And of course, Sub Pop 'discovered' Green River, from which, one day, mad butterfly-like, Pearl Jam would emerge.

Even without the value of squillion-dollar hindsight, though, it's not difficult to see how easily the venture could have failed. Had Pavitt been left to his own devices, it's doubtful any of us would have come to know the Sub Pop moniker in quite the same weird way we all eventually did. First – though he certainly wouldn't have thanked you for saying so at the time – what Bruce Pavitt badly needed was a partner; someone to bounce his quasi-headcase ideas off of. Someone who not only understood what he was babbling on about but could contribute something Pavitt himself was simply unable to do at that point; inject some much-needed cash into the operation.

9

Originally from Toledo, Ohio, Jonathan Poneman moved to Seattle to attend the University of Washington at about the same time that Bruce Pavitt was getting ready to leave Chicago. An aspiring musician himself, Poneman played guitar in a notably obscure college band called the Treeclimbers that excelled, in his words, in 'mid-Eighties twinkie pop',[29] and also hosted his own evening show on KCMU, eventually hanging around long enough to become the station's promotions director in 1983.

Flexing his newly developed entrepreneurial muscles, he began booking a weekly KCMU showcase at a local club, which is where he first encountered a particularly shit-kicking gang of low-fi noise merchants with a penchant for spot-on Led Zeppelin piss-takes called Soundgarden. 'It was one of the most riveting shows I had ever seen,'[30] gushed Poneman later. Indeed, the occasion seemed to represent something of a personal turning point for him, immediately deciding to lay aside his own demi-musical ambitions and offer the band his services as manager. 'I felt more creative and adventurous marketing others. The energy was something I wanted to tap into.'[31]

Having already released five thousand copies of *Sub Pop 100*, Pavitt had turned his attention to working on the Green River EP; they were the happening local band, it was only fitting, he reasoned, that they should cut their first substantial recording for the most happening local label. The band didn't take much persuading; nobody else was begging them to do anything. Pavitt instructed Skin Yard's Jack Endino to go ahead and record five tracks with the band on his little 8-track machine at Reciprocal Studios and to forward the tape-and-burger bill to him later, then turned his laser-beam mind to the problem of what to do about Soundgarden and their distractingly ardent manager.

Pavitt had stayed in touch with guitarist Kim Thayil, who had played with hs brother in a local Park Forest band and had also put in some time as a DJ at KCMU. Pavitt's problem was that he'd invested all his money on the Green River EP, and though Soundgarden were keen to become a part of the burgeoning Sub Pop roster, they weren't about to start paying their own studio bills for the privilege.

Poneman, with a supply of ready cash and a Rolodex of useful biz-wise contacts he'd developed through his work in college radio, seemed like the obvious answer. Kim Thayil thought so, anyway. 'Bruce had a lot of ideas, he just didn't have the money to work them,' Thayil recalled. 'And here was Jonathan, very interested in these same bands, and he had money. Jonathan was very confident in his own ability to get a record out, but we weren't as confident. We knew he could make a record, but we also knew that Bruce could get it noticed. And Bruce was kind of into the idea of Jonathan having money . . .'[32] 'We actually started the company on about $19,000,' Poneman remembered. 'And we spent it on space, a little bit of advertising, and putting out a couple of records, basically.'[33]

It was this attitude – where the guys in charge were far more aware of what the bands themselves were talking about than the major label honchos were ever likely to be – that attracted bands like Green River and Soundgarden to the label. Soundgarden had already been tentatively approached by several majors (including A&M, who they eventually signed to) whose cash-register antennae had been tweaked by all the New Zeppelin stories the local Seattle pundits had been putting out. Cornell and Thayil preferred to start small. 'We were more interested in working with Sub Pop because it was more exciting,' said Thayil, simply. 'I was confident that their taste in music was good, the bands were good – in fact, everything about their style was interesting and unique. I thought it could be a huge phenomenon. I didn't think it would be, just that it *could* be.'[34]

Though initially reluctant to become partners, Pavitt and Poneman eventually saw sense and agreed, and in July 1987, over a year late, Green River's *Dry As A Bone* EP was finally released; the initial pressing of two thousand copies coming in lurid 12-inch green vinyl. (In keeping with their policy of limited editions but long shelf-life, Sub Pop have subsequently run through several different pressings of *Dry As A Bone*: the original and most collectable 12-inch edition comes with a tell-tale yellow insert.) As a semi-companion piece, the first five hundred copies of Soundgarden's début Sub Pop single, 'Hunted Down', were released almost simultaneously in sea-blue vinyl. 'We thought about putting it out on blue vinyl in a blue envelope just to be sort of a lost brother to Green River's single,'[35] joked Kim Thayil. The first six hundred copies of Soundgarden's next 12-incher, the six-track *Screaming For Life* EP, were released on orange vinyl by Sub Pop two months later. 'It was a process of evolution, really,' said Poneman pragmatically. 'We were trying to capture the public's imagination, create the idea that there was all this music in Seattle, trying to create a Seattle invasion. And if it meant trickling out singles and limited editions, then so be it.'[36]

Jack Endino, whose sound was an integral part of the early Sub Pop identity, had originally played guitar in Skin Yard with C/Z Records' Daniel House, and was the natural choice to become Sub Pop's 'house producer'. His first official project under the Sub Pop auspices was taking charge of the *Dry As A Bone* sessions. Slated to become the second ever release on the label, Green River's pill-tempered metallic mewl was built around Mark Arm's overwhelming preening, scowling personality, his impotent rage spilling over convincingly in 'Unwind', a twisted acid-blues that builds until it slams into unabashed Green River-style thrash, centred around Arm bawling, '*I CAN get ya THINKING anything I WANT!*' until you almost plead for him to stop. Their version of Tales of Terror's 'Ozzie' is something of a poor taste anthem, too, with its key line, '*I know the secret of the river*', referring to the infamous Green River slayings from which the band only half-jokingly took its name. The 'current Kings of Noise in Seattle', *The Rocket* crowned them when they finally got to hear it, and not even Chris Cornell would argue it otherwise.

10

In terms of straightforward cost-and-return, Sub Pop had made a lot of small change for Pavitt and Poneman very quickly. They may not have had any million-selling albums, but then they had none of the outrageous expense that producing a million-selling album entails. Endino's same small 8-track studio was used to record everything; Pavitt designed all the sleeves himself (he had a penchant for blur-armed, hair-flailing live shots); there were no such things as 'budgets' or 'advance fees', meaning very little money down, so that whatever they sold was almost immediately translated into instant profit, which they then plunged back into the next thing that caught their roving, increasingly more ambitious imaginations.

In July 1987, with *Dry As A Bone* finally out, Green River returned to Endino's cramped Reciprocal Studios to begin work on the nine tracks intended for the first Green River album proper, already titled *Rehab Doll*, which Sub Pop hoped to have out in time for the string of return dates along the west coast the band were planning for the autumn. The only track from those initial sessions that ever saw release, a blitzed and stoned version of David Bowie's 'Queen Bitch', was originally included only as a 'bonus' track on the early *Rehab Doll* cassettes. Though working with Endino pleased Mark – perhaps finding in the young producer the untroubled, punk-conscious perspective he had lost when Steve Turner left – the rest of the band, in particular Jeff and Stone, were in a hurry to upgrade what they saw as the overtly garagey sound of *Dry As A Bone*, and instead looked to the comparatively more luxurious 24-track facilities offered to them by Bruce Calder of Steve Lawson Productions, who they would record with, on and off, until the end of the year.

All was clearly not well; angry disagreements were becoming the norm. With Steve Turner's anti-everything influence long since expunged from the rehearsal room, the business of coming up with the tunes had fallen squarely on to the more rock-steady shoulders of Stone Gossard and Bruce Fairweather. Alex Vincent was always given a joint songwriting credit as well, though for what exactly is anybody's guess as his drumming is one of the least remarkable aspects of *Rehab Doll*-era Green River. Presumably, he just raised his sticks aloft and *insisted*. Never a prolific songwriter, Jeff Ament made himself useful getting involved in all the odious tasks the band didn't have other people to do for them yet. 'I went and worked a day-job for eight hours a day and then went to practice,' he recalled. 'We didn't have a manager, so we did everything ourselves. I booked all of our tours [and] I did all the artwork for the band . . .'[37] 'Basically, we just got together, played really loud and drank a lot of beer,' Bruce Fairweather shrugged. 'But Green River was more fun than organized – that's basically why we broke up. Stone, Jeff and I wanted to be more professional.'[38]

Green River split up on Halloween, 1987. Mark and Jeff had begun to clash incessantly over how best to deal with what Mark referred to as 'the major-label menace',[39] and what Jeff saw simply as the next step up the slippery slope to stardom, the pair of them conducting a painful feud which came to a messy head when Green River supported Jane's Addiction at The Scream club, in Los Angeles. Mark wanted to put some friends on the guest-list for the show, but Jeff insisted on giving the limited guest-tickets they had been allotted as support band to some record company A&R people he had invited along. There was a row: Jeff got his way but when only two of the A&R men turned up and one of those didn't even arrive in time to see Green River play, an even bigger row broke out in the dressing-room, which resulted in Mark first threatening to punch an apparently unrepentant Jeff out, then promising to leave the band; a promise he kept that same night. Green River practically disintegrated on the spot . . .

'Some of the other musicians started getting the idea they could be popular, and began to think, "Well, I'm getting to be twenty-four, what am I going to be doing the rest of my life?"' said Arm, in a pointed reference to his former bass player. 'So Green River got into the idea of signing to a major, and that's how *Rehab Doll* was recorded, with that idea in mind. But for me . . . I was listening to far simpler stuff, such as basic Stooges. In the end . . . I formed Mudhoney and the others became Mother Love Bone and signed to Polygram. So I guess we both got what we wanted.'[40]

When Green River broke up, Mark Arm immediately sought out his former partner-in-grind Steve Turner . . . starting a new band together seemed like the best idea either of them had come up with in a long time, especially as Steve was by then already jamming with ex-Bundle Of Hiss drummer Dan Peters. Thus, along with bassist Matt Lukin – back in town following the temporary break-up of The Melvins – Mudhoney was born. Mark and Steve have always insisted there was no relation between the name of the new band and yet another previous 'sludge-punk' Arm/Turner creation that lasted just a few pre-Green River gigs called The Thrown-Ups, who had a penchant for spreading sacks of earth all over the floor, adding a bucket or two of water, then rolling in it naked before going out to play their set, as they first did in the men's toilets at the Central on one memorable occasion. The true inspiration behind the name Mudhoney, they claimed, is that it was filched from a 1965 Russ Meyer movie of the same name that none of them had actually seen, they just dug the name. Their first single, the wilfully anthemic 'Touch Me, I'm Sick', was released to universal acclaim on Sub Pop (first eight hundred copies on puke-brown vinyl) in August 1988.

11

Once again, there was a long delay over the actual release of *Rehab Doll*. *Dry As A Bone* had been nominated for a North American Music Award (NAMA) at the beginning of 1988, and the band were understandably anxious to make the most of their growing reputation regionally. But Mark's departure had thrown the whole concept of Green River into disarray. There was no way Stone, for one, was going to continue under the same name; it had become too much associated with its former singer, who'd lost no time in decrying the mainstream direction the others seemed to be content to drift in to anyone who would listen.

Some deep thinking needed to be done. First off, whatever Jeff and Stone and Bruce (they'd decided to drop Alex as soon as they'd decided Green River was effectively over) called themselves in the future, the most important thing was to find a new frontman; preferably someone a lot less earnest and a little less afraid of the idea of becoming a famous rock star than his *louche* predecessor. They found what they were looking for in the twenty-two-year-old singer of Seattle's other less popular glamsters, Malfunkshun. Hitting even the tiniest of backroom stages in white-face, glittery jackets and spray-painted motorcycle boots, sometimes with platform heels nailed on for extra effect, yodelling 'Helloooo Seattle!' and camping around like Freddie Mercury's long lost much kissier younger sister, Andrew Wood appeared to be the answer to Jeff, Stone and Bruce's most weed-ridden prayers. On the surface, at least.

In the mean time, *Rehab Doll* did finally appear, issued as an eight-track mini-album on Sub Pop (the first thousand on goblin-green vinyl) in June 1988. As a PS, it was a telling one. Intelligent but savage rock, with Mark's impassioned vocals screeching over Stone and Bruce's mega-drive guitars, six years on tracks like the spiteful 'Swallow My Pride' (which dated back to the Steve Turner era), the panicky for-real 'One More Stitch', or the lumbering, jacked-up title track itself (music co-written by Stone and his guitar guru, Paul Solger), serve as a strangely poignant reminder of what might have been . . . if.

Yet when one considers that there would have been no

Mudhoney, no Mother Love Bone, perhaps no Temple Of The Dog, and certainly no Pearl Jam – all of whom surpassed the original template in their own fashion ten times over – if Green River had *not* broken up when they did, it is perhaps best to save one's tears for more deserving cases, of which there would certainly be more than one over the coming years. 'I loved Green River,' says *Rocket* editor Charles Cross. 'I would say they were the best, musically, of that era. If I remember, *Dry As A Bone* and *Rehab Doll* really brought a lot of attention . . . It was like nothing else happened for a long time.'

Green River's final, posthumous release was to have a track from *Rehab Doll* included on the neo-legendary *Sub Pop 200* compilation. Initially released on vinyl in December 1988, originally it came in a numbered limited edition of five thousand comprising three 12-inch EPs, showcasing the nefarious talents of twenty more or less 'local' Northwestern acts, only nine of whom were actually on the Sub Pop roster at the time. Alongside contributions from by now established Sub Pop mastheads as Green River, Soundgarden, Tad and Blood Circus were tracks by a variety of Northwestern artists including power-drone trio the Fastbacks, singer/songwriter Terry Lee Hale, art-school rockers Beat Happening, a spoken-word piece by underground poet Jesse Bernstein and the acoustic punk of the Walkabouts. An epochal set which has since been released on CD, it garnered a lot of attention for the label in America; while in the UK, revered Radio 1 DJ John Peel wrote an influential piece in the *Observer* proclaiming: 'It is going to take something special to stop *Sub Pop 200* being the set of recordings by which all others are judged.'[41]

But by then Green River were well and truly history. For a while, it looked as if they had left everything to Soundgarden, whose next Sub Pop release, the *Fopp* EP, recorded in 1988 with Steve Fisk producing, was Soundgarden's first stone cold classic; the first track, 'Kingdom Of Come', a more than gentle nudge-nudge in the direction of vintage clown-face Kiss; plus two versions – 'dub' and 'straight' – of 'Fopp' itself, the Ohio Players' floor-packin' Seventies funkmeister, here transposed into a natural glam-metal groove that the band camp up with extravagant bad taste.

Back in the basement, Stone and Jeff and Bruce were busy learning all about their new singer and the boy-man that would help make some of their corny dreams come true, plus one or two nightmares they thought you only read about in books like this. They had already decided on a new name for themselves: Lords Of The Wasteland. Andy had come up with it after their first rehearsal. Or something . . . And if that didn't fit then Andy would think of something better . . . OK? It was gonna be all right.

CHAPTER TWO

LOVE ROCK

'I've been training for this all my life, I have always been a frontman. I remember when I was nine or ten, in my bedroom I'd wait till my folks were gone, then I'd put Kiss's Alive! *on really loud and I'd use my bed as a drum-riser and a tennis racket for a guitar. At the end of the album I'd smash my tennis racket – my guitar – start the album over for the encore, and walk out on stage with a brand-new guitar. You should have seen it! The Andy Wood Band! We were really big in the Seventies . . .'[1]*

– Andrew Wood, *The Rocket*, January 1989

'I traded life for instant satisfaction
I tipped the scales at twenty-two
These eyes broken for ever
Lost my soul and I never knew . . .'[2]

– From 'Death', a poem by Andrew Wood, February 1988

'Died: Andrew Wood, 24, lead singer of the Seattle-based rock band Mother Love Bone, Monday in Seattle, of what appeared to be a heroin overdose . . .'

– Obituary Column, *Seattle Times*, March 21, 1990

1

Andrew Wood was born in Columbus, Mississippi, January 8, 1966. The youngest and most naturally outgoing of a family of three boys, because his father, David, was an officer in the US Navy, the Wood family moved incessantly throughout young Andy's childhood – first Mississippi, then on to Washington, DC, Maine, even West Germany for a brief spell. Finally, in 1978, David Wood found himself stationed on Bainbridge Island, one of several small residential dots just off the coast of Seattle.

Marin (Toni) Wood was a young housewife and mother finding it increasingly difficult to cope with the lonely family life a naval spouse is sometimes forced to lead. Now divorced, Toni and David Wood had married when they were barely out of their teens. Most of the time he was on exercises with the Navy, and she would be left to deal with the boys on her own. Toni felt no cleverer than the youngsters she was supposed to be in charge of and she always felt that she had been unable to provide them with the disciplined and secure family atmosphere young children require. All three sons – Brian, Kevin and Andy – would battle at some point against chemical and alcohol abuse and to this day, Toni Wood holds herself responsible for the history of drug dependency in her family.

Growing up being allowed to do pretty much as he pleased, Andy Wood spent most of his teens hanging out with a circle of like-minded young Bainbridge mascara tykes, usually passing around joints or indulging in 'beer and keg parties' at the home of his best friend, Regan Hagar, playing the same albums over and over – anything by Queen, Kiss, Aerosmith or Elton John – and thinking up cool names for the ultimate rock band. It was the Seventies, back when sex was supposed to be free and drugs meant enlightenment and Andy Wood grew up drinking, toking, tooting and poking anything his grimy teen-sage heart took a fancy to.

His next older brother up, Kevin Wood, remembers an Andy who was always 'running around singing . . . trying out stage moves in the mirror'.[3] Andy had grown up a big sports fan – he was always an ardent Dallas Cowboys football fan – but from the age of eleven, his 'main event' was always rock music, rock stars and how to go about becoming a rock star. David Wood had to work very hard with his errant son to get him to stay on at high school. 'He almost didn't graduate . . . He couldn't see how anything they had to teach him could help his singing career and in rock 'n' roll.'[4] But graduate Andy did, with the not inconsiderable help of his father and several private tutors, in 1984.

'Andy was always a performer,' sighed his father. 'When he was about ten his uncle gave him a microphone that transmitted through the radio. He'd go around after dinner interviewing everyone in the family.'[5] Kevin Wood recalled the night in 1977 he took his baby brother to see Kiss at the local Coliseum. 'The opening act was Cheap Trick [and] right after the set Andy turned to me and said, "I want to be a rock star." I looked at him and said, "Yeah, I want to be a rock star, too," and that was pretty much it from then on.'[6]

2

Kevin and Andy decided the best way to get started was by most of all sticking together. Andy would be the outrageous singer, of course, and Kevin his trusty co-conspirator and guitarist. There was just the two of them to begin with and as Kevin was already fairly adept on the guitar, Andy took occasional piano lessons and harassed his father into loaning him the money for a cheap second-hand bass. Thus equipped, the brothers recorded the first of several 'Malfunkshun' tapes together in Andy's bedroom. Not long after, when Regan Hagar revealed that he had begun taking drum lessons, Malfunkshun stopped existing solely in the frenzied imaginations of the starstruck Wood brothers and became something like a real band. 'We played together for about eight years and people were always taken away by Andy,' Kevin recalled. 'He wore the most outrageous clothes he could find and he wore face-paint . . . He was insecure about playing when we first started, which is the reason he wore all of the face-paint, [but] you didn't really have to know how to play your instruments, you just had to have the guts to go out there and do it.'[7]

A connoisseur of masks and a skilled mimic, it wasn't long before

Andy had invented a whole new 'persona' for himself. In future, he told everybody, he wished to be known on stage as L'andrew. All the early flyers for Malfunkshun's earliest gigs contained the immortal line: *'L'andrew, mythical love child from Olympus, now resides in Seattle where he fronts a band called Malfunkshun . . .'* His aim, Andy said, was to turn Malfunkshun into a band that would transcend what he saw as the staid local metalcore scene in favour of a fresher, funkier, more futuristic rock sound. He even had a name for it: 'love rock', the most important component of which was something called '3-Power', a symbol of the trio's spiritual unity, he would say without blushing. 'We had a mission to spread the word of love,' Regan Hagar explained wryly, years later. 'We were the odd eccentrics because of that, the opposite of all the bands that were all heavy and Satanic.'[8]

'We were an anti-666 band because that's when the Satan thing was becoming really big,' Andy told *The Rocket* in his first proper press interview, in December 1986.[9] 'So we were a 333 band and did anti-devil songs. But it's just called "love rock" because we love to play it. I thought of what to call it today at work – we're a deranged gypsy hard rock band,' he boasted, joking and not joking. 'Love rock' was rooted in the Seventies with its flamboyant funk edge, roaring big-gig guitars and bitchy glam vocals. Andy would smile and nod his head approvingly when Malfunkshun was compared to the New York Dolls, but it was always more for the look than the Dolls' own peculiar brand of collapsible punk pop. Andy wanted Malfunkshun to be tight; he wanted it to work.

While his usual street clothes consisted more often than not of plain tracksuit pants and an old football jersey, his long blond hair which he had not cut since 1981 coyly hidden in a ponytail and baseball cap, Andy Wood's best live performances were the ones where he pranced around in a ripped fur coat, sporting unfeasibly large sunglasses and strangely shaped hats. Andy admired and adored the pop showmen who knew what it meant to be glamorous, no matter how unpromising their surroundings . . . Freddie Mercury, Marc Bolan, David Bowie, Prince, Elton John . . . these were the stars Andrew Wood aspired to explore and emulate. No stage was too small, no venue too modest for L'andrew the Love Child.

One night he performed in a bar dotted with less than twenty people in attendance and so he began by pretending there was an invisible balcony on one wall, which he serenaded and addressed throughout the entire performance in his raspy, sing-talk style, not dissimilar to that of a pint-size David Lee Roth, self-regarding and deeply nervous. 'How you people doin' up there in the balcony?' he called out ecstatically to his invisible fans. 'I robbed the theatre department in my high school and one night Kevin and I were playing with all the make-up I'd stolen,' Andy recalled with glee. 'The first face I put on, I decided this is it. We were the only band who looked like that at the time . . . We'd come out with our wild hair and make-up and people thought we were a novelty comedy band.'[10]

But what made Malfunkshun big, as they say, is what unfortunately kept them small. Their homemade contribution to the same *Deep Six* compilation that Green River first appeared on (an early Andy Wood pulpit-thumper – and the only surviving Malfunkshun recording from those days – called 'With Yo Heart Not Yo Hands') was, he confided in that first interview with *The Rocket*, about taking heroin and catching hepatitis. All too aptly named, all three members of Malfunkshun owned up to drug problems at various times. Andy announced that it had been only a few months since he and the others had shaken off the worst of their addictions. Wise to the allure an illicit four-letter word like 'drug' confers on any rock personage, he also stressed that it was OK to print that.

It is generally reckoned amongst the people he knew best in those days that Andy Wood began taking drugs intravenously the year after his graduation from Bainbridge High. He had begun seeing a lot of a new girl he had met who came from Seattle. It was assumed amongst his closest friends that it was she who introduced Andy to the dubious pleasure of mainlining cocaine and heroin in the summer of 1985. Andy was not yet twenty, and according to Kevin Wood his brother's shooting habit was soon so out of control he had track marks up and down both arms. When his new dopefriend returned to Seattle, Andy insisted on following her but his stay was brief and not in the least pleasant. Within weeks he had contracted a severe case of hepatitis after injecting heroin into his veins with infected syringes – 'dirty needles' – and he had returned, tail dragging on the ground, to stay at his father's home on Bainbridge Island while he recuperated from the illness. Alarmed at the sight of his stricken son – Andy's eyes and skin had turned a sickeningly bright yellow, his jaundiced body terribly thin and bowed – David Wood eventually persuaded him to check into the casualty department of nearby Cabrini Hospital. He later told friends that his son had gone in voluntarily but it's clear that Andy had been left with little choice at that point, not unless he wanted to die . . .

3

Originally, following the break-up of Green River, Stone Gossard and Jeff Ament had talked about moving down to Los Angeles. They felt they had played Seattle out. They had saved a little money and would have done it if they hadn't started thinking seriously about Andy Wood first – the singer they had seen in Malfunkshun who dressed like a cross between a biker and Ziggy Stardust. By then, of course, Andy Wood had well and truly made his presence felt on the select Seattle club scene. He always incited a response; audiences either loved or hated Malfunkshun. Seldom did anyone come away from their high-octane performances indifferent.

After eight years, however, Andy was starting to believe Malfunkshun had run its course, and had begun to give occasional performances simply on his own around Seattle's clubs and bars. Billed ostentatiously as 'L'andrew the Love Child', Andy's solo shows were unusual, precariously balanced showcases for his moon-age piano ballads, multi-tracked taped backing tracks, and increasingly larger doses of his over-achieving stage personality. He was a prince on-stage, regal as a brothel keeper, seduced by his own nefarious beauty, constantly flirting with the audience, building their expectations up for the next moment of hoped for 'outrage'. But not so out there as to forget to tell them where they could pick up a cassette of original 'solo' acoustic material he had put together in his bedroom, and which the Love Child advertised and sold sporadically as a mail-order item. 'Andy had a very giddy charm,' said Stone. 'He was always so funny, so disarming, that it was hard not to like the guy. He was totally captivating . . .'[11]

Although he recognized that the opportunity he was being offered represented a big step forward for himself, Andy was unsure at first what to do. As Mark Arm would later write of his successor, 'I think he felt he was ditching his brother Kevin . . . [But] no matter how great they were – and they were often amazing live, as well as pretty awful sometimes – Malfunkshun weren't exactly the most easy-listening band.'[12] Disillusioned by his failure to find a band to play in after Green River broke up, Alex Vincent eventually gave up the idea of being a drummer and turned his back on the music business altogether. The last anybody had heard of him he was working in the darkness at a local Seattle cinema. But guitarist Bruce Fairweather was still around and willing to give it another shot under a different name. So to begin with, the new drummer was going to be Regan Hagar. But that was always more Andy's idea than Regan's and soon Jeff and Stone were calling on another well-known Seattle scene-stealer from those days, Greg Gilmore, who had drummed in Ten Minute Warning and just then recently returned from Tibet. Jeff credited Greg with getting the new band members to clarify their musical direction, defining what was important to them as a band.

All of which only made Andy feel even worse about finally leaving Malfunkshun behind. Most of all, it meant leaving Kevin behind. His way around the problem was typical of Andy Wood. Green River had been the best-known band then crowding the underground Seattle scene and Andy wasn't about to pass up his chance to become better known. But Andy swore to Kevin that once he was a success, which naturally he was convinced he would be before too long, he would return to help get his brother's career off the ground properly.

At first Mother Love Bone (Andy thought up the new name – a snatch from his lyrics to 'Capricorn Sister', one of the first songs he wrote with Stone – while working at his day job as a delivery driver) kept themselves out of the spotlight. The most openly eccentric and almost proudly self-indulgent of all the Seattle bands from that time (including Mudhoney, whose self-conscious anti-star trip too often got in the way of a good tune), a little like early Guns N' Roses, only more deliberately psychedelic, but easily as tongue-in-ear as The Cult, 'We knew what we wanted to do,' said Bruce Fairweather. 'It took about two or three months to really gel, but once it started getting together it took off really quickly. We were really prolific with the songwriting.'[13]

Andy wrote all the lyrics and collaborated on the music. 'Any word Andy liked he'd work into a lyric in some strange way. He was a very amusing guy, constantly putting on a show. He's absolutely one of my favourite lyricists of all time. If he could have been anybody, he'd have loved to have been Freddy Mercury,' said Stone.[14] 'Our songwriting perspective was – make things weird enough to interest ourselves, but if they didn't groove let them go,' said Jeff. 'We knew it would take a while for people to get where we're coming from – there was always a lot of tongue-in-cheek stuff. Anybody who took us – and especially Andy – seriously could be seriously offended.'[15]

4

Once he'd got used to his new surroundings, Andy's performances with Mother Love Bone started to catch fire. Assuming the role of a finger-pointing fire-and-brimstone-preaching minister of love, the stage his sky-wide pulpit, Andy would relentlessly pitch his audiences on the importance and redemptive power of love. No one ever really knew if he was kidding or not. One of their first shows was at the gaudy Kent Skate Ring, a wonderfully appropriate place to launch the new band . . . a touch Seventies, somewhat seedy and debauched, but a magnificently lurking sense of humour. In Mother Love Bone, Andy Wood finally came into his own as an artist. He left behind the white-faced stage persona of L'andrew and became, in his words, plain Andy Wood, 'world's greatest rock 'n' roll frontman!' At his most relaxed in front of an audience with his new band, he catwalked around the stages of Seattle's few nightspots like he was already striding the big arenas, which in his head he always was.

'Andrew Wood had so much presence to him on stage,' says Kate Ellison, music director and local music coordinator of Seattle radio station KXRX, who was too young to go to clubs when Green River were happening but remembers her one and only glimpse of Andy Wood and Mother Love Bone vividly. 'He had the audience in the palm of his hand, and people were just awe-struck by his ambience.' 'All that was very exciting. In fact, that . . . was the moment when I think everyone began to realize that something very big would happen,' remembers Gene Stout, music writer for the *Seattle Post-Intelligencer*. 'Andy Wood, he had the charisma, the showmanship, to be somebody. So at that point I started paying attention to the band because there was a long point after that when nothing happened . . .'

In fact, Mother Love Bone played less than a dozen gigs together in 1988, most of them at the Central Tavern, which had recently begun featuring live music more prominently again, before they were signed by Polygram Records in November. Realizing better than anyone that they wouldn't be able to play enough gigs in Seattle to keep things moving and keen to capitalize on the posthumous attention Green River's *Rehab Doll* album was getting, they had resolved to make a demo and send out as many tapes as possible. The immediate aim was to try and get some shows in LA, hoping as always that someone influential would see them and help them take things further.

'I thought this woman who worked at Slash Records, who I'd met a couple of times, could maybe help us get some shows. So I sent her a tape, and like two days later she calls up at nine in the morning, screaming over the phone that she loves the tape,' remembered Jeff. 'I didn't know what to think because people in those positions can say, "I really love your band, I think you're the greatest," and then you never hear from them again . . . But in this case she kept calling me all week, every day.'[16] Jeff's contact at Slash Records was Anna Statman, who had worked as a junior rep in the A&R department. While at Slash, Statman had been involved with the signing of the Bo Deans, the Del Fuegos and the Violent Femmes. By the time Jeff had contacted her again, though, Statman had left Slash to begin working in the A&R department at Geffen. So suddenly it was Geffen Records that was calling Jeff Ament and yelling at him about how great his tape was – a horse of a very different colour indeed. This was big time.

Frustrated in her earlier attempts to sign Soundgarden, Statman was determined to move quickly on this one. Thinking quickly, she called up an old acquaintance, Kelly Curtis, then working at Mark Allen Productions in Seattle, to see if he would go with her to see the band at an upcoming date they had scheduled for The Vogue. Curtis was by then already familiar with the Mother Love Bone name because the ever-thorough Ament had already sent a tape to his office. The timing – next to luck, the most important ingredient in any success story – could not have been more perfect. Curtis, who had worked during the early Eighties as personal assistant to Heart, the only arena-sized, locally-based Seattle act in those days, was about to take the leap into independent management along with his colleague

Susan Silver, who had just begun to look after the business affairs of Soundgarden.

The photographer Ross Halfin remembers that Kelly Curtis 'basically did the PR for Heart, like if you wanted a photo pass you dealt with him' and that 'he was always very charming, but distant, you know'. Curtis's initial involvement with Mother Love Bone was equally courteous but arm's length. 'We weren't originally intending to work with each other as a management thing,' Kelly admitted. 'I wasn't that interested in it and I didn't think the band was that excited about having me do it. But we were willing to help them out and . . . as things started to progress it worked out, it clicked.'[17]

Statman, accompanied by Curtis and Silver, met up with the band for the first time backstage at The Vogue, where Statman told them she had liked what she'd seen enough to offer Mother Love Bone $5,000 to record another, more professional demo-tape, from which, Statman suggested, Geffen would be in a position to base a favourable offer of a deal to the band. Time was booked at Lawson Studios – the same 24-track studio where the *Rehab Doll* sessions had taken place – in Seattle in June 1988. Kelly Curtis, in his role of 'acting manager', flew down with the band to LA in early July, ostensibly to hear what Geffen thought of the new tape and to begin negotiations on the band's behalf with company president Ed Rosenblatt.

While in LA, Curtis and the band 'worked the building', calling in personally on agents, publicists and well-known music industry attorneys. As their legal counsel they retained Stan Diamond, who then represented, amongst others, Iggy Pop and David Bowie. Pleased with their first meeting with Geffen and the new contacts they had established, fledgeling band and manager returned to Seattle at the end of the week waiting for what they thought would be a first-draft contract from Geffen.

5

What happened next depends on who you ask. Whether it was merely the original batch of tapes Jeff had sent out in his initial hunt for gigs, or the combination of that and the endless networking they embarked on while in LA, but word was suddenly going around that Geffen was on to something hot and overnight every musclehead A&R shark in LA looking to score points wanted to talk to Mother Love Bone. The band's next two gigs at the Central looked more like an annual record company convention. 'Suddenly people were flying up here to take the band to dinner who had no idea as to what it was about,' Kelly said. 'They heard I don't know what . . . but this was not the type of band that was going to sign with the big schmooze guy.'[18]

At which point, the band's relationship with Geffen began to cool before quickly breaking down into open hostility. The problem, as Kelly Curtis saw things, went back to when Anne Statman had been obliged to hand over responsibility for negotiations to her boss, Tom Zutaut (the man who signed Guns N' Roses and okayed the Nirvana bid). 'At first he wasn't sure he would sign us, then he was sure, and then he wasn't again,' Kelly huffed. 'Geffen never really made an offer until mid-September on the street outside the Central.' By which time it was, he said, 'a whole new ball game'. There were a lot of other labels there to see the band for the first time that night. 'We felt we owed it to all these people who had come up to listen to their rap. The last time we talked to Zutaut we told him we were calling him in a week; we called to tell him we were signing and we never heard back from him.'[19]

'Their britches became too large for their body very quickly,' a heated Geffen source complained to *The Rocket*. 'They tried to get as many labels, as many booking agents, as many scum-bag parasitic people as there are in this business, to be as interested in this band as possible and they blew the whole thing out of proportion.'[20] After that, there began what Andy laughingly dubbed 'the Mother Love Bone Restaurant Tour' during which he and the band met extensively with reps from as many major labels as wanted to know. Geffen, Island, Capitol, A&M, Polygram and Atlantic all actively sought out the signatures of the band at some point in 1988, a situation which resulted in a mini-bidding war the ever-smiling Kelly Curtis did nothing to discourage. Whether Mother Love Bone were really as good as they kept telling everyone they were was neither here nor there. Less than twelve months after forming, the band was in the ultimate position of power, choosing whose calls to return, whose expense account to dine out on.

The man whose calls they did finally return were those of Michael Goldstone, then the newest gun in the Polygram Records A&R department, and after a seemingly endless round of lunches, meetings and midnight discussions, Mother Love Bone signed a lucrative seven-album contract with Polygram Records on November 19, 1988. The deal was for a reported advance of over $250,000, making it one of the year's largest signings and a record for a local Seattle act. Critics and industry insiders alike viewed the news very much as the Northwest's entry into that year's Guns N' Roses sweepstakes and they were not far off the mark.

Goldstone and the band agreed that an EP ostensibly marketed as being on the band's own indie label, released prior to their major-label album début, would have the double benefit of being a good cheap ice-breaker for the first-time buyers out there and adding a bit of much-needed street cred to their image: it didn't do to give the impression that they had merely been scooped up and sucked into the record company sausage-machine. 'It was important to let the world know that there was more to these schmucks than bucks,' as one Polygram employee inelegantly but accurately put it. So during Thanksgiving weekend 1988, Mother Love Bone began work on their first record at London Bridge Studios, in Seattle, with former AC/DC producer Mike Dearnly flying the faders.

Shine, as the five-track EP was called, was timed for release in March 1989, when they would embark on a gruelling forty-date tour, opening some nights for the Dogs D'Amour – 'English drink rock,'[21] Jeff christened it – headlining their own shows the closer they got to the Northwest. Packed inside a van, hitting spots from Boston to New York and back to Seattle via Washington, DC. Meantime, Mother Love Bone ended 1988 continuing to hike good local gigs where and when they could, opening for Jane's Addiction at The Paramount in November and then headlining the *Backlash* first anniversary party at the Central Tavern the following month.

6

The only fly in the ointment remained Andy's strange and unpredictable nocturnal habits. Like a lot of junkies, Andy loved to convert non-junkies occasionally. One of his many girlfriends from those days, Wendy Watson, claims that, early in 1989, Andy Wood introduced her to heroin. Andy would drive over to her apartment, she said, and Wendy would phone a dealer and arrange to have the smack delivered like pizza. Or when that didn't work she'd find herself, at Andy's behest, dealing direct with the lowlifes of First Avenue and Pike Street, the quickest and most dangerous score of all. Once Wendy brought the stuff home, Andy would cook it up in the spoon in front of her but would always turn his back when he came to actually taking a shot.

One long hot summer night in 1989, Wendy spotted a stoned Andy weaving around with some of his junkie friends at the Central. He claimed he had run into them on his way to a band meeting and that they had asked him if he'd wanted to get loaded. Andy, of course, did not believe in just saying no. He made Wendy cross her heart and promise not to tell anyone that she'd seen him. Later that same night as they sat together in a corner café, sipping espresso and chainsmoking, Andy looked at her and said self-pityingly, 'I bet you don't know why we do it.' Wendy thought she did. 'Oh yeah? Why?' Andy scrutinized her. 'Because there's so many feelings. You don't have to deal with the hurt. It's just so easy to do heroin and not feel.' There was a pause while he appeared to be listening to something Wendy could not hear, or waiting for some signal inside to turn from green to red, perhaps. 'So you do understand,'[22] he whispered, at length.

7

Elsewhere in Seattle in 1989, things were not standing still, either. Word was out. When The Cult played the Seattle Arena over the New Year's holidays, singer Ian Astbury ended the show by telling the audience: 'Seattle, you've got the best bands in the country right now! Mother Love Bone, Soundgarden and Mudhoney! Get out and see 'em and support 'em!' he cried to deafening cheers. Meanwhile, Bruce Pavitt was flying in music journalists from England and telling them all the same thing: Sub Pop and Mudhoney were 'the true heirs of mid-Sixties Northwest punk'.[23] Mark Arm and Steve Turner had certainly gotten off to a mud-flying start. While Mother Love Bone were learning to do the dance of masks with the multi-faced major record companies, Mudhoney released their first six-track EP, *Superfuzz Bigmuff*, on Sub Pop in October 1988; the first run of a thousand came with a free poster and later editions were released in 'splattered purple' vinyl.

Even after Mother Love Bone had announced their record-breaking deal with Polygram, Arm and Turner continued to enjoy a higher public profile, Mudhoney's fortunes continuing to rise when they formed a mutual appreciation society with Sonic Youth, supporting them on their 'Daydream Nation' tour, and even appearing together on Sub Pop's first single of 1989; a double A-side featuring Mudhoney covering the Youth's 'Halloween', and Sonic Youth returning the favour by tackling 'Touch Me, I'm Sick'.

Over at Sub Pop, the inauguration of the much-cherished 'Singles Club', in October 1988, was a major turning point for the still struggling label. An idea that would soon be taken up by every other wild-minded rock indie the world over, the Singles Club began as an occasional series of album-length collections of 12-inch singles from the multifarious artists Sub Pop were then becoming involved with. They even sold subscriptions, like *Reader's Digest*; sprinkling each edition with high-profile bands not necessarily all on the Sub Pop roster, tempting potential buyers and subscribers with the usual small, limited runs and polychromatic vinyl. As a result, Nirvana's 'Love Buzz', the first ever Sub Pop Singles Club release, is currently worth £150 complete with its original numbered sleeve – if you can find anyone desperate enough to want to part with it. (Collectors should beware that bootlegs of this single have been manufactured in America and the UK, though domestic fakes are relatively easy to identify, with slightly blurred sleeves, glossier labels and no attempt to number the edition.)

The logic was simple: within twelve months, most Singles Club releases were limited to five thousand copies. With five thousand members paying $35 a year to join (with a few 'taster' copies going into the stores) Sub Pop would realize approximately $175,000 in up-front, interest-free capital. Indeed, it was singles – those seven-inch slabs of buzz and wonder that all the major American labels had just decided to stop issuing because they were now, post-CD, judged 'unprofitable' – that not only kept Sub Pop in business in those early hand-to-mouth days, but were what helped to define the anti-mainstream image Sub Pop coincidentally wanted to manufacture. According to Daniel House, Sub Pop 'almost single-handedly man-aged to revitalize interest in independent singles'.[24] There was also an increasing number of records released by Sub Pop from bands outside the Northwest region, and Singles Club releases included Cincinnati's Afghan Whigs, and Rapeman from Chicago (Steve Albini's first post-Big Black combo) . . . a partial response to popular perceptions of what the 'Sub Pop Sound' actually was, according to Jonathan Poneman, who said he intended 'to mess with that a little'.[25]

8

But the main focus of attention, as always, remained right on their own doorstep, in Seattle. After Mudhoney, Soundgarden and Mother Love Bone, the next hottest name in Seattle at this time was Alice In Chains, who opened for Mother Love Bone when they celebrated the release of *Shine* with a show at the newly opened Oz club, in April 1989. The origins of Alice In Chains go back to the night vocalist Layne Staley was introduced to guitarist Jerry Cantrell by some mutual acquaintances and ended up offering him a place to crash. Cantrell, son of a Vietnam war vet, and an all-American extra-cheese-with-everything rock-and-sports fan, instantly sized up his new acquaintance as a likely looking recruit to the band he was then trying to get off the ground. Staley, who was fronting his own funk-metal outfit at the time, was reluctant to commit himself at first but allowed himself to be pulled into a 'side project' with the guitarist, whose outward-bound enthusiasm contrasted perfectly with Staley's own broodingly introspective character.

They formed a 'joke band' together and called it Fuck, mainly so that at gigs they could hand out condoms to the crowd marked 'Fuck The Band'. Ho, uh, ho . . . By the beginning of 1989, the joke band had stopped being funny and so they changed their name to Alice In Chains; a more consumer-friendly moniker that perfectly mirrored the band's gothic, manacled-but-unrepentant attitude. Indeed, it was the band's name as much as their music that caught the attention of the fly-eyed A&R men from LA and New York who had already begun to descend on Seattle in 1989. Alice's first attempt to impress an invited audience of record company big wheels almost finished them. 'We were all on coke, high as hell,' Cantrell recalled years later. 'So Layne comes out with this fuckin' Mohawk and this punk jacket. And the first line of one of our songs is, "You say you don't like the way we look, fuck off!" So Layne does it and the label people said, "All right" and walked out.'[26]

All except Nick Terzo, A&R man for the giant Columbia Records, who duly signed the band to the label in 1989. They recorded and released their first album, *Facelift*, and for the next two years toured with anyone that would have them – Iggy Pop, Slayer, Anthrax, Bonham, Megadeth, Extreme. The album slowly went gold; a year later it was platinum . . .

And then there was Tad. The Meat Loaf of Grunge as he too quickly became known was originally from Boysie, Washington. Tad Doyle first rolled into Seattle as drummer for avant jazz-punks H Hour. The group were booked to play by Jonathan Poneman in his pre-Sub Pop radio programmer days. Now Tad fronted his own band whose début Sub Pop album, *God's Balls*, was choked with song titles like 'Sex God Missy (Lumberjack Mix)', 'Pork Chop' and 'Satan's Chainsaw'. Tad was a joke but one told in a very loud voice by a lunatic that delights in growling 'muthafucker' every third word . . . A butcher by trade ('There's nothing bad about it. It's kinda pleasurable, the feel of keen metal cutting into raw flesh'), Tad actually went to college to learn music theory. 'I'm sophisticated,'[27] he would grunt. He wasn't.

So far, however, the reputation for having 'cool bands' hadn't translated into concrete successes like Top 40 chart placings (aside from college charts) or six-figure record sales, both of which local heavy metal outfits like Queensryche (a million plus for their 1988 *Operation: Mindcrime* album) or Metal Church (over five hundred thousand for *Blessing In Disguise*) managed to achieve as a matter of course. All told, by the middle of 1989, The Young Fresh Fellows were the best-selling independent Seattle-based band, with around fifteen thousand copies sold of their eponymous début album, and they weren't even on Sub Pop. Green River's *Rehab Doll* had notched up about a third of that amount (including cassettes); Mudhoney's 'Touch Me, I'm Sick' single had sold a modest three and a half thousand, and Soundgarden's 'Screaming Life' EP a shade more at about four thousand. Nobody was giving up their day jobs yet.

Shine had little to do with Sub Pop's genius-dumb aesthetic and much to do with traditional American big buck rock 'n' roll . . . yes, it appeared as though Polygram had signed The Next Guns N' Roses. Under the slick, tricksy production of Mike Dearnly, the five tracks on *Shine* paid homage to everyone from T. Rex ('Capricorn Sister' and 'Half Ass Monkey Boy') to the Red Hot Chili Peppers ('Thru Fade-away') and early Hanoi Rocks ('Mindshaker Meltdown'). But the stand-out cut was the eight minutes plus Wood opus, 'Chloe Dancer/ Crown Of Thorns', Andy's cigarette-stung vocals weaving like a blind man in a fire over a haunting marriage of piano and guitar. The one spot on the EP where the band took themselves seriously enough to come up with something genuinely moving, the personality and potential are unmistakable.

Mother Love Bone got the star treatment in two rock publications on the stands in the summer of 1989, both featuring lengthy interviews with Andy. The first, the *Alternative Press*, a Cleveland-area specialist publication, characterized Andy and Mother Love Bone as 'a motley assortment of blues-rock mystics' and called *Shine* an 'admittedly flawed approximation of a middle ground between marginally funky good-time guitar rock and outright psychedelia'. Andy is quoted as saying he had 'a total sore throat' while making the EP, while also revealing that he had written 'some of the best stuff I've ever written under the influence of marijuana'.[28]

Seconds, the New York based rock tabloid, called *Shine* 'almost a great record, possessing the inconsistencies of many young just-signed bands', and reported that 'there's lots of animosity toward them in their home town'.[29] Responding to the snide comments made about the apparent enormity of the band's deal with Polygram, Andy said, 'Especially in Seattle, people think we're millionaires now. The rumours are crazy.' All he said he wanted to do was make a living out of music. 'I don't ever want to have to get a job again. Washing dishes was hell, and I did a lot of that. We're all products of Seventies rock, and that's what's big right now, so we're gonna ride that train, hopefully to fame and fortune.'[30]

9

Mother Love Bone spent the late summer and early autumn of 1989 recording their first album, *Apple*, at The Plant in Sausalito, California. It was produced by Terry Date, whose work on Soundgarden's recently completed major-label début for A&M, *Louder Than Love*, had impressed them. While everybody was excited by the sounds that were beginning to emanate from the giant Plant speakers, it was during the recording sessions for *Apple* that it became apparent to the others that Andy was up to his old tricks again. When they returned home, Andy was once again persuaded to enter a treatment programme. It had been decided at a band meeting as soon as they got back to Seattle: with the album finished and tour dates being finalized, they needed Andy in good shape to make the thing work. The band would pay for Andy to undergo his second attempt at rehabilitation in five years, and through much of November and December 1989, Andy was incarcerated in Valley General Hospital Alcohol and Drug Recovery Center in nearby Monroe.

During his thirty-day stay there, Andy took to documenting his painful personal struggle, his insane cravings and the uncertain feelings that drove him into that state by filling pages and pages of a red spiral notepad with self-analytical poems and jagged surreal lyrics. He was a man 'angry too long', he wrote. A man that ran from his 'crippled state' and had 'locked emotions'. He confessed that he sucked his thumb while he wrote his songs and how now he toiled in 'toxic shame'. He saw his rehab programme, he wrote, as 'a new way to show love and a new way to feel', as a way of finally being able to 'pull off the mask' of his addiction.[31]

The most important relationship in Andy Wood's short but special life, after Mother Love Bone, was with his live-in girlfriend, Xana LaFuente. Like the sleeping beauty who awoke from her hundred years of sleep and promptly fell in love with the first person she clapped her bleary eyes on, Andy Wood met and fell in love with Xana LaFuente not long after he had been released from his first stay in a rehab clinic, at Cabrini Hospital in 1985. His dream girl, he often described her to his friends, one of whom had first told him about seeing a girl working in a downtown vintage-clothing store who perfectly matched Andy's oft-recited physical description of his ideal female companion: dark eyes, darker hair and the body of a cat. Andy didn't believe it but went to see for himself and a month later they had moved in together.

A bundle of camp energy with the ability to make her laugh or cry at the drop of a dope deal, Andy both delighted and dismayed Xana. She loved him and believed him when he told her about how one day soon he was going to take his 'love rock' to the top of the charts. But she deplored his drug use. It wasn't enough that he wanted to be constantly drunk and stoned, he wanted to take things much further, regularly scoring coke and eventually heroin, then snorting or injecting it in front of her. Worse, much as he craved the sensation, heavy drinking and doping always had a disturbing physical effect on his body. He got blotchy hives and trembled with sweat; he became bad-tempered and hyper-active or completely listless and still. And yet he always wanted more. Andy marvelled at his father, who could drink a single glass of beer and say enough. There was never enough of anything for Andy.

During one fight, he screamed at Xana, 'Haven't you learned yet? This is who I am. This is what I do!'[32] Then, when the gear had all gone up his nose or into his arm, when he was coming down and the remorse arrived like daylight after dark, he'd cry and beg for Xana's forgiveness. 'You're my only friend,' he would weep pathetically. 'The only one I can talk to . . . I want to stop! I don't know what to do!'[33] Then, a few days later, sometimes only a few hours later, tearful confession over with and forgiveness won, he'd slip out and score some more, only this time he'd take it somewhere else where Xana wouldn't be there to hassle him.

After another particularly nasty fight, Xana decided she'd had enough and actually moved out. She packed her things and caught a cab over to a friend's apartment. Later, regretting her haste, she returned. She was expecting an important phone call from her mother and Andy's number was the only one her family had. By four in the morning, Xana was dozing fitfully in a closet with the phone by her side when she was woken by the sound of Andy returning home. He had turned on all the lights and begun blasting out music from the stereo. Xana crept cautiously from the closet and snuck into the kitchen where she found Andy probing for a vein to shoot the coke he'd just scored into. Ashamed, he began crying and yelling that he was afraid Xana was going to take his stuff off him. On the contrary, she was fearful he might get violent if she tried such a thing; Andy wasn't known as a hitter but his mood-swings could be terrifying and unpredictable. She didn't know what to expect ever from Andy. It was part of his wicked charm, his attraction; and it was the reason he frightened her.

'Go ahead,' she cried. 'Do it in front of me! Show me how sick you are!'[34] So he did. Not just once but seven times that night. Andy had looked like a madman, she said, repeatedly plunging the needle into his arm and watching hypnotized as the syringe bloomed like an evil rose with his blood; the act as much a part of the kick as the effect of the injection itself.

10

Andy's first show clean for more than a year and practically his last ever appearance on stage with Mother Love Bone was at the tenth anniversary party for *The Rocket*, held at the Paramount Theater on December 29, just a week after Andy had left Valley General. The impressive line-up included Beat Happening, the Defenders, the Fastbacks, Girl Trouble, Mother Love Bone, the Posies, the

Walkabouts and the Young Fresh Fellows, and though still physically weak, Andy positively glowed on stage that night, making lyrics up as he went along, whipping the audience into a genuine fury.

Then, two weeks before *Apple*, the first and – not that anybody could have known it then – last album Mother Love Bone was to have been released, a strange and unexpected thing occurred. It was around 10.30 p.m., Friday, March 16, when Xana returned home to the Queen Anne apartment she shared with Andy. His car was parked outside but she had not expected to find him home. Andy was supposed to be meeting the band's new tour manager – a 'recovering addict' who specialized in road managing for musicians also 'in recovery' – over at Kelly Curtis' office that night. But when Curtis phoned, Andy cried off, claiming he was too ill to make it and suggesting they reschedule for some time the following week. But he wasn't ill; not in the sense that he'd given his manager to understand, anyway.

Whether it was the thought that once his new drug-wise tour manager was on the payroll there would be no getting away with any surreptitious 'occasional' joy-banging (one former addict unfailingly able to tell when another addict is even thinking about getting high) or whether it was merely the typical junky-logic of wanting to 'celebrate' four straight months without it, but whatever the reason the action was undeniable: Andy Wood took a drive out on his own to First Avenue and Pike Street that night and bought himself some heroin. There has never been any evidence to suggest that anybody else accompanied him on his final journey to the floating world. Indeed, it is more likely that he really did intend to make this a strictly private, one-off occurrence. As lapsed recovering junkies are inclined to think they can do, of course. Despite guidance from two drug-treatment programmes and despite keeping up his regular sessions with a therapist as well as attending weekly meetings of Narcotics Anonymous and Alcoholics Anonymous, Andy Wood had relapsed after exactly a hundred and sixteen days, clean and sober.

The apartment was strangely quiet as Xana closed the door behind her that night. The lights were on but there was no music or TV blaring; unusual for Andy. She called out to him that she was home but there was no reply. For a moment she thought maybe he had gone out after all. Then she walked into the bedroom. Andy was lying face-down and unconscious on the bed, his arms sprawled out at his sides in a grotesque mock-crucifixion pose. At first, Xana simply did not believe what she was seeing and she tried to wake him. When she noticed the blood oozing from his lips and the blue tinge of his expressionless face, she ran to the phone and called for an ambulance. Thirty minutes later Andy's comatose body had been rushed to nearby Harborview Medical Center. Later, at the hospital, waiting for news of his condition, Xana told David Wood that there had been a fresh needle mark on his son's arm and an empty syringe on the floor next to the bed. Later, she would find Andy's favourite T-shirt mysteriously ripped to pieces in the washing-machine. Nothing made sense.

For all his vivacity and apparent cleverness, Andy, it seems, had fallen for the oldest junky trick in the book that Friday night, when he filled the spoon with not much less than he had the last time he'd had a shot four months before, at a time when his habit was so severe he was shooting up three or four times a day. The effect of the powerful opiate on his newly clean metabolism was instant. Andy lay motionless in a coma, barely breathing, for the rest of the weekend. Without the artificial aid of the hospital's life-support systems, the doctors told his horrified family, Andy would have been dead already. The chances of his ever coming out of the coma were, they said, almost non-existent. His brain had been starved of oxygen for too long before he had been admitted to Harborview, and they estimated that if Andy did ever regain consciousness, he would be mentally handicapped, in all probability little more than a vegetable, for the rest of his life.

After wrestling with their emotions for three days, Toni and David Wood gave their permission to the doctors at Harborview to switch off the life-support systems on the afternoon of Monday, March 19, 1990, three days after Andy's fatal last fix. As a mark of love and respect for the 'hard-rock gypsy' life their son had chosen to live, the lights were lowered in the hospital room where he lay, the way Andy always liked them to be when he was relaxing or making music, and a cassette of Queen's *A Night At The Opera* was played on a portable ghetto-blaster. Everybody in the room – his family, his band and his girlfriend – stood around his bed holding hands and cried as the doctors pulled the plugs. Andy died peacefully, still asleep and no doubt dreaming the dream, the same afternoon. Andy Wood – 'world's greatest rock 'n' roll frontman!' – was just twenty-four years old.

11

In the last year of his life, Toni Wood had begun the habit of passing self-help books and self-awareness tapes that she herself had found useful on to her son. 'I'm not totally together now,' she admitted. '[But] I could relate that [Andy] was fighting a battle that I was beginning to win.'[35] During his last ever conversation with his mother, Andy agreed to see his therapist with her for a joint session, which they had provisionally scheduled for March 20, the day after he died. Toni Wood had gone to her bed that night thinking, 'I can save that beautiful boy.'[36]

Almost a thousand faces, most of whom neither the band, Xana, nor the huddled Wood family would have been able to put even a first name to, attended a memorial service held for the deceased singer the following Saturday evening, March 24, at the Paramount Theater, in Seattle; the scene of so many of Andy's real and imagined triumphs. Dr Richard Fields, the Valley General consultant who had overseen Andy's latest rehabilitation programme, agreed to get up and speak briefly on substance abuse; some of Andy's more reflective songs were played; donations were collected for an anti-drug video; and David Wood also got up to utter a brief eulogy of his own to his son's memory.

Friends still insist that Andrew Wood was no junky. Junkies are desperate people; out of luck and out of time. They shoot up every day and their deaths are preordained. 'There was a great deal of pressure on Andy,' Xana pointed out. 'He had me counting on him for things to work out with us. He also had the band counting on him to stay sober and he had Polygram, his family and his friends counting on him also.'[37] 'He was never a junkie,' Regan Hagar insisted. 'He liked getting high because it made him float that much higher, maybe, than life already did, and he really did like to float.'[38] Andy's death was accidental, they insisted. David Wood disagreed. Barely able to speak through his grief into the microphone at the Paramount, he began by wishing his son's bandmates every success, urging them to go on television and have hit records. Fighting back tears, he said the best thing they could now do was to find themselves a new singer. 'But whatever you do,' he sobbed, 'make sure he's not a junky.'

'There were tons of people there who didn't know him, who were just, like, fans, and that were coming up to me and saying that they knew how I felt and how awful it was. It was really ridiculous,'[39] sighed Soundgarden vocalist Chris Cornell, whose apartment Andy had crashed at for months at a time when he first moved to Seattle. 'They didn't know how I felt, they didn't know anything. They were just rock fans, basically, going to a show ... The idea that Andy was perfect, you know, is pretty laughable. I mean, he had a lot of serious problems, like we all do. But something about a person dying, especially someone from the entertainment industry, always elevates who they were and what they did into this other space.'[40]

Stone admitted his own outlook on all forms of drug use had changed dramatically since Andy's death. 'When one of your closest friends dies, you have these feelings about your own limitations as a human being. It's frightening. At the same time it makes you confront things in your own life ... The whole process has been one where it's made me say, "Fuck if that's going to happen to me." That's the main thing ... aside from the total tragedy of losing my best friend.'[41]

'The only thing about drugs and rock 'n' roll that I ever really knew for sure about and noticed and understood was back when guys like Andy were getting into it,' said Chris. 'I've seen a lot of guys in music doing it because they thought that was part of how you became a rock star. That's definitely why Andy started doing drugs. He was that guy and that's all he wanted to be.'[42] Stone's outlook was perhaps the most philosophical: 'I don't think [Andy's death] was inevitable at all. Everyone was aware that Andy had a drug problem. He had been fighting it for as long as we knew him ... He just broke down. Sometimes you break down and get bad heroin – and that's it. Andy always knew he was an addict and it was never anything that he thought was cool. He really felt ashamed of it ... it wasn't very glamorous.'[43]

As Jeff said, 'Andy was a troubled guy. He tried to hide it from us, say he'd cleaned up his act and then he wouldn't turn up at rehearsals. Andy just turned to drugs to get away from the pressure of it all ... I've always been against hard drugs but Andy's death did affect me. I wouldn't stand up and preach about it, it's like telling a kid not to pinch cookies, as soon as your back's turned he'll be there! I'll just say there are other ways of education in more creative ways.'[44]

Film director Cameron Crowe and his wife, the Heart songstress

Nancy Wilson, had been close to Kelly Curtis for many years and were amongst the first people he turned to the day Andy died. 'Cars lined the street,' Crowe later recalled in a piece he wrote for *Rolling Stone*. 'Inside were Andy Wood's friends, bandmates and members of other bands throughout the city and still they kept on arriving.' Acquaintances for the most part more than friends, in the coming years many of the musicians in that room, some then just barely out of their teens, would see success far beyond their dreams; beyond even the arena-filling dreams of Andy Wood. 'But that night it was mostly about staying warm, pulling together,' wrote Crowe. 'And I thought about Los Angeles where musicians would have already slipped demo tapes into Kelly's pocket.'[45]

On Tuesday, March 27, eight days after his death, the King County Medical Examiner's Division made it official when they announced that the death of Andrew Wood had resulted from an acute and accidental overdose of heroin. There were no suspicious circumstances involved, they added. Dying, it seems, like singing and writing, was one of those rare things Andy Wood could do all on his own. And of course, he still managed to draw a crowd doing it. The irony would no doubt have brought a smile to his painted lips.

12

When Andrew Wood died so did Mother Love Bone. 'It wasn't openly discussed right away. When your friend is lying there in a coma you're thinking a million thoughts,' said Stone. 'The situation right now is, Mother Love Bone is not going to be around any more. There's no reason to continue with the name . . . What we stood for is on [*Apple*] and I'm not going to try and recreate what made us great with some other singer. I'm not into it. When something is over you've got to let it die.'[46] Or as *The Rocket*'s editor and publisher, Charles R. Cross, puts it: 'Mother Love Bone was a great group that gained a lot of local attention and they had a really unique sound but a *lot* of that was Andrew Wood. It wasn't like anybody saw Mother Love Bone and talked about any of the other guys in the group.'

'Mother Love Bone as a band is history,' agreed Jeff. 'Us going out and using the name, pretending in a sense that Andy's still there, was never even a consideration. As far as us going on in another musical direction and starting something new, that's definitely being looked at, with at least some of the remaining members. Me and Stone aren't trying to force the next step . . . I'm really proud of what we did and just from Andy's end of it, people should know that he existed, that he made critical music for critical times . . . [But] getting out on the road as a band and promoting it with a singer pretending to be Andy would be a terrible waste. It would be just total prostitution.'[47]

From a purely fan-worshipping point of view, the sad part is that *Apple*, when it was finally released in July 1990, proved that underneath all the overhanging scarves and low-slung attitude, Mother Love Bone were more than capable of wringing fresh and startling ideas from the heard-it-all-before grunt-speak of hard rock. What stuck in Stone's mind most after Andy's death, he said, were tracks like the bombastic send-up 'Stardog Champion', or the thrillingly self-parodic 'This Is Shangrila', Andy turning the room cold as he begs, *'Doncha die on me, babe . . .'* And 'maybe "Heartshine" and "Man Of Golden Words" . . . I've always been a huge fan of Andy's lyrics. They're vague, but at the same time, very colourful and imagery-conscious. He could really hit you with emotion.'[48]

Of course, the 'world's greatest rock 'n' roll frontman' eats up hard rockers like the revamped 'Capricorn Sister' or 'Holy Roller' (with its humorous 'love rock rap' tacked on to the end) and spits them out in kiss-shaped thought-bubbles. But where the love child really excelled was on slower, more enigmatic tracks like the mournful and grandiose 'Bone China' ('Andy's [Marc] Bolan tribute,' according to Jeff[49]), 'Stargazer', Andy deadpanning cutely over a tittering country twang, or better still, 'Man Of Golden Words', whose theatrical *'words and music – my only tools . . .'* refrain could have been penned by Andy as his own epitaph. Best of all though was still 'Crown Of Thorns', regrettably shorn of the original 'Chloe Dancer' passage that preludes it on *Shine*, but still smoking with an incandescent flash that lingers long after the track has slunk off back to whatever sad corner it had crept out of.

There were plenty of other great moments on the album – stink-fingered grooves like 'Half Ass Monkey Boy', or 'Captain Hi-Top', 'a Zodiac-Mindwarp-meets-Magic-Johnson tribute', according to Jeff[50]

– but none quite as transcendent as 'Crown Of Thorns'. It is perhaps Andrew Wood's greatest, most revealing moment. Proof that he had a greater grasp of his own predicament than anybody.

13

The question everybody always asks, of course, is: would Mother Love Bone have been as big and as popular as Pearl Jam have become? Would Andrew Wood have had the *impact* of the guy who replaced him? 'I don't know . . . when somebody dies, all of a sudden they're so much bigger,' says Kate Ellison. 'I don't know if Mother Love Bone would have been *as* popular as Pearl Jam, but just by the quality of [*Apple*], I can guess that it would have been big.'

As Jon Hotten, the editor of *RAW*, says: 'No one can say for sure, of course, whether they would have been as big as Pearl Jam had Andy lived. But yes, I think so. I don't think Mother Love Bone were as immediate as Pearl Jam. You don't know what their second album would have been like. And Mother Love Bone, if you're not a rock fan, are a lot harder to listen to . . . But yes, I think they would have made it. However, I do think it's more interesting to look at why Stone Gossard and Jeff Ament were so intent on *not* keeping the name.

'If Gossard had been clinging to the idea that this was his one chance of glory, he obviously would have done. He's obviously some-one who's just led by the music. So he just started again. I think he displayed courage in doing that. It's an honesty you don't find often in the rock business. He must have great faith in what he does, to think that he could start again. But when you think he struggled for a long time, through Green River and then Mother Love Bone, finally got a record deal with a major label, and they've cut a great album, and then the singer goes and dies on him! That would have finished most people right there. But he walks away from it. He surely could have gone and got a replacement. I mean, he could have got the guys he did for Pearl Jam and still called it Mother Love Bone, but he didn't. So that's real courage.'

And of course, they had learned a great deal from the experience. 'There wasn't a lot of touring, or opportunity to really enjoy being in a band,' Stone reflected. 'Dealing with being on a major label for the first time and new people who had their two bits' worth to say; not being able to go out on tour, waiting for nearly two years and thinking you're on a major – that pressure kind of fucked us up.'[51] 'The whole thing had fallen to pieces, anyway,' said Jeff. 'It had got to the point where there was friction and a lack of communication, so the band separated into two camps. Me and Stone ended up with Pearl Jam and the other two formed Blind Horse, who [later] split. I think they're doing session work now . . .'[52]

Michael Goldstone, who signed the band to Polygram, once described Andy Wood as a visionary. 'He was an amazing talent. He had a lyrical depth that goes beyond what most bands in the marketplace are doing right now.' He added that the band's commercial potential had, in his view, been unlimited. 'A lot is happening on the Seattle scene now. This was one band that was going to explode it wide open.'[53] Frustratingly, as is so often the case in these circumstances, Andy had entered one of his most creative periods just before he died. 'He was showing me new melodies and harmonies,' Stone remembered. 'A lot of new piano stuff . . . There were so many songs that we had just begun to write, it's devastating to know that nobody will ever be able to do them, that no one will sing over the top of them like that.'[54]

But then, as Jon Hotten remarked, you don't know what the second album would have been like. Andy had already confided to Xana during his thirty-day stay at Valley General that what he really wanted was to get what he called 'the band thing' over with. Once Mother Love Bone had sold a million records, he said, he would have a famous name and be free to go solo, concentrating on his ethereal piano music. He couldn't wait for the day he could cut his long rock star hair short, he told her earnestly. But then he also told her that if he ever had to make a choice between his career as a rock star and staying clean and sober, he'd choose the latter. A promise he was utterly unable to keep.

14

The face paint had long been dispensed with but there were still many who were close to Andy in those last days who still had difficulty penetrating the emotional mask he continued to wear, on stage and off, to the very end. The conviction he espoused in his lyrics, in the healing and visionary power of love, came from another kind of addiction: an imperfect belief in a perfect world. But the deep-end inspiration for so much of his best work came from a much darker, emotional place hidden like a dungeon inside his baby-food heart. 'For years I tried to somehow help him,' Jeff lamented. 'He would do stuff like . . . last year in the middle of winter, ten below, he slept in Ivar's parking lot one night, a block from my fucking house. I was like, "Dude, you don't know me well enough, you don't have the confidence to come to my door and say I need a place to stay, I need some help?" That really hurt a lot . . .'[55]

Rock star to the very end, Andy Wood gave his last interview just the day before he died. Speaking to writer Michael Browning in an interview that was eventually published in the December 1990 issue of *RIP* magazine, Andy was touchingly open about his drug problems. 'I'm lucky to be sitting here,' he said prophetically. He talked of his time in rehab, insisting that now he was clean he was determined to stay that way. 'I was a druggie until I went into treatment. I'm not doing it any more.'[56] A quirky companion piece, written retrospectively, featured an interview with Xana LaFuente. 'It's really cool and weird, 'cause he wrote so much religious stuff in the weeks prior to his death,' she is quoted as saying. 'All these songs about heaven and dying.'[57] 'Andy had been struggling with having an addictive personality most of his life, having started drinking and smoking pot and stuff when he was really young,' Jeff pointed out. 'He had a lot to live for, he had a lot to be clean for. But then if you know an addictive person you can understand how powerful that is. It's not something you can just give up and forget about. It's always there.'[58]

'As far as coming to terms with Andy's death, I don't really know if I have yet or not,' Jeff Ament said in an interview two years later. 'I miss him a lot and think about him all the time, but at the same time, I feel he might even be better off and a lot more happy where he is than he was in real life. I think he suffered a lot. In some ways, I can't help but think that, whether it's sick or not.'[59]

Or in the words, nearly four years after his death, of the manageress of the Musicland record store in Westlake Centre, downtown Seattle, where Andy would sometimes buy his tapes and records: 'Andy Wood was such a showman. If he were alive today, he would be number one. No problem. That boy was just a born star . . . I guess he died like one too, didn't he?'

CHAPTER THREE

ALIVE

'San Francisco moved to Oregon and Washington . . . The whole thing is psychedelic. You can see it in the T-shirts and tie-dye. It's all hippies. These are the hippies' kids or something . . .'[1]

– Bob Pfeifer, director of A&R at Epic Records

'When you see Ann and Nancy Wilson at an Alice In Chains gig or Chris Cornell at a Heart concert, it's pretty exciting. I don't think that would have happened last year. It sounds weird, but Andy's death has a lot to do with it. It brought a lot of people together.'[2]

– Kelly Curtis

'I haven't really had a lot of faith in any sort of God or anything in a long time, I was always like, well, if it exists, I'll know it when I die. But somebody's definitely been making sure everything's OK. I know that everything that led up to this, all the stuff that was really painful at the time, happened for a reason . . . Somebody's looking out for us. Because there's no other way to explain this.'[3]

– Jeff Ament

1

The Eighties had been a rotten time for mainstream rock music. Ever since Johnny Rotten coined the term 'boring old farts' in relation to cloudy beanstalks like Pink Floyd, and Rat Scabies complained he fell asleep watching *The Song Remains The Same*, Led Zeppelin's self-indulgent fantasy-concert film, heavy metal had been reduced to the role of cultural leper in the trend-driven realm of popular music. Where once a plugged-in, amped-up guitar had been a weapon to wave in the face of the old and reactionary, by the beginning of the Eighties, *après* punk, the most talented and influential hit makers in Britain and Europe – Human League, Spandau Ballet, Ultravox, Culture Club, Depeche Mode, Japan, New Order – all spurned the face-pulling, hip-thrusting egocentricity of the electric guitar in favour of the poker-faced, asexual tides and perfect rhythm blips of the new user-friendly synthesizers that had just then alighted on the market. Even Paul Weller – a direct descendant of Pete Townshend's guitar smashing iconoclasm – finally put the lid on The Jam and swapped his fuzz-toned Richenbacher for the *café-crème* keyboards and muted gloss-horns of the Style Council. Anyone left in Britain still chugging away at blur-fingered guitar solos in the early Eighties was either in their thirties or Iron Maiden. It was only the advent of The Smiths in the mid- to late-Eighties that inspired bold new British tykes like the Manic Street Preachers or Suede to return to the seedy glories of the six-string razor.

In America – where the stagecoach mentality has never been allowed to die out properly – the situation was somewhat different. American punk sneered at many of the same figures and things as its older, gob-eyed Euro-cousin, but still stood back and applauded loudly when one of its own, like Blondie or Talking Heads or Patti Smith, broke from the gantry and made an impassioned dash for the US Top 40. In America, success was the *reward*, not the problem. Throwing away your guitars would have been like giving up your guns; it went plumb against the national character, as though there was something frankly un-American about a synthesizer.

Inevitably, after the worst excesses of party-hearty heavy metal monsters like Mötley Crüe, Ratt, Quiet Riot and Poison, it was left to

America to come up with the first vaguely credible stars of the trad-metal genre. But while Guns N' Roses, Metallica and Anthrax were busy in the late Eighties replacing the flabby put-your-hands-in-the-air order with a leaner, street-conscious metal rock that relied less on babes and more on bathos, the lines of credibility had become blurred again. Ads for Sex Pistols bootlegs began to appear in metal-credible UK magazines like *RAW*; Seattle's premier heavy metal stars, Queensryche, enjoyed an astonishing critical success for their thought-provoking *Operation: Mindcrime* concept album (the concept was totalitarianism in the twentieth century); fascination grew for punk-metal hybrids like Sonic Youth, Dinosaur Jr. and Big Black; Faith No More and the Red Hot Chili Peppers proved that you could put the funk in there with the punk and the metal, too, and come out with a whole new sound-sensorium, the bits of which might belong else-where but the whole as such was made entirely your own.

1990 had begun with the astonishing news that a record nine Seattle-based artists had been nominated for awards at the thirty-second annual Grammy Awards gala, held on February 21st that year at the Shrine Auditorium in Los Angeles. Alongside Seattle Sym-phony Orchestra saxophonist Kenny G and avant-jazz singer Diane Schuur stood hard rock Seattle stalwarts Queensryche and Sound-garden. Though nobody actually won anything, as the *Seattle Post-Intelligencer* noted, 'their presence at the prestigious music-industry awards heightened interest in Seattle and its music at a time when the city was topping livability polls across the country'.[4]

Certainly the 'Seattle scene', as such, had begun its ascendance on to the front covers of the world's rockzines. No longer the exclusive property of a few small labels and their even smaller bands, by the middle of 1990 there were at least twenty new indie labels in Seattle all vying with Sub Pop for position in the grainy hearts of the no-wave congnoscenti . . . Big Flaming Ego, Black Label, The Cruddy Record Dealership, C/Z Records, eMpTY Records, Ensign Productions, Estrus Records, Green Monkey Records, Horton/Reflex, K, Nastymix Records, New Rage Records, Overkill Records, The Parkland CoOp, Penultimate Records, PopLlama Products, Regal Select and Sun And Steel were just the ones that lasted longer than their first few adrenalin-riven releases.

Rolling Stone, as usual, led the way for the print establishment, when they brought out their Seventies cover story issue, in September

1990. An in-depth look into what was going on in Seattle and thereabouts, focusing specifically on the Posies, Alice In Chains and Mother Love Bone, the story, written by Dave Di Martino, announced that 'the major labels are coming because amid the city's lush greenery, they smell money'. Mother Love Bone had 'all the markings of a superstar band', except, it sadly noted, its chance now appeared to have been lost with the death of Andy Wood. *Billboard* also ran a cheery profile on Seattle in September 1990; and *Spin* ranted and raved about Alice In Chains, sending the band ceilingwards in its annual list of top new artists in its December 1990 issue. 'I talked to somebody at CBS in New York last October, and he said, "You're from Seattle. Just find me *any* Seattle band. I'm *dying* to sign a Seattle band – I'm so mad I didn't sign Alice In Chains",'[5] claimed one industry insider with strong Seattle connections. It was a situation that was hardly unprecedented in the place-name history of American rock music – Detroit, San Francisco, Cleveland, Boston, New York, Athens, Austin, Minneapolis . . . where hadn't there been a regional musical scene of some significance in the US these past fifty years?

Still some weren't sure what to make of the rapidly growing Northwest scene. One typically sceptical voice was that of *New York Times* entertainments writer David Browne, who turned a review of four Seattle bands – Mother Love Bone, the Posies, Alice In Chains and the Screaming Trees – into a decidedly downbeat analysis of the impossible to define 'Seattle Sound', in November 1990. 'Seattle, the city that brought us Jimi Hendrix, Quincy Jones and Heart, is now home to a different breed of rock band – loud, hardened and musically ugly,' Browne trumpeted. 'The city may be saddled with an image of yuppie tranquillity and lush woodiness, but its upstart musicians trample that stereotype with grim determination.' Praise was heaped, though, on *Apple*, which Browne prophetically described as 'one of the first great hard rock records of the Nineties'.[6] True or not, the biggest selling album from any of the Seattle rock bands that year was Queensryche's *Empire*, which took the band into the US Top 10 for the first time in October 1990.

2

But not all was well in the grunge garden. Despite the huge profile they now enjoyed, almost without warning, Sub Pop had begun to feel the pinch financially and for most of 1990, though Pavitt and Poneman were loath to admit it, Sub Pop were in serious trouble with their creditors. As Bruce Pavitt put it: 'Basically, we got caught up in trying to compete with major labels . . . giving advances to groups that were much larger than we really should've contemplated, simply because A&R people were crawling all over Seattle and we had to protect our interests.'[7] The relative success of the *Mudhoney* album (first three thousand with fold-out sleeve and poster, followed by later editions in creamy yellow and clear vinyl) and new signings – the Dwarves, whose 1990 *Blood, Guts and Pussy* album was notorious for its sleeve featuring two naked women smeared with blood, a début solo album from Mark Lanegan of the Screaming Trees, and seminal Singles Club releases from Soundgarden, Babes In Toyland and L7 – are what kept the creaking Sub Pop ship afloat during this period.

Rapid growth in any business is always difficult to manage, but this was chaotic book-keeping by any reckoning – bands, friends of bands, journalists and DJs came to visit the bands and their friends all regularly waltzed out of the Sub Pop portals at the Terminal Sales Building with armloads of records and CDs that were rarely, if ever, accounted for. Poneman admitted that the label put out at least a dozen records before he and Pavitt had even the most rudimentary agreement in writing with any of their increasingly sought-after bands. 'They had lots of money and they blew it,' Daniel House said matter-of-factly. 'I think Bruce is a creative mastermind. I really think he's brilliant in a lot of his ideas about marketing and packaging [and] I think Jon is a master of hype. The one thing I don't believe either of them are is businessmen.'[8]

But while they admit to having spent money freely, neither Poneman nor Pavitt were apologetic after the fact. 'I have no regrets in doing the grandiose gestures and coming up with these schemes which were a lot more potent and a lot higher profile than we probably could have afforded at the time,' said Poneman. 'If we had been fiscally more restrained we wouldn't have gotten a tenth of the hype.'⁹ It was a good promo man's argument, but as Sub Pop were becoming a household name, Pavitt and Poneman's cash-flow problems intensified; unpaid bills began to pile up. The furore surrounding the release of the Tad *8-Way Santa* album, in February 1991, was typical of the times. The original sleeve, which featured a picture of a young man playfully holding his girlfriend's bikini-covered breast (the photo had come from an album bought at a garage sale), resulted in a threatened lawsuit when the new husband of the woman in the photo spotted his wife's picture on the album whilst browsing through the racks at Tower Records. When her outraged spouse brought her attention to it, the woman moved to sue the recalcitrant record company. Although the controversy would, in time, create another red-hot collector's item, Sub Pop initially lost money after being forced to recall all copies of the record and hastily replace the original sleeve with a tamer group shot.

When, towards the end of 1989, Island Records had approached Sub Pop about the possibility of working out a mutually beneficial distribution deal, Pavitt and Poneman listened politely but refused to commit themselves. The idea Island proposed – that the smaller label become a subsidiary of the larger, retaining a proportionate measure of artistic control over the product they issued but with the safety-net of the major label's massive marketing and distribution network – was certainly tempting. But the primary drawback for the smaller was that it feared becoming so dependent on the larger label for advances that its say over the final product would be increasingly diminished. Sub Pop continued talking to Island right through to the middle of 1990, then backed out unapologetically at the last minute.

By the summer of 1991, however, with the world recession biting much harder than the severest financial analysts had predicted, Rough Trade, a veritable flagship of the indie scene and long considered one of the most reliable independents in the business, had gone horribly belly-up in America in a matter of weeks and sunk without a trace, and Pavitt and Poneman had begun to drum their fingers nervously over their dwindling chequebooks, wondering for whom the bell would toll next time.

Some say they were approached; some say they went looking. Whatever the initial spur, talks began between Sub Pop and Columbia Records, for a distribution deal very similar to the one Sub Pop had just turned down from Island, at the end of 1990. Disney's

Hollywood Records division also became involved in discussions at this point; both labels were intent on capturing what they saw as the nursery of the 'Seattle Sound'. 'The whole naïve notion that you could have an independent label and have major distribution was very appealing to us,' claimed Pavitt, somewhat disingenuously. 'Putting out a Dwarves record on Disney was the ultimate concept.'[10] But instead of finding a suitable 'big brother' partner, Sub Pop merely accumulated inordinately large legal bills. And of course the moment the acts heard that Sub Pop were talking money with the serious labels, 'a lot of bands that we had flimsy contracts with said: "Major distribution? Well, instead of giving us five thousand dollars for our next record, give us twenty-five thousand",' claimed Poneman. 'That's what fucked us,' said Pavitt.[11]

3

The five members of Mother Love Bone had hoped to be a part of the exciting times the pundits were all predicting lay just ahead, but the death of Andrew Wood had left the others looking on impotently, not entirely sure whether to carry on or not, or even how. The only thing they were certain of was that Mother Love Bone was over. It also meant the end of Stone Gossard and Jeff Ament's relationship with Bruce Fairweather and Greg Gilmore. None of them wanted to attempt the impossible: recreating Mother Love Bone with another singer. So traumatized were they by the grisly manner of Andy's death that for a long time none of them would want to play at all. Jeff, ever the pragmatist, who had returned to his other love, graphic arts, for solace in the empty weeks following Andy's death, was the first to remember he used to be a musician. He began playing on a part-time basis with a group called the War Babies which, in turn, led to a loose band of casual, floating members called Love Co., one of which was another former aspirant young guitar hero by the name of Michael McCready.

Michael McCready was born on April 5, 1964, in Seattle, where his mother was an art teacher and his father worked for the city. An only child, his first musical experience was rat-tatting out a beat with pencils on his dad's bongos. His first guitar was a cheap and cheerful electric Mateo Les Paul copy that he still owns today. 'I used to play "Smoke On The Water", and I remember my dad coming in and yelling at me because I was getting feedback out of the amp; I just thought it was really cool.'[12]

Unusual for a 'feel' player who never learned to read music, his earliest influences as a guitarist were the telegraphed, classically informed guitar solos of arch heavy metallists like Deep Purple's Ritchie Blackmore and UFO's Michael Schenker. As he progressed on his instrument he would grow to appreciate and learn from the steamier, less cluttered R&B styles of Stevie Ray Vaughan, Keith Richards and Johnny Winter. But to begin with, Mike's biggest idols were the same as every other cola-slurping pinhead's of his generation. 'I started playing guitar because of Kiss. I was eleven. I had the Kiss lunch-box, everything,' he always admitted with a broad grin.[13] 'Every kid at that time was into Kiss, with all the fire-breathing and stuff. We used to leap around the couch with brooms and strut in front of the mirror. Actually I still do that . . .'[14]

'Mike always seems to be the forgotten one. He's very much on the quiet side,' says Kate Ellison, music director of KXRX. 'Wonderful guy, very good musician . . . He's not the one that needs to be in the limelight maybe as much as Jeff and Stone do.' Mike McCready first met Stone Gossard in 1984 at a Shadow gig. Shadow was an exceptionally young five-piece. Mike was sixteen when he joined; the youngest member was drummer Chris Friel, fourteen, who had formed the band when he was nine. At first they were called Warrior and they did covers . . . Def Leppard, Kiss, anything simple and bitchin' . . . Switched to the less hubba-hubba Shadow a year later and began performing their own songs. They chanced their arm, like so many others, in LA for a while, in 1988, and Mike worked for a time at Aaron Records in West Hollywood, a haven for vinyl junkies and independent record enthusiasts.

Unfortunately, the nearest Shadow ever came to making a record was the four-track demo they'd brought with them from Seattle, where they returned after thirteen months of disillusioning gig-hopping and label-seeing. Shadow broke up six months later. It was 1989 and Mike enrolled in a high school diploma course at the local community college, took a part-time job in a video store and forgot all about playing the guitar seriously. Apart from a few glad-hand appearances with a short-lived psychedelic blues band called Love Chile, Mike had all but given up on ever making a fist of the music business. When Stone and Jeff came upon him, wailing away on his own at a party on a borrowed amp, he had cut his hair short and was reading a book by arch-Republican right-winger Barry Goldwater as a result of his utter disillusionment with the way things were.

The fun they had together in Love Co. was enough to coax Mike out of the protective shell he had retreated into after Shadow fell apart. 'I had known Stone from Shadow days,' Mike said. 'We used to trade rock pictures and stuff like that.'[15] Soon Stone had invited Mike and Jeff to come by his parents' house and jam together in the upstairs attic room; the same room he had first found the haunting riffs to so many Green River and Mother Love Bone songs in. 'He had tons of songs – the beginnings of "Alive" and "Black" – and I was like, shit yeah!' Mike recalled.[16] Still without a permanent drummer, Soundgarden's Matt Cameron offered to step into the breach for them while they began work on a demo together. An early Gossard instrumental built around a riff that sounded like a sob called 'Dollar Short' was the key. An unfinished track he had begun and then dropped when he was still in Mother Love Bone, the riff had returned to him again and again in the days that followed Andy's death, when Stone had turned to his guitar to help him blot out the pain and frustration. Mike McCready would later say that he knew that they had a band when they started playing 'Dollar Short' . . .

Eventually, New Bohemians drummer Matt Chamberlain, who had also been filling in for them occasionally, introduced them to Dave Krusen, an old pal of his from Dallas. 'Dallas is so incestuous!' Jeff declared. 'Everyone's played with each other . . . Dave Krusen played with us and fitted in perfectly. There were none of the usual problems we'd had with drummers; Dave was really motivated and diverse. He also plays guitar and writes songs, so he provided an extra input into the band, which was great.'[17] All they needed now was what they had needed all along: a singer. Not just a replacement for Mark this time, nor a cleverly remodelled Andy, but somebody who wore his skin in a totally different way. Stone and Jeff began passing their demo-tape around; five instrumentals in need of a voice, a vehicle looking for a driver.

One of the first people they sent a copy to was former Red Hot Chili

Peppers drummer Jack Irons, who they had met back in the days of Green River and who they had offered the drum slot to in the new band. Irons had turned the gig down, but, impressed by what he heard on the tape, he told Jeff about a guy he threw hoops with on a Friday night, not a drummer but a singer, lived out San Diego way, that Jack thought was maybe looking for something new to do . . .

4

Edward Louis Severson Junior was born in Evanston, a northern suburb of Chicago, two days before Christmas Day, 1966. The eldest of four stepbrothers, he only discovered his real name years later; his mother had separated from his biological father when Eddie was still a baby and he had grown up as plain Eddie Mueller, believing his stepfather's surname was his own.

An autodidact who dropped out of high school, Eddie has always kept the cards of his childhood close to his chest. He has spoken privately of waiting tables in Chicago, of moving to San Diego and buying his first cheap stereo . . . of briefly studying music in Boston ('all those guys getting really proficient with their musical knowledge . . . having to study so intensely that their inspiration was getting lost'[18]). But always with the details kept vague, as though he was never too sure of the real story himself, which in a sense, of course, he never was. Eddie never knew his real father. And he didn't get along with his stepfather. They were always fighting and bickering. Eddie had been on his own as long as he could remember.

When Eddie was five years old, his parents took charge of a group-home for parentless children for a year. 'I went from being the oldest to being like this little punk amongst these other big punks. All of a sudden, most of my brothers were older, and black and Irish, and all those intense, diverse cultures. We were like foster brothers,'[19] Eddie recalled. 'A totally mixed bag of youths . . . their musical tastes rubbed off on me. That's when I got into Smokey Robinson, James Brown, Otis Redding, the Jackson Five . . . To this day, when I pull out a record with the blue Motown logo of the map of Detroit on it, I get the chills.'[20]

The first record Eddie remembers owning is 'Puff, The Magic Dragon', which his folks purchased for him when he was three. 'But "Puff" didn't make me want to sing and dance like "ABC" by the Jackson Five did.'[21] Always a quick learner, when the Mueller family moved to San Diego in 1974 the city kid instantly metamorphosed into a perfect-wave obsessed surf punk. Inspired in his teenage years by the Sex Pistols, early Talking Heads and most especially The Who, Eddie would later claim that the father-figure he turned to for comfort and advice most as he was journeying through the rough seas of adolescence was Pete Townshend. 'The Who's *Quadrophenia* album basically saved my life. I thought it was so amazing that this guy who lives thousands of miles away in another country could totally explain my life. It was really intense, and obviously I wasn't the only one who felt that way.'[22]

When his family moved to Chicago in the early Eighties, Eddie stayed behind in San Diego with his new live-in girlfriend, Beth Liebling. He immediately swapped the 'Mueller' in his name for 'Vedder', his mother's maiden name, and contrived from that moment on never to speak to his stepfather again. Eddie was still living in San Diego when his mother arrived unexpectedly one day with some earth-shattering news for him. His father – his real father, she now revealed – had died of multiple sclerosis. Eddie was appalled. More a distant family friend than a close relative, his real father was someone he had met only a few times and remembered only vaguely.

Edward Louis Severson Senior had been an organist-vocalist of the type who sang in restaurants and at weddings. He would doubtless have been proud of the successful career his estranged son made for himself in music. Dealing with the anger of not being told the truth about his father while he was still alive, though, was to scar the already troubled son deeply. He was a big secret and Eddie had come to learn that secrets were bad news.

Eddie became known around the San Diego scene as 'the guy who never sleeps'. For four years, Eddie pumped gas at an all-night garage from midnight till eight in the morning, then went surfing. 'People think of sun and sand and girls, but surfing's not really like that. At eight in the morning, it's foggy and cold; you drag yourself into the ocean and you can't even see the waves through the fog . . . the still water's like glass. It's a good time to think.'[23] He usually spent his days writing and demoing material on his own portable 4-track, which he had saved up for, working occasionally in between stints at the garage, often for no more than a T-shirt and free admission to the gig, as a roadie at the nearby Bacchanal Club, humping gear. 'I was a mad-scientist character. People thought I'd either do really big things some day or just . . . die.'[24]

For a time, he fronted a band called Bad Radio, who played intermittently and even recorded a half-decent demo (Echo and The Bunnymen meets Bruce Springsteen) but broke up, as Eddie put it, 'mostly because of the lack of ambition on the other members' parts'.[25] At the time of being given the cassette marked 'Stone Gossard Demos 1990', Eddie Vedder had been considering shopping for a solo deal. But then his buddy Jack, whose taste he respected, had handed him this tape one Friday night and told him to play it. Eddie had been aware of Green River but not so much Mother Love Bone. 'I think that was good because when I got the tape I really didn't know where they were coming from and so I just did my own thing, and the next thing I knew I was part of their thing.'[26]

He took the cassette with him to work that night and spent the long hours before dawn when business was slowest listening to it, wondering. The next morning, as usual, he went surfing. 'It was a great feeling. A combination of sleep deprivation and being very excited by the coldness of the water with this music floating around in my head. I got out of the water, walked into this little run-down shack on the beach I was living in and laid down three songs . . . My feet were still wet and sandy. It was such an honest thing.'[27] The demo from Seattle contained five instrumentals . . . one in particular kept repeating itself in Eddie's mind as he waded out into the fog. When he got home, he immediately recorded himself singing the words that had come to him in the surf that morning, the morning 'Dollar Short' became 'Alive' . . . Eventually he had enough words, just like that, to fill three of the five instrumentals, which he now retitled 'Alive', 'Once' and 'Footsteps'. The resulting 'mini-opera', as he labelled it, Eddie quickly put down on to a cassette, which he packaged up with some homemade graphics and a swank new obscurantist title: *Mamasan.*

5

Back home in Seattle, Jeff played the cassette Eddie had sent him all the way through three times, then picked up the phone and hurriedly dialled Stone's number, barely able to keep the excitement out of his voice. 'The songs of ours that he sang over we thought were the closest thing that we had heard to really turning any one of us on,' Jeff explained. 'It felt right.'[28] Stone agreed. Jeff called Eddie that same night and invited him up to Seattle to see if he could recreate the mood he had captured on tape live with the rest of the band there to see him do it. Coming straight from the airport to the rehearsal room, as Eddie had insisted they do, the first song they played together was, fittingly, 'Alive'. Phantasmagorically speaking, Pearl Jam began their career the first time Eddie Vedder opened his mouth to sing. A wounded, guttural sound that wraps itself around you like a shroud, when Eddie hits his stride, eyes closed, head tilted forward, his whole body convulsed and quaking as though there were volts of electricity going through him, the voice railing against the impossibility of it all, the mind apparently gone as the heart opens up and lets it all come down ... A little reminiscent of a swaggering young Jim Morrison in places, or a folksier, less sullen Tim Buckley in others, on a purely technical level, Eddie made someone like Axl Rose sound like a hysterical schoolgirl, Kurt Cobain a flaccid Johnny Rotten clone. He perhaps lacked some of their brutal charisma, but he had a much better voice than any of them. 'I can't really take credit for a lot of this because it's this in between thing where I'm just focusing on this space,' Eddie would intone solemnly when pressed on the subject. 'The best shows are the ones I don't remember at all.'[29]

Apart from the blazing sun of his voice, the most intriguing thing Jeff and Stone noted about Eddie on that first trip was how very different he was as a frontman and singer compared to either Andy or Mark. Where they had always been upfront and larger than life, Eddie was remarkably introverted, very little eye contact let alone make-up, speech soft and punctuated by long pauses ... his lyrics luminous with emotional pain and neglect. Eddie claimed he was never aware of how much Stone and Jeff wanted to take things away from the Mother Love Bone vibe – 'It wasn't something that was ever discussed. It just kind of happened. I think they trusted the fact that Andy and I [were] different.'[30] By the time he'd got to Seattle, Eddie had already written the lyrics to another Gossard riff that had been hogging his mental turntable: 'Black'. When he sang the words for the others at that first rehearsal, it gave Stone chills. Jeff and Mike were simply in awe. If they had sincerely been looking for someone different, they had definitely stumbled upon the genuine article.

'As a writer ... I observe a lot of what goes on around me; I always have since I was a toddler,' said Eddie. 'I even tried to write songs back then ... I remember locking myself in the bathroom so I could think, and writing words with arrows over some where you'd go up if you were singing. I was a pretty weird kid, I guess.'[31]

One rehearsal together was all it took for them all to decide, although initially they tried to keep it cool and told each other they would stay in contact and get together again in a couple of weeks' time. 'We were prepared to compromise a little but, fortunately, that never happened,' said Jeff. 'It's definitely one of those instances that seems to happen from some outer-worldly reason, and only a very few times in my life has that ever happened.'[32] 'The first week when we got it together, it was really intense,' Stone said. 'I'd go home and try to do something else, and I couldn't. I had to keep picking up my guitar and carry on playing what we had been doing that day. Couldn't wait to get up the next day and start again.'[33] 'I just remember the coolest thing playing "Alive". That was the first thing we played together,' said Eddie. 'We were all in this little basement of this art gallery – so the vibe was really cool – and here were these guys, and I finally had this music that I felt like, there was something about the music . . .'[34]

When Eddie returned a month later, the new, still unnamed line-up went at it even more intently. They were a band now. During breaks, they would go across the street to buy soft drinks and trade basketball cards. Mookie Blaylock – then of the New Jersey Mets, now the Atlanta Braves – was always a favourite. As a gag, once they had a demo ready to be sent out, a Mookie Blaylock card was included with each cassette. Their first gig was the day before Eddie's twenty-fourth birthday, December 22, 1990, opening for Alice In Chains (returning the favour Mother Love Bone had done them just a few months before) at the Moore Theater, in Seattle. The new band needed a name to add to the handbills and posters. They chose Mookie Blaylock.

Interestingly, and despite cameo appearances by Soundgarden's Chris Cornell and Matt Cameron, the *Seattle Times* reviewed that first gig without much enthusiasm, writing that 'Alice In Chains gave a better representation of the Seattle Sound than those that should have: opening band Mookie Blaylock, [whose] music leaned more towards bad Seventies' country rock (Bad Company came to mind) than the punk-metal angst of Green River or the flamboyant grooves of Mother Love Bone . . .'[35]

6

On the day Andrew Wood died, Soundgarden had been preparing to leave for an important European tour. The depression that descended upon Chris Cornell at the news of his former flatmate's appalling demise was further compounded by the usual rigours of the road and the vocalist retreated into a songwriting stupor, penning two new songs in his hotel room that were almost entirely inspired by Andy's death – 'Reach Down' and 'Say Hello To Heaven'. As time crept by, other themes suggested themselves, other songs that weren't strictly Soundgarden material, but weren't strictly not, either. In the end, he talked his new record company, A&M, into allowing him a creative outlet for his confusion; a project that would be clearly separate from and yet intrinsically a part of the Soundgarden catalogue. Chris wasn't asking that A&M spend any money on promoting the work – that could wait for the next Soundgarden album proper – he just wanted them to put it out. He even had a name for the project – *Temple Of The Dog*, a line lifted from one of Andy's most dreamily autobiographical songs, 'Man Of Golden Words'.

The eponymous album teamed Chris Cornell and Matt Cameron with Stone, Jeff, Mike and Eddie. Originally it was just going to be a four-track EP, but as recording began, on weekends, in between recording the first Mookie Blaylock demo, the idea grew in all their minds until they found they had enough material for an album.

As the *Melody Maker* would later write of the resulting album, released without fanfare in May 1991, 'Maybe it's a cleansing process, for by the end, *Temple Of The Dog* sounds battered but triumphant. Uncomfortable but unabashed, this is a very real dose of heartbreak . . .'[36] A far superior collection to either the glorious irreality of *Apple*, or the laughable by comparison *Louder Than Love*, with music more like early Free or Humble Pie in its earthy sensibilities than the self-conscious punk-neon of Mudhoney and Nirvana, *Temple Of The Dog* was unique to the hard rock ghetto of the times; this wasn't Jon Bon Jovi weeping at the altar of Bruce Springsteen, or even Bono on one knee, a hand pushed wearily through the hair in the practised gesture of the ham actor, this was the real cooked-up-in-the-spoon thing, baby . . . The only easy comparison, as *The Rocket* noted, was 1990's remarkable Lou Reed and John Cale collaboration, *Songs For Drella*, inspired by the death of their former friend and mentor, Andy Warhol.

The sheer atmosphere surrounding the *Temple Of The Dog* sessions was amazing, said Eddie, who was deeply impressed with the dignified manner in which Chris Cornell had set the whole thing up. 'We were rehearsing during the day and *Temple Of The Dog* were rehearsing at night. Can you imagine how inspiring that was? I came up and we were going to coffee shops, fuelling up and going into this dank basement, playing this music with the band that had a magical intensity about it.'[37] 'While we were making the album, feelings were pretty strong that it was just a side project – a collaboration that we were all happy to do,' Chris reflected. 'Once the record was made and mixed and we knew it was going to be released, then I think the tribute aspect of it started to creep back in on everybody. The songs had a big effect on us. I mean, we've known each other for a long time, but we never ever talked about doing anything like this before.'[38]

Chris denied that the sordid manner of Andy's death had hardened his own resolve not to get tangled up in the drug-obsessed tentacles of the music business. 'I pretty much had my course set for my career before Andrew's death, so there hasn't been much room for hardening my resolve any more,' he said. 'The only thing that might've changed is my tolerance for relationships with people who aren't as amazingly creative as Andy was. I've found it more important to surround myself with people who have genuine talent instead of those who pretend to be creative. I also realized that having people like Andy as a friend shouldn't be taken for granted. He was a creative inspiration to me, and I definitely took that for granted. I would rather not let that happen again . . .'[39]

'*Temple* was my first experience in the studio, so it was a little weird, but it went by way too fast for me,' said Mike. 'We didn't analyse anything, we just did it. Music's always been an emotional thing for me, just to get the shit out of my head.'[40] 'It was a victory . . . a huge victory for me and Jeff and Mike to go in there after struggling to make that Mother Love Bone record for three months,' said Stone. 'To go in with confidence and make a record with Matt and Chris that we thought was the best thing we'd ever worked on was nothing short of joy. And it deserved to be huge because it's a great record.'[41] Not for the last time, Eddie, the new dick on the block, would put it best. 'It was something that was done in a real low-key natural way. It took a couple of weekends and that was it, and all of a sudden you had this lasting statement of what was going on at the time . . .'[42]

7

It seemed the repercussions of Andy's death were endless. Filmed in March, April and May of 1991, the catalyst for the idea behind the *Singles* movie was also spawned the night Andy Wood died. 'I always liked Green River and Soundgarden,' said director Cameron Crowe. 'The Mother Love Bone thing I kinda liked, even though Andy Wood was more flamboyant, and headed for the arena more so than any of those other bands. I really liked Stone and Jeff as guys. I remember going to the Virginia Inn with [them] and . . . I was telling them that what I wanted to do was this movie. It started at that point. That's how I veered into the Pearl Jam/Alice In Chains/Soundgarden realm, a realm that ended up being more successful than I ever thought.'[43]

Cameron Crowe is Mr Right Time Right Place. He was born there – in Southern California, in the mid-Fifties. His father sold real estate; his mother taught sociology and English. Both were strict God-fearing WASPs who didn't allow rock 'n' roll music to be played in the house, and young Cameron had to wait until he won tickets from his local radio station before he could attend his first rock concert, Iron Butterfly. No good with girls, no better at contact sports, he found he could write though, contributing reviews of favourite records to his school magazine. It was an activity he enjoyed and better still it helped him build up his meagre record collection as the already biz-wise young journo began canvassing record companies for review copies. His first free record was *Sunshine Of Your Love* by Cream. He couldn't believe his luck. 'I remember getting Steve Miller's *Rock Love* in the mail. It was like, yeah! I want to do this for ever!'[44]

Soon he was sending reviews in to an underground paper in San Diego called *The Door*. His break came, as so often happens, quite by accident. He and *Rolling Stone* staffer Ben Fong-Torres happened to be visiting the same public relations office in Los Angeles when, as Fong-Torres later recalled, 'He shyly offered to let me see a couple of reviews and a story or two. They were good enough that I felt like there was something there. He had facts down, not too gushy, not too teen-magaziney . . .'[45] Emboldened, Crowe dropped out of San Diego college and began to rack up an impressive array of by-lines, including a piece on the US leg of The Who's *Quadrophenia* world tour for *Playboy* at a time when he was still legally too young to buy a copy. *Rolling Stone* added the name Cameron Crowe to its masthead in 1974 and agreed to pay him $400 a month for first dibs on anything he chose to submit. Crowe would turn in fan's-eye pieces for *Rolling Stone* on artists such as David Bowie, the Eagles, Linda Ronstadt, Fleetwood Mac, Boston and Peter Frampton throughout the rest of the Seventies. He genuinely enjoyed meeting the most popular rock stars of the day at a time when many of the magazine's more senior writers had given up on the music business altogether.

Then, at twenty-two, a publisher approached the young scribe with the idea that became the best-selling novel, *Fast Times At Ridgemont High*. The spiel was that Crowe would go back to high school under cover, attending the local public school in Redondo Beach as Dave Cameron, transfer student, where he would collect first-hand material for his docudrama. Only a few teachers and administrators were allowed in on the secret, and Crowe kept a hidden tape-recorder whirring during classes and at breaks, or he'd overhear something usable and slink off to the toilet, where he'd scribble down whatever it was that had caught his attention. Remarkably, his cover remained intact right up to graduation day, after which Crowe went back and confessed who he was and what he had really been up to all these months to the teenagers who had unwittingly become the models for the book's chief characters. When *Fast Times* was published in 1979, its witty, unflinching depiction of the everyday lives of a group of high school students was so pinpoint accurate that many parents simply refused to believe it: that teenagers had sex with multiple partners, got pregnant, had abortions, got drunk, took drugs and didn't give a shit what anybody thought about it – except, of course, other teenagers.

His introduction to writing for the screen came when film producer Art Linson shrewly suggested that Crowe himself write the script for the movie version of *Fast Times* and handed him two screenplays to look at and try to obtain a rudimentary grasp of modern screen-writing techniques from – *Chinatown* and *Raging Bull*. 'It was a little intimidating. I'm not a film-school guy. I loved movies, but I didn't know the language . . . Art walked me through the first step,'[46] Crowe admitted bashfully. Luck played her hand in things when a little-known actor named Sean Penn was cast as stoned surfer Jeff Spicoli, and turned out to be brilliant as the hunched-up, squinting, Valley-yakking boy-doll, and the film eventually earned a box-office take of about $30 million. The studio, as is the way of Hollywood studios in sight of a swift buck, insisted he make a sequel.

Crowe refused and instead his second screenplay, *The Wild Life*, was, in his own words, 'a disaster . . . It wound up being what *Fast Times* was a reaction against – an exploitative view of youth.'[47] An over-ambitious exploration of an unfulfilled Eighties teenager who befriends a spaced-out Sixties Vietnam vet, the film is remembered mainly for one cringe-inducing scene in a topless go-go bar intended no doubt as a satire but, in effect, serving the same base instincts it purports to subvert; all tits and no squeeze. Nevertheless, producer James L. Brookes (*Broadcast News*, *Terms Of Endearment*) believed in Crowe's somewhat bruised ego enough to persuade him to go for bust and write *and* direct his next movie, *Say Anything*. Released in 1989, and spray-gunned with purple bits of Soundgarden and Mother Love Bone, it starred, somewhat improbably, John Cusack as a kick-boxing student who recklessly decides to devote the rest of his life to the cleverest girl in class (Ione Skye), who, fortunately for kickhead, just happens to be the most beautiful too. It was pap but well-crafted pap and though it earned much less than *Fast Times*, it helped reestablish Crowe's faltering career as a film-maker in an industry where second chances are something that usually only happen to characters on screen, not off. He was back and this time he was going to make sure he stayed there, or at least die on his own terms.

Rolling Stone photographer Neal Preston, who also worked with Heart as their tour photographer, had shared a house with Crowe for six years in the Seventies. It was Preston who introduced him to Heart vocalist Ann Wilson. As the photographer had long predicted, the pair made an easy couple and within twelve months they were married. The budding film-maker kept his place in California so that he could be near to the studios when he was working, and moved into a new house with his bride in Seattle, where Heart were and still are based today. 'I just always liked the environment in Seattle,' he commented on his new home. 'It's been a passion of mine to do a whole movie based there for a long time.'[48]

8

The first time the cast members of *Singles* met each other was at an Alice In Chains/Mookie Blaylock gig at the Off Ramp, in Seattle, at the end of February 1991. Director and cast nabbed a corner booth and sat back and watched. Originally, singer Paula Abdul had auditioned for the part of Cosmo girl Debbie, but had to pull out at the last minute due to the commitments of her recording career. 'Basically, she was doing herself as a Laker Girl with four roommates, and it was funny as shit,' Crowe reckoned. 'If I'd hired her, it would have been your favourite part of the movie.'[49] A young unknown by the name of Sheila Kelly, whose only previous screen credit had been on TV in the cast of the final series of *LA Law*, was allotted the role instead. Christ Cornell had auditioned for the part Matt Dillon eventually played, that of the obnoxious Cliff, singer in Citizen Dick. Chris had flown down to Burbank to read scenes for the watchful Warner Brothers execs, who were impressed, they said, by the newcomer's improvisational acting ability, but not by his box-office potential.

Singles had been allotted a not inconsiderable $18 million budget and the studios were looking to make a profit, not a prophet. (Chris ended up appearing in the movie with Soundgarden performing as themselves.)

Of the two hundred or so zealously shot scenes the final movie contains, most memorable are the ones between Steve (Campbell Scott) and Linda (Kyra Sedgwick), as an over-cautious new couple, each already anticipating the other's betrayal; and Janet (Bridget Fonda) as the hopelessly downtrodden girlfriend of singer Cliff (Matt Dillon) – 'I'll see you Saturday, then!' she calls after him at one point, as he walks away, barely listening. 'And I'll help you with your speakers!' 'I just wanted to approximate the whole experience of when you're single, and the town feels like it's your town, and you go out and meet twenty people in one night and maybe you'll meet 'em again, but probably not,'[50] Crowe explained. Some of the locations filmed in Seattle included the Off Ramp, the OK Hotel – the Java Stop, in the movie, where Bridget Fonda works. And of course, Capitol Hill – where the apartment house where the characters all live is situated.

In the spirit of authenticity Crowe set out to purvey, the band Matt Dillon's character fronts – Citizen Dick – comprised Stone on guitar, Jeff on bass and Eddie on drums. 'The one time you hear [Cliff/Matt] sing, it is his voice. He got all the way into it,' Crowe told reporters. 'He hung out with Eddie, Stone and Jeff . . . they went out in New York together and had a "bonding experience"! And that was before Matt had even committed to the part. He really got what the character was supposed to be . . .'[51] One of the funniest scenes in the film is when Citizen Dick are sitting around reading the music papers and they come across a review of their last gig and start to read it out loud. 'I don't wanna hear nothin' negative!' Cliff/Matt tells his bandmates, and is thereafter forced to sit in silence as the rest of the band huddle around the paper to read the slew of invective the imaginary reviewer has hurled their singer's way.

Crowe studiously tried to avoid turning the movie into an *A–Z* for trend-tourists. 'Matt was most comfortable wearing Jeff Ament's clothes,'[52] he said. 'The clothes in the film are all pretty much stuff from either my or Pearl Jam's closets.'[53] Cliff/Matt's cramped untidy room was also based on Jeff's own. 'I think Matt Dillon's character is based more on the type of things I've done,' Jeff admitted. 'He works in a coffee place, it shows him screening T-shirts and doing a lot of the band's artwork, which I do. A lot of my posters and things are used for his apartment. But his love interest and the way he goes about it, that's not me.'[54]

Erroneously represented as Seattle's *Saturday Night Fever*, the only thing *Singles* had in common with John Travolta's Seventies knee-trembler was its fearsomely one-eyed soundtrack. Pearl Jam contributed two previously unreleased tracks ('State Of Love And Trust' and 'Breath'), as did Soundgarden ('British Ritual' and Chris Cornell's solo effort, 'Seasons'), Mudhoney ('Overblown'), and Anne and Nancy Wilson in the guise of The Lovemongers (a live 'Battle Of Evermore'), plus extras from the likes of Alice In Chains ('Would?'), Smashing Pumpkins ('Drown'), Mother Love Bone ('Chloe Dancer/Crown of Thorns') and Jimi Hendrix ('May This Be Love').

9

Stone, Jeff, Eddie, Mike and Dave played about fifteen shows under the Mookie Blaylock moniker before changing the name to something less obscure. 'The joke kinda wore off and we didn't want to be known as a joke band,'[55] Jeff explained. The alternative they came up with – Pearl Jam – was suggested by Eddie. 'Great-grandpa was an American Indian and totally into peyote and hallucinogenics,' he told his incredulous bandmates, 'and Great-Grandma Pearl used to make this hallucinogenic preserve – Pearl's jam – that's just legendary. Shame we don't have the recipe . . .'[56] The sudden change of name was prompted, as much as anything, by the sudden interest being shown in them by Epic Records, who had just picked up Alice In Chains. As luck would have it, Michael Goldstone, who'd signed Mother Love Bone to Polygram and stayed in touch ever since, had moved over to Epic at the start of 1991. It also helped that their attorney, Michael Anthony, also worked a great deal with Epic's parent company, Sony. The band had been together as Pearl Jam less than three weeks when, as Jeff put it, 'Through a lot of magic and a lot of hard work on their part, we ended up getting out of our contract at Polygram and we ended up signing with Epic.'[57]

Working out of London Bridge Studios in Seattle with producer Rick Parasher, *Ten*, the first Pearl Jam album (named after the number of Mookie's Mets shirt) was completed over March and April 1991. Sticking closely to the original template of Mookie demos, the songs were recorded as live, the way the band had been doing them for months. Very little embellishment took place. 'Mother Love Bone in a lot of ways, toward the end especially, was a creatively stifling experience for the people involved,' said Stone. 'In that sense, I think similar ideas that we would have had in Mother Love Bone that never came to fruition are actually being finished at this point . . . there are moments on the record that we have right now that aren't perfect, which is great. That's the kind of record we wanted to make.'[58] 'I don't think it was anything that we were aware of at the time,' said Eddie, 'but after the record was done all of a sudden we realized there was almost a running theme about the appreciation of life. Songs like "Porch" that talk about how . . . randomly our lives can be taken. And obviously there's "Alive" and "Deep", which is about substance abuse and people maybe not appreciating their life and being decadent in the way they live it.'[59]

On straight-ahead stompers like 'Even Flow', 'Why Go' or 'Deep', Pearl Jam didn't sound so much 'Seattle' or 'grunge' as a lip-smacking amalgamation of the most dramatic moments from the collected works of The Who, Led Zeppelin or early Aerosmith, while the exotic twin-guitar thrust of 'Oceans' or 'Alive' reminded older heads of vintage pre-smack Allman Brothers or Lynyrd Skynyrd. What was 'Seattle' was the sheer bare-faced power the new five-piece exuded. Coupled with sensitive, biographical lyrical sketches like 'Jeremy', a remarkable song about mental and physical child abuse, and Stone and Eddie's descent into the void, 'Black', these were anthems of yearning and loneliness that zillions of people who didn't necessarily all wear baseball caps and feel misunderstood by society would be able to relate to.

In May 1991, as the band travelled to Ridge Farm Studios in Dorking, England, where they would oversee the mix of the eleven tracks that would comprise *Ten*, 'Alive', destined to be the band's first single and the first track they had finished, was pre-released in America as part of the recently launched *Coca-Cola* Pop Music Cassette series.

Specially marked 'Pop Music' packs of *Coke* products contained either a free 3-inch CD or a certificate redeemable for any of ten cassettes. 'Alive' was featured on 'Rock Cassette Volume 1'. Then, in August, just prior to its release proper, as the band prepared to take the road for the first time as Pearl Jam in earnest, a three-song sampler of *Ten* was issued to US radio stations and interested music-biz pundits. Reaction was favourable and the band nudged things along with a specially bright-eyed launch-party performance at the RKCNDY (pronounced: rock candy) club in Seattle, with Sweet Water opening.

But there was consternation for Eddie at the band's post-gig record-release party; a harbinger of the delights in store for the still determinedly individualistic singer. 'We'd just played this amazing show and it was real. Then you go into this, like, disco with Pearl Jam posters everywhere and people shaking your hand – "Hey, this is Barney; every time you see your record, Barney put it there" – that lasted for hours,' he complained. 'I had friends who were laughing at me from the corner, and I was like, "Dude, fuck you, this isn't funny."'[60]

10

Dave Krusen departed shortly after the band were in England mixing the album. He later returned to his pre-Pearl Jam band, Son Of Man, but at the time of his disappearance from Pearl Jam, there were whispers that the drummer had fallen victim to the same kind of ill-advised self-abuse that finally dragged Andy Wood down, and that the band summarily dismissed him when they found out. Close friends now refute this. 'Their original drummer, like in the middle of their first tour, had problems with his girlfriend and bummed out on the road,' said one. New Bohemians drummer Matt Chamberlain filled in once again briefly before coming up with the name of yet another young sticksman he knew of from Texas called Dave Abbruzzese.

The middle child of three brothers – 'I'm the only person in my family who was ever really involved with music'[61] – Dave Abbruzzese was born in Stamford, Connecticut, on May 17th, 1968 and attended grade school in East Hartford and Manchester before he and his family moved to North Carolina when he was eleven. A year later they moved to Texas where he lived for the next twelve years. He dropped out of high school early because, he said, compared to his devotion to drumming and making music 'nothing else mattered. My theory at the time was that I could always go back to school, but I couldn't always seize the opportunities that were at my door [as a musician] ... I had no sense of the gamble I was taking at that time. Music was the only thing that made me happy.'[62]

He was living in Dallas with his girlfriend and their cat, when Chamberlain called up out of the blue one day and asked if he was interested in going on tour. 'I asked him why he was leaving and he said it was like being in a fight with Mike Tyson every night.'[63] Chamberlain had also just been offered a steady job with the house band on *Saturday Night Live*. Dave had been playing in a funk band called Dr Tongue and co-hosting his own radio show, *Music We Like*, in Houston, at the time of Matt's call. 'At first I said no, I was happy playing with my friends,' he recalled.[64] But after his second gig with the band he went out and had the sickly stick-figure drawing by Jeff that graced the cover of *Alive* – a grinning, shaggy-headed stoner, his bleary eyes upturned, bony fingers clawing the sky – tattooed on his shoulder. 'I saw the drawing as this symbol of everything that I feel right now ... I wanted to remember that second for the rest of my life.'[65]

The appeal Pearl Jam went out of their way to nurture on *Ten* derived not from the trad-codpiece posturing of Mother Love Bone but rather from an abiding affection for the cacophonous revelations of late Sixties music – rock's first truly progressive phase – and an ironic, caustic take on post-adolescent cares here in the red-faced, white-knuckled Nineties. With Pearl Jam, you didn't just get what you paid for, you got more, extra, double overtime; a socially aware, riff-laden monstermash, busy redesigning the cock-rock embarrassment of metal decades gone, while still cranking it up to eleven ... Eddie standing perfectly still one moment, folded into himself while 'Once' or 'Jeremy' bucked and swirled about him like a stormy sea. 'I'm kind of a cynic about these guys who cross their arms when they sing,' said Soundgarden's Kim Thayil. 'But there were songs that Eddie sang that sent shivers up my spine.'[66]

With the new Ament/Gossard/McCready/Vedder/Abbruzzese

line-up firmly in place and *Ten* about to hit American stores for the first time, Pearl Jam began to take their music to the people outside Seattle. Supporting the Red Hot Chili Peppers on their 'BloodSugar-SexMagick' tour, as well as stretching out with some high-profile headline spots of their own in such media-friendly hives as CBGB's in New York, most nights they faced sceptical audiences unfamiliar with their material and impatient for the headliners. Winning them over was a task they faced with considerable relish, for by now they needed no one else to tell them; they knew they were good.

Live, where Andy had been never less than flamboyant, Eddie was dark and glowering. Where Andy would curl his pock-marked arms around an audience and want to kiss them where it counted, Eddie's main stage habit seemed to involve climbing the scaffolding, then dropping like a stone on to the (hopefully) waiting hands of the sometimes genuinely frightened crowd below. At one point, Eddie had both hands wrapped in plaster to protect the wounds he had incurred from crowd-surfin', and was taking medication to kill the pain. He was spotted a month later with his arm in a sling – still willingly plunging himself into the mosh-pit every night with the rest of the body-slammers. 'It's like stand-up comedy,' Jeff pondered. 'You either come out strong or fall flat on your face.'[67]

They had intended to give the home-town audience a chance to see what they were missing with a show with the Chilis at the Seattle Center Arena on January 3rd, 1992, but were forced to cancel at the last minute when Chilis' mainman Anthony Kiedis was laid low with heavy flu. Meantime, *Ten* was beginning to steadily catch alight on the *Billboard* Hot 100, boosted in no small measure by MTV's heavy-rotation of the 'Alive' video; a straight-to-camera performance piece shot at the Moore Theater in front of an invited audience.

11

At the start of 1991, Sub Pop had begun selling a T-shirt with the legend WHAT PART OF 'WE HAVE NO MONEY' DON'T YOU UNDERSTAND? emblazoned across its front. But help was at hand – though not, as

Above: Bruce Fairweather, Stone Gossard, Andrew Wood, Greg Gilmore, Jeff Ament: the late lamented Mother Love Bone, 1990. (*London Features International*)

Left: Jeff Ament and Bruce Fairweather: Mother Love Bone, 1989. (*London Features International*)

Mother Love Bone graffiti on the wall of The Vogue, a principal venue for the band in Seattle. (*Laura Wurzal*)

Jeff Ament. (*Redferns*)

Out-take promo shot of Pearl Jam, August 1993.
(*Retna Pictures*)

Dave Abbruzzese. (*Redferns*)

Left: Mike McCready goes native in Holland, February 1992. (*Redferns*)

Below: Eddie gets a good tongue-lashing from Red Hot Chili Peppers frontman, Anthony Kiedis, 'Lollapalooza II', 1992. (*London Features International*)

All live shots from 'Lollapalooza II', 1992. (*Retna Pictures*)

Above: Eddie and rock babe backstage, 1992. (*Redferns*)

Above right: Shooting the hoop: Jeff Ament, Stone Gossard (standing) and Dave Abbruzzese in publicity shot for *Ten*, 1992. (*Retna Pictures*)

Right: Eddie in typical hand-wringing pose on stage, 1992. (*Retna Pictures*)

Pearl Jam Unplugged, recorded New York, March 1992; since repeated on MTV countless times. (*Retna Pictures*)

Above left: Jim True, Bridget Fonda, Matt Dillon, Kyra Sedgwick and Campbell Scott in the Warner Brothers film *Singles* (1992). (*The Kobal Collection*)

Above right: Jeff and a newly shorn Stone on stage, summer 1993. (*Retna Pictures*)

Right: Eddie Vedder in one of his many full-head masks. (*London Features International*)

Below: MTV music video awards, September 1993. Pearl Jam swept the board winning four awards. (*London Features International*)

Left: Eddie on stage, 1993. (*London Features*)

Below: Roger Daltrey, Eddie Vedder and Linda Perry (singer in 4 Non-Blondes) at Carnegie Hall, 23 February 1994, for Roger Daltrey's Fiftieth Birthday Bash. (*London Features International*)

they had envisaged, in the shape of a white knight label coming to their financial rescue. The answer to all Sub Pop's perverted dreams came from the least expected source: massive record sales by an artist they actually had under contract; a possibility that seemed so remote at the start of 1991 they had not even considered it. Ironically, the help even came from the artist direct, when Nirvana bassist Krist Novoselic had pounded drunkenly on Bruce Pavitt's door late one night before the first Nirvana album, *Bleach*, was released in 1989, and demanded he write out an agreement of some sort between Sub Pop and Nirvana. Poneman duly put together a contract, which the band signed straight away. Consequently, when the newly set-up 'punk division' of Geffen Records, DGC, wanted to sign the band in 1991, they first had to buy them out of their hastily drafted agreement with Sub Pop. Pavitt and Poneman ended up with a tidy $75,000 in cash plus three points on each subsequent Nirvana album sold. The nine million plus copies of the band's début DGC album, *Nevermind*, would ensure that Sub Pop never had to go cap in hand to the bank again. Demand for their back catalogue alone nudged *Bleach* into the *Billboard* Hot 100 for the first time, in 1992 – the first Sub Pop record to do so. But of course, by then, they had re-issued *Bleach* in a variety of different coloured 'limited editions' no less than seven times.

Once memorably described by his future wife, Courtney Love, as looking like one of these tacky paintings of the little boy with too big eyes and a single tear trickling down his face, sweet and innocent on the surface but with something sinister lurking underneath, Kurt Cobain's songs could be described as something similar. Staccato and charred at the stumps, but smeared in the reassuring sheen of a thousand half-remembered pop choruses, the bittersweet refrains of early Nirvana classics like 'About A Girl', 'Floyd The Barber' or the unsettlingly blue-in-the-face 'Reciprocal' weren't so much North-west punk as pure uncut Sixties American pop. It could have been the 1910 Fruitgum Company on acid or the Chocolate Watchband not on acid ... except Cobain had never heard of them. He was strictly into the Beatles. 'We're just babbling idiots, wise-dickers, opinionated white trash,' he told whoever wanted to know. 'I decided when I was seven that all my surroundings sucked, there was no sign of anyone who would be into art or music ... I listened to the Beatles' records every night religiously. That's all I did when I was a kid. After I reached my teens, I decided I didn't want to hang out with anyone. I couldn't handle the stupidity.'[68]

Cobain and Krist Novoselic, a first-generation Yugoslav, were both from Aberdeen, 'a really dead logging town on the shores of the Pacific Ocean ... If we hadn't done this band thing, we would have been doing what everyone else does back home, which is chopping down trees, drinking, having sex and drinking, talking about sex and drinking some more,'[69] Cobain deadpanned. The band's slogan, 'Fudge packing, crack smoking, Satan worshipping motherfuckers', was, he said, 'a joke on anybody stupid enough to believe in any of that shit'.[70]

As an anti-Eighties icon, Kurt Cobain was perfectly suited to his role. Quotable, cute, not afraid to say yes, not in a hurry to say no, not afraid to be his own inadequate, bad-mouthed, talented self, Kurt Cobain began to grace the covers of so many magazines in 1991 that if he had suddenly declared the sky green, millions would have rushed outside to see what he meant and *still* agreed with him. Which is why, when he accused Pearl Jam at the end of 1991 of being 'responsible for this corporate, alternative and cock-rock fusion,'[71] the taunt hit home. As Mudhoney guitarist Steve Turner could confirm, 'When I met Stoney, he liked commercial hard rock. He was a metal dude and I was, a punk. He'd play me early Alice Cooper and Motorhead records, and I'd play him Black Flag'[72] – none of the members of Pearl Jam came from a particularly radical musical background.

But if comparisons between Pearl Jam and Nirvana were inevitable, ultimately, they were irrelevant; the two bands had nothing in common but geography. While *Ten* was still struggling gamely for a foothold on the American Top 40, *Nevermind*, released a month earlier, in September 1991, had entered the *Billboard* charts at a safe No. 144, then jumped to No. 109 the following week, made another long hop to No. 65 the third week, kept going at No. 35 the fourth ... and by the seventh week of release, *Nevermind* had bludgeoned its scary way to No. 4, snapping at the expensively coiffed tail of the much bigger hyped *Use Your Illusion II* album by Guns N' Roses. By January 1992, however, it had displaced Michael Jackson's *Dangerous* from the No. 1 spot in the US and was fast on its way to achieving worldwide sales of over nine million. The first single from the album, 'Smells Like Teen Spirit', also became a huge worldwide hit.

Though he would expend much useless energy over the next two

years refuting the suggestion that his band were somehow manufactured by the record company to look and sound like this year's model
grunge band, at first Eddie was too busy expressing his own doubts
about Pearl Jam's own apparently imminent success to over-concern
himself with the jibes starting to come his way from potential rivals.
'I'll tell you right now and the band will probably hate me for saying
this, but I feel it's getting a little too big too quick,' he confided to
RAW magazine. 'Believe me, I'm really trying to keep it small, these
songs are really intimate songs . . . Some people are saying let's go
with it, let's ride the wave to see how big it can get. It's a ride, but you
can only go so high before you start sounding silly. In many ways I
can almost feel sorry for Kurt Cobain, I don't know what he's going
to write about on the next record. How frustrating can it be, having as
much money to do whatever you want to do, you know? How's he
going to sing to punk rock music?'[73]

Certainly, you couldn't question Eddie's commitment to making
music that had a focus beyond mere sales figures. On New Year's Eve,
1991, Pearl Jam opened the bill below both Nirvana and Red Hot
Chili Peppers at the Cow Palace, in San Francisco. Every year for
twenty years on New Year's Eve, San Francisco's famous Haight
Street had been overrun by tie-dyed Grateful Dead fans – 'deadheads'
– on their way to the annual Dead show at the Oakland Coliseum.
'Want to hear some songs by the Dead?' Eddie taunted the six
thousand fans at the sold-out Cow Palace show. The audience booed
loudly. Eddie drowned them out with an a-cappella rendition of
Fugazi's anti-rape song, 'Suggestion'. 'Don't go partying on other
people's pussies unless they want you to,' he solemnly advised the
crowd. Later, once the music had started up, as a mark of respect, he
dutifully climbed the lighting rig and, at the set's close, leapt blindly
into the maw of the crowd.

But the night belonged to Nirvana. The band had that special light
around their heads that said they had just reached No. 1 for the first
time in their lives and the world was a suddenly much newer, stranger
place to live in. When the Peppers appeared – bassist Flea lowered to
the stage upside-down by ropes tied to his ankles – even they seemed
to have trouble matching up . . . fire-eaters, naked day-glo smeared
dancers and enormous explosions of light and sound timed to go off at
midnight – nothing looked or sounded quite the same after Nirvana.
Simply, this was their time and next to them everything was bound to

look somehow out of sync; a comedy with the wrong laugh-track. Not that that stopped the final stage-diver of the night, Eddie, from taking the leap during a shared encore with the Chilis, an over-the-top rendition of 'Yurtle the Turtle'.

'This is the future. And this is only the beginning. Pearl Jam will reach these shores by January; murder anyone who tries to stop you from seeing them,' catcalled the *Melody Maker* bravely.[74] 'Our Christmas wish is to come over as support for the Chilis,' Eddie told *MM*. 'Cos the Chilis don't really get naked on stage, but we get naked . . .'[75]

CHAPTER FOUR

TOP TEN

'The whole hype thing is stupid, but it's great for all the bands in Seattle. You call up your friend – "Hey, d'you get a record deal today? I got one." "I'm on the cover of a magazine!" "All right! So am I!" "Let's eat dinner tonight!" "Sorry, Time *magazine's coming to my house . . .!"'*[1]

– Dan Peters of Mudhoney

'To some people, a punk ethic would be just getting sloshed before, during and after a show, staying up all night fucking and shooting heroin. But to me it's more punk to be in control, strong and able to do things with your body that you wouldn't be able to do if you were weak, or weak of spirit . . .'[2]

– Eddie Vedder

'Pearl Jam = Journey'[3]

– graffiti seen on a wall in Washington, DC, 1992

1

By the time *Singles* was released, in the late summer of 1992, the whole situation had changed so much in the Northwest that Citizen Dick, if they had been a real band, would probably have been signed by a major label. The breakthrough had undoubtedly been Nirvana's stunning

Nevermind album, but elsewhere the word 'Seattle' was already becoming synonymous with a new breed of American rock music that laboured haphazardly though not entirely inaccurately under the 'grunge' *nom de plume*. After Nirvana, the name the rest of the world knew best was Mudhoney. Both were Sub Pop artists, of course, but insiders always knew that the most popular *local* Sub Poppers were Soundgarden. One of the first Seattle bands to record for the label and one of the first to leave for a major, their second album for A&M, *Badmotorfinger*, released in the autumn of 1991, had followed *Nevermind* into the US charts less spectacularly but just as fulsomely. A lot of the new-found success Pearl Jam were starting to enjoy, said Eddie, had 'a lot to do with bands like Nirvana and Soundgarden'. Stone agreed. 'Both their new records are so great I think they've totally come into their own,' he said. 'In that way, they are totally inspiring, especially Soundgarden.' 'There's no pointless guitar solos, and no gratuitous, meaningless lyrics,' Eddie pointed out. 'I think Cornell's lyrics are amazing.'[4]

When Pearl Jam arrived in England for their first live dates in Europe, on February 3rd, 1992, Nirvana had already sold their first million albums and Soundgarden were not far from doing the same. *Ten*, boosted by MTV's shrewd decision to put the grainy 'Alive' video on their 'heavy rotation' roster in the wake of the response they had already received from videos by Nirvana, Soundgarden and Alice In Chains, was hovering around the quarter-million mark in America. Healthy but not heavy – not yet. The success of their contemporaries reflected well on the new band's chances but it also made their task more difficult. From their inception, Pearl Jam had always had a lot to live up to, but now, following Kurt Cobain's comments in *Musician* magazine – 'They're going to be the ones responsible for this corporate, alternative . . . fusion,'[5] snidely comparing the band to Poison – they suddenly had a lot to live down, too. It was an off-the-cuff remark that was to have lasting consequences for Eddie and the band's credibility in the UK.

'Every article I see written about them, they mention us,' moaned Cobain to his biographer, Michael Azerrad. 'I would love to be erased from my association with that band and other corporate bands like The Nymphs and a few other felons. I do feel a duty to warn kids of false music that's claiming to be underground.'[6] With the exception of Eddie, who was deeply hurt by Cobain's continual put-downs, the rest of the band shrugged their lean shoulders and went back to doing what felt right: playing. 'I don't know what I did to him; if he has a personal vendetta against us, he should come to us,' said Jeff, more puzzled than shocked. 'To have that sort of pent-up frustration, the guy obviously must have some really deep insecurities about himself. Does he think we're riding his bandwagon? We could turn around and say that Nirvana put out records on money we made for Sub Pop when we were in Green River – if we were stupid about it.'[7]

'I can see why the Nirvana camp wouldn't like Pearl Jam's music because it's not really related to that punk tradition,' says *Record Collector* editor Peter Doggett. 'If you were growing up in Seattle with the punk/hardcore scene and there were these people came up who'd turned their backs on it and gone with a very mainstream tradition, you can see that there'd be a sense of betrayal. I mean, if someone like Courtney Love had been fronting Pearl Jam, they would sound very different. Eddie Vedder's vocal syle bears no relation to Andrew Wood or Green River . . . singing about the homeless on 'Porch', for example, even though he's very sincere, he does it within a tradition that's so totally insincere that you can't take it seriously.' 'There is no really controversial figure there,' concluded Geoff Barton, managing editor of *Kerrang!*. 'Also with Pearl Jam, they undoubtedly have that Seattle heritage of Green River and Mother Love Bone, but a lot of people still perceive them to be the band who is part of a big corporate rock 'n' roll machine. Which, obviously, Nirvana are too, but with Cobain being the kind of guy he is that kind of nullifies the situation.'

The first Pearl Jam single, 'Alive', was released in Britain in February 1992. The four different formats it came in (white vinyl 7", 12" poster bag, picture CD, and cassette), in tandem with the wealth of attention their visit attracted in the music press, did little for their punk cred. It did ensure that 'Alive' would sail straight into the UK Top 20, though. Accordingly, MTV Europe rotated the video like a spit on a well-done barbecue and the band arrived with a smile on their faces ready to glad-hand anybody that was willing to give them five minutes of their time. However, not everybody was waiting to be smitten. In the *Los Angeles Times*, reviewer Chris Williams had compared 'Alive' in an early review to The Who's 'My Generation'. Reviewing the same record six months later in the *NME*, sour-faced Julie Burchill wannabe Barbara Ellen wrote that Epic was 'sinking a lot of moolah into these Seattle also-rans in the hope that they might emulate the success of current music industry saviours Nirvana. I think ramming them anus-first on to the end of a cannon may be quicker and more heartening.'[9]

Chastened, when Pearl Jam played their first UK date, at the tiny Borderline club in London, on February 3rd, 1992, they did not know what to expect. Stoically, they sauntered on stage trying to ignore the press of faces in the darkness around the molecule-sized stage, strayed into 'Wash', a B-side no one recognized, the crowd still talking, oblivious. Then Stone struck the first chiming chords of 'Once', Eddie opened his mouth to roar and the crowd were suddenly very aware indeed. The talking had stopped. 'Why Go' found Eddie crouching, swaying, hugging the mike like a drunk friend being helped down the street, urging the front rows to move some more, before standing on tiptoe in mock-crucifixion pose, then falling, a sleeping Christ, safely into the arms of the strangers about him . . .

2

After the Borderline appearance, Pearl Jam crossed the channel for a handful of promotional dates on the Continent. When they returned to Britain a fortnight later, the short tour began inauspiciously at the modest International 2 club in Manchester, on Friday, February 21st, 1992. 'This isn't what I thought it was like!' Jeff remarked to a journalist from the *NME*. 'We thought there'd be clubs on every corner and people raving on the streets . . .' Stone explained, only half-joking.[10] At the show Eddie introduced 'Deep' as being 'about homo-sexuality'. 'Fuck off, you faggot!' someone in the crowd shouted. 'Oh, really?' Eddie responded, surprised not at all. 'That's a pretty typical response. That says a lot . . .' Earlier in the evening, the band's tour bus had been robbed by a surprisingly organized gang of youths, some as young as thirteen, holding tour manager Eric Johnson at knife-point while the band were inside the club eating a meal, removing gear and personal belongings from the bus. 'At first, I thought they were just local lads helping out the roadies,' said one of the Epic reps who was there. 'Then when I walked round to the front of the van, I saw that they were lifting stuff over a fence to a chain of their mates on the other side . . .'[11]

The incident was not reported to the police. Instead, they wove their way the next morning to Newcastle and the Riverside club (22nd), and from there to Glasgow's Cat House (23rd), the Rock City, Nottingham (25th), Edwards in Birmingham (26th), the Queen's Hall, Bradford (27th) and finishing back in London at the University of London's Student Union hall on the 28th. As one over-eager kid swept past him to leap off the stage at the final show at the ULU, Eddie yelled after him, 'You may think you look like Jesus Christ when you see yourself on MTV, man, but when I see you I just want to crucify you.' He seemed in a bad mood. He verbally abused the stage-divers all night, saying, 'Those are people's heads, not casaba melons!' And yet how many times had he himself fallen on to the melon-like heads and hands of the faithful? By the encores he had lightened up enough to tell the crowd that there was a record company party upstairs after the show, but that 'I ain't gonna be there – I'm gonna be in Russell Square and you're all invited!' The show ended with Eddie clambering up the PA stack, before leaping from the giant speaker-amps to the long heavy curtains draped over the ULU's windows, turning, as the *Melody Maker* noted, 'from Edmund Hilary to Tarzan'[11] as he started to swing across the wall, using the curtains as tree vines, the crowd watching open-mouthed below . . .

3

When *Ten* appeared in Britain at the end of February 1992, it didn't need any heavy-handed marketing. Initially available on import, its reputation had preceded it and the accompanying clutch of live dates had been eye-opening for both band and fans alike. Nevertheless, reviews for *Ten* were mixed, to say the least. The specialist metal mags like *Kerrang!* blew the trumpets; the even more 'specialist' rags like the *NME* dismissed it as yesterday's cheese. The *Melody Maker*'s editor, Allan Jones, was the most genuinely baffled by the album. 'Listening to this remarkable record,' he wrote, 'I can hear echoes of Neil Young & Crazy Horse, REM, The Replacements, and – unlikely, I know – Tim Buckley. These people worship in the broad church of American music,' he decided, eyebrows raised, before coming down unequi-vocally on the side of positivity. '*Ten* is rock the way she was meant to be rolled . . .'[13]

The chief quality *Ten* offered the first-time Pearl Jam buyer was its raw, worldly atmosphere; the sense that what the singer with the voice like old wine was singing about had been lived . . . 'Why Go' was written about a real friend of Eddie's who was hospitalized after being caught smoking pot; 'Release' was written as Stone was playing and tuning up, the rest of the band just teasing out the melody, burring along, Eddie putting down the phrases as they stole into his mind . . . everything kept deliberately raw, the opposite of the contrived, no-rough-edges approach of Mother Love Bone. 'We wanna do some more of that ambient stuff,' said Stone prophetically, referring to the space-trance instrumental that opens and closes the album. 'Again, that's away from rock music rules, the whole ambience, that whole wash, it floats you away,' Eddie explained obliquely. 'I was, like, singing vocals through a headphone plugged into an amp, and Jeff was playing his twelve-string bass with a violin bow through a wah-wah pedal. And I hung upside down on gravity boots, while Jeff put a microphone at the bottom of a swing and just pushed . . . it was just Jeff and I at four o'clock in the morning . . .'[14]

Most of Eddie's lyrics appear as riddles; even the lyrics printed on the *Ten* sleeve are only partial. Indeed, the most he ever gave away about any of his songs was when he told Cameron Crowe that the story of 'Alive' was far from being the life-affirming message of hope as interpreted by everybody from REM's Michael Stipe to the kid in the back row in the Anthrax T-shirt. Loosely related in the chorus to a half-formed stream-of-consciousness bit of nonsense called 'I'm Alive' that he used to sing in Bad Radio, the real story behind the song was so personal, so deeply rooted in the singer's own psyche that even the lyrics are only expressed in scattered half-thoughts, spluttered, con-fused and deeply angry. 'There are people who have got the *Ten* album because they love the tunes and it's just another good album in their collection. And there are the people that look on Eddie as a bit of a God,' says *Raw* editor Jon Hotten. 'Part of Eddie's credibility is that he's not at all self-centred. He's best when he looks outward. Whereas someone like Kurt Cobain or Axl Rose are always turned in on themselves. That kind of introspection is only interesting for a certain length of time.'

There was certainly some deranged stuff in there . . . 'Once', Eddie confessed, was almost autobiographical. 'Don't get me wrong,' he said, 'I wouldn't want to do it. But there's a sense of – and again, I frighten myself by relating so much – a sense of "Fuck it, if I'm going down, and it's not my fault, and I did everything I fucking could, and I worked with these hands, and I didn't do drugs, if I'm out of here, then I'm taking a few people with me." There's no logic there, but that misplaced passion . . .'[14] And of course, there was 'Jeremy', based on the true story of sixteen-year-old Jeremy Wade Delle, a loner from the small town of Richardson, Texas, who put the barrel of a .347 Magnum pistol into his mouth in front of his English class one morning after being told off for missing classes, and pulled the trigger. The incident, which occurred on January 8th, 1991, was reported widely in the American press at the time and it was a story that had deeper, unknowable resonances for Eddie, who identified with the tragic victim's confusion so strongly that every lyric he came up with for weeks afterwards seemed to reflect his thoughts on the incident.

'It's a good story,' Eddie would say. 'A kid blew his brains out in front of his English class. That probably happens once a week in America. It's a by-product of the American fascination, or rather perversion, with guns.'[15] 'Parental neglect and abuse is the source of many problems that the Earth has today,' Stone commented solemnly. 'Childhood is such a critical time of a person's development, the critical time. Many of the things that happen to you as a child resurface. Some of the inspiration for 'Jeremy' came from a Texan newspaper article, but you can tell that some of the elements are out of Eddie's own experience.'

'The thing that surrounds Pearl Jam is the recession,' says Jon Hotten. 'They've got a very dark undertone to their music which the youth of today respond to. Eddie Vedder was an itinerant. The society he came from had nothing to offer him, and that's what he writes about. That's sort of the difference . . . Mötley Crüe and Guns N' Roses and all those guys lived in LA and had all this party scene buzzing round them constantly, and that's what their music sounded like. Vedder, who comes from a completely different world, had none of that.'

'Two days ago I got a package from some guy who had interviewed me for his college newspaper. I'd told him I'd talk to him if he'd climb up on the edge of this bridge overlooking the water. This guy and a friend did it and it was totally memorable, better than most interviews I do,' Eddie told *Kerrang!* on the eve of the band's departure for London. 'Anyway, inside the package was the article and a tape of the interview. I went to put them back inside the package and found a letter. I pulled it out and read, "Here's the interview that we did with the assistance of Michael, my friend. In the newspaper, you'll also notice a memorium to Michael because he died in a fatal car accident on December 15th". In the letter it told me how they were playing 'Alive' on the college radio station and how they had broadcast the interview . . . That gave me such an inescapable feeling of how suddenly things can change. That's just another reason to do something new each day. Either way, you'll end up doing one thing new to you in your life and that'll be dying.'[16]

4

Returning to America in March, Pearl Jam found themselves booked into increasingly larger venues, as *Ten* started to climb the charts seriously, its complicated tentacles curling slowly around the neck of the US Top 10. Of course, Eddie had his reservations but there was no doubt that things were moving now. 'I'm wondering if they're coming because they feel good things about this band or because they want to be shown the latest thing,' he pondered. 'Because that's not where I'm coming from.'[17]

At the annual Northwest Music Awards in March, Pearl Jam won three awards: New Group of the Year, Best Rock Album, for *Ten*, and Mike McCready was named Best Electric Guitarist. In April, they made their first appearance on the prestigious *Saturday Night Live* show. At the end of the performance, Eddie turned his back to the camera and revealed a message printed on his shirt. The director moved quickly to pull the camera out of range but the shirt was clearly inscribed NO BUSH '92. On the front was just a coat-hanger – a symbol for Pro-Choice, the coat-hanger as symbol of the typical back-street abortionist's tool-kit. 'That is the only cause that I will go public with,' Eddie explained later. The band had just returned from playing with Fugazi in Los Angeles at a Pro-Choice benefit called Rock For Choice, persuading people to sign petitions supporting the recently launched French abortion pill. 'You get a chance to say something on national TV, and I'm not gonna keep my mouth shut. I try to do it in a subtle enough way.'[18]

The effect of their *SNL* appearance boosted album sales, which were, by now, starting to emulate Nirvana and Soundgarden's success, moving *Ten* inexorably towards platinum status, with total sales in America by then of around eight hundred and seventy thousand. In April, the second Pearl Jam single, a re-recording of 'Even Flow' from *Ten*, was released: this time the big promotional gimmick was a 7" vinyl single with a special competition on the sleeve – the prize being the chance to meet the band and see them play live in Seattle. The bonus cut on the 12" and CD was a somewhat spurious ode to the band's 'colourful' tour driver, a self-explanatory ode entitled 'Dirty Frank'. That month, the band were also spotlighted in a *Superstar Concert* syndicated radio show in the States, alongside former college radio stars the Smithereens, and MTV added the 'Even Flow' video (another no-frills performance clip, though in colour this time) to its 'Buzz Bin'. Among the new fans that the band had picked up were U2. All of U2 except Bono had attended a Pearl Jam nightclub appearance in Chicago that spring, and the two bands had spent some time together getting acquainted afterwards. When the Edge and Adam Clayton hosted *MTV's 120 Minutes* in April, the new 'Even Flow' video, replete with quaking hand-held shots of Eddie climbing to the top of the room and jumping down, was among the videos the two singled out for special praise.

At 10.00 p.m., on Wednesday, May 8th, 1992, with their first album still less than six months old, MTV paid the band their highest accolade and aired a special *Pearl Jam Unplugged* performance. Taped in March at a midnight session at a New York studio, surprising many previously unimpressed observers with the power and emotion they were able to summon from the songs without the back up of arena-sized amps or the indoor fireworks of a modern computerized light-show. They played 'Alive', 'State of Love And Trust', 'Black', 'Jeremy', 'Porch', and the current single, 'Even Flow', the magic between Eddie and Stone and the others as visible as the glint of wonder in their nervous, smiling eyes. 'Up to that point, Pearl Jam had been very much this *heavy metal* band – even if they had been lumped in with the word "grunge". That acoustic set alerted the HM sceptics to how well constructed the songs were that Stone and Eddie were writing,' says former *Sounds* child prodigy Peter Makowski. 'After that, a lot of people rightly stopped giving a shit whether it was grunge or whether it was this or that. They just dug the groove, the lyrics . . . Eddie's amazing voice . . . you know, the *music* . . .'

5

A week after the *Unplugged* session aired, the band returned to Seattle for what was supposed to have been the crowning glory of their success so far: a free show, ostensibly as part of a voter-registration drive for newly eligible teenagers – 1992 was an election year and George Bush vs. Bill Clinton was already shaping up to be the boxing match of the year in America. When the concert, to have been held in Gas Works Park, was cancelled just four days before the event was supposed to have taken place, Pearl Jam held a noisy press conference, frustration and anger apparent on their faces. The show had been in planning for over five months, they said, and the producers had obtained approval from City Hall. Eddie then claimed that at the last minute the Parks Department suggested the event be held on Wednesday, May 27th, at noon, a date the band could not make because of their tour schedule. 'I'm not sure if Mayor Rice had planned to sign excuse notices to every kid in town, but in case he didn't notice, Wednesday is a school day for a lot of our fans,' Eddie added with an unconcealed contempt. 'If we hit another smoke-screen there'll be trouble,' he warned. 'We're not going to get into a pissing match with the city, but I think they'll find that a lot of people are going to be up in arms about this.'

The line up was not the issue so much as the size of the crowd. Initially estimated at the planning stages that about five thousand people might show up, since then the band's burgeoning success had inflated demand for tickets to such an extent that revised estimations now put the figure expected to turn up at closer to thirty thousand. A prospect that plainly unsettled the mayor. Eddie pointed out that Gas Works Park has been the site of Fourth of July celebrations with crowds far larger than that. Several large outdoor classical music concerts had also been held there. According to *The Rocket*, the Parks

Department decided to cancel the show because of political back-stabbing by other Seattle promoters. 'This was a free concert and since other people couldn't make a buck out of it, they didn't help get it approved,' one source said. 'The Parks Department is an old-boy network and you have to have the connections to work with them and only a few people in this town do. It's ridiculous and it has to change.'[19]

Eddie ended the press conference with the same message he said he would have given from the Gas Works Park stage, delivered straight-faced to the crowd of sceptical reporters present. 'Get your bodies into the trenches and empower yourselves. You have to do this. Silence equals death.' There was to have been a special skateboard ramp built alongside the main stage in Gas Works Park to display the skills of some of America's best-known skateboarders that the band had paid to come along. When the show got cancelled, Eddie went ahead and had the fifteen-foot-high ramp built anyway on land away from the park. 'Skaters have this weird cosmic energy,' he explained enigmatically. 'When they're catching air [flying off the top of the ramp] it's like they're feeling nature. It's like when you surf, when you feel the power of the ocean, the rhythm of the waves.'[20]

In June, the band were scheduled to depart for another five-week tour of Europe, including dates in England, Ireland, France, Denmark, Germany, Sweden, Belgium and Italy. Two nights before their departure, Eddie took Kim Neely of *Rolling Stone* to the top of the Space Needle, where he showed her the view and pointed out the huge star-like light-bulbs that ring the Needle's uppermost circumference. 'From the ground they look like stars or Saturn's rings,' Eddie told her. He was just starting to suss out his chances of sneaking through the suicide nets to procure a light-bulb when the writer announced that she had no wish to watch Eddie convert himself into pizza from a height of thirty storeys just on her behalf. Eddie acquiesced and Neely breathed a sigh of relief, but the next night he went back with a friend ('It was much windier, too,' he boasted), wriggled through the wire, edged out along the bars, and knocked off not one but two of the luminous prizes. One sits on his mantelpiece at home right now, a bizarre trophy to his courage, ego, stupidity and imagination. The other he sent to Neely.

'Eddie keeps things bottled up until it just spews out, and he gets very emotional about it,' said Jeff. 'You rarely see a singer that's willing to really open himself up. You often see singers pretending they're doing it . . .'[21] 'Eddie gets so intense sometimes, I mean it literally scares me,' said Stone.[22] 'We just found out we sold a million records [and] it doesn't matter,' Eddie was fond of telling jealous reporters. 'It doesn't change how you look at music, or how I'm going to play tonight. Getting a gold record was cool for about two and a half minutes . . .'[23] Thankfully, not everybody in the band was quite so tense about encroaching stardom, Jeff and Stone in particular had come too close to the flame to worry about getting any more burned now. When *Ten* had sold its first five hundred thousand copies, thereby qualifying it for a gold record, Jeff had sent Mookie Blaylock a copy in gold with the taken aback basketball player's name on it. 'I got to meet Mookie a few weeks ago and I was excited out of my shorts,' Jeff said.[24] A month later, when *Ten* passed the million mark, Blaylock sent him a congratulatory pair of sneakers, spray-painted platinum . . .

6

June 1992 found Eddie Tarzaning around the surprised stages of Europe again. 'The audiences aren't this good in Seattle,' he told the audience in Copenhagen as he clung like Spiderman from the corner of the ceiling above the stage. The tour paused in Germany, where they shot the video for 'Jeremy', their first 'narrative' video. Directed by the highly rated Mark Pellington and, as MTV never tired of retelling their viewers, based on the true story, 'Jeremy' was the first of their videos not to centre itself entirely around a group performance – indeed, blink and you miss the band, pictured just twice in black and white. 'Jeremy' was considered 'high concept' by MTV standards. Colour shots of Eddie sitting down and looking mournful as he mouths the ugly words, cut to flashing images of 'Jeremy' fighting with his parents . . . ending with a pile of dead schoolmates shot in a classroom . . .

A few days later, they returned to London where, on Sunday, June 6th, the band were second on the bill to The Cult at their 'In the Park' festival, in Finsbury Park. Below them on the bill were Red Kross, L7 and Therapy?. Despite some rather nasty sound problems, which meant that Eddie's vocals were drowned beneath the guitars for the first couple of numbers, 'Once' and 'Why Go', 'Alive' was rapturously received, and a deeply moving performance of 'Black' hypnotized the main area in front of the palatial stage. Eddie dedicated 'Even Flow' to L7's guitarist Dee, who had apparently missed her last two periods, and 'Porch' struck a queer subdued note on an evening of otherwise light-hearted grooving. In an attempt to enliven proceedings, Eddie did his usual disappearing act, dropping into the crowd from the none-too-sturdy-looking frame of the stage, his voice continuing, disembodied, from somewhere near the front, as he dodged the over-zealous security men, who gave him just as hard a time of it as they did everyone else that day, at one point even trying to prevent him from climbing back on stage, believing him to be just another stage-diver. It was a set that earned the first encore of the day the hard way, a royal rip-through of Neil Young's 'Rockin' In The Free World' with all the irony of the original still gloriously intact . . .

The band set off for the Continent again straight after the Finsbury Park show; the plan was to return to London the first week of July for dates at the Astoria and the Brixton Academy. On June 25th, after packed dates in Germany and Holland, they reached Sweden; that night they were to headline a tiny club in Stockholm. It had been a sweltering day and the band had spent most of it milling around the picturesque Old Stockholm part of the city. Everywhere they went they were recognized sooner or later, but it was never a hassle – unless it was other Americans, so different from the whispish, mellow Swedes, in which case there would be a lot of ducking for cover and hailing of taxis. They wanted to relax and look around without constantly being reminded of 'home'. They succeeded. It had been a beautiful day.

That night, when it transpired that through a mix-up by the promoter there was to be no opening act, Eddie and Mike volunteered to go out and do a number acoustically, as a warm-up for the already warm. 'Today it just feels good,' Eddie explained to the astonished crowd as he and Mike settled themselves on stools and rearranged the mike-stands. 'It's a little different thing. So we thought we'd have some fun with it . . . I'm just going to play one, fast or slow, what do you want?' Catching up at last, the crowd called out suggestions and started clapping out a spontaneous beat Eddie and Mike seemed to improvise on, before Eddie started to sing and the riff turned into

'Driven To Tears', the old Police chestnut. Stone and Jeff could be seen dancing in the wings. Grinning broadly, surfing on it inside his head, as the number ended and the crowd stamped their feet and cheered, Eddie leant into the mike and said, 'Lets's try one more song. I was trying to think in my head what song I could play that felt like today. It's like a song that's just like summer and outdoors . . .' Several members of the audience shouted suggestions, not all of them songs. 'Whoa, surfers in the audience, look out everybody!' Eddie chortled. 'Those are surfers, you should be warned!' The crowd started clapping again and Mike began picking out the spidery opening chords of an old Hunters and Collectors tune, '(Throw Your Arms Around Me) We May Never Meet Again'. As the number melted into rapturous applause, before the crowd had even realized it, Eddie stood up and with the mumbled words, 'Thanks, we'll see ya in a minute,' he had disappeared like a vampire into the dark cloak of the stage curtain . . .

A long sustained howl of feedback announced his return to the stage with the rest of the band fifteen minutes later. 'Let's just have fun tonight,' he shouted as the band pounded into the angular, head-first riff of 'Even Flow'. At the end of the song, Eddie, clearly enjoying himself, threw his arms out wide and looked the audience crowded around the lip of the stage straight in the microphone. 'You OK, you're all friends now, all right, yeah?' 'YEAH!' They answered as one. 'Wait . . . This guy's making a tape-recording, everybody be careful not to make too much noise,' he joked, pointing to an American kid who was indeed holding aloft a small Walkman. The kid tried to hide the equipment and turned to go, but Eddie implored him. 'No, keep it out, I like that idea.' Then, to the muscled and serious-faced security men that had already begun to move, crablike, in on the kid, 'No, he's OK, let him tape the show, he's OK.' Everybody froze. 'We wanna remember this, right?' Eddie asked the audience. The cheer was overwhelming. The tape-recorder went back on and the band hit the play button on 'Once' . . . '*Once upon a time,*' Eddie crooned, '*I could control myself* . . .' but for once you could see his mind wasn't quite on it. He was having too much of a good time. At the end of the number, he shook his head and appeared to say something to himself, then turned to the crowd and said, 'I'm crazier than any of you fuckers . . .' 'Fuck you!' yelled a voice from the crowd, American accented. 'I'm crazier than you . . .'

At the end of what turned out in the end to be nearly a three-hour set, the band returned to the dressing-room elated, euphoric; it had been the perfect end to a rare, almost perfect day. The feeling lasted right up until they actually closed the dressing-room door behind them and they discovered that they had been burgled. While they had been on stage, someone had broken into the dressing-room and made off with clothes, money and any personal knickknacks they could fit into their swag bags. Almost all of it was replaceable. All except one item, which was in every way irreplaceable: Eddie's dog-eared journal in which he kept all his diary notes and scraps of ideas for songs and lyrics. The one item that never left his possession – except for when he went on stage. When he found out, Eddie's mood changed from one of startling euphoria to almost fathomless horror. No one was allowed inside the dressing-room for over an hour after the show was over. 'He almost lost his friggin' mind,' said one bystander who did not want his name mentioned. The rest of the band could only stand back and wait and pray for the storm to pass. It never did . . .

The following afternoon, at the Roskilde Festival, in Denmark, Eddie was still deeply upset about the loss of his journal and the rest of his personal belongings. His fearful anger and terrifying shouts had subsided into an even more worrying silence, punctuated by moans and mumbled curses. He was so rattled he ended up punching a security guard in the face when a stage-diver got attacked by the bouncers. After the show Kelly Curtis put out an official announcement that was duly reported in the *Melody Maker*. Pearl Jam had been forced to cancel their two London shows when Eddie 'was diagnosed as physically exhausted and ordered to rest by a doctor. [He] had been complaining of chest cramps during the band's Roskilde Festival in Denmark the weekend before.' . . . 'It's a combination of things, a lot of it to do with not having been home for more than a week in the last year,' the *MM* quoted Jeff as saying. 'If we hadn't been doing the "Lollapalooza II" tour in four weeks' time we might have kept the European shows on. But if we'd done it all I seriously don't think the band would be in existence by the end of the year . . . Just tell 'em I'm real sorry, man. But we had to do it or there wouldn't have been a band any more.'[25]

Dramatic stuff. But the truth came out, as with Eddie it usually did, in his very next interview, six weeks later, with Radio One DJ Tommy Vance, backstage at Riverbend Amphitheater, in Cincinnati, where 'Lollapalooza II' was bedding down for the night. Although he had been 'sick in some ways' the truth was, he confessed, Eddie simply 'didn't have anything else to give and you know what it stems from? The last show we played in Sweden, someone broke into the dressing-room, while we were playing. We played a very long show that night, I won't forget, it was like, three hours, and we played, like, five encores. I played acoustic and sang some songs because there was no opening act, to start. We'd never done that before. It felt like we gave a lot . . .' After the show, they 'went back to the dressing-room and all of our stuff had been pilfered. To my horror I found that all this was stolen; including, like, two books, all these lyrics, everything I'd worked on the first time we were in Europe and the next time we were in America to this last time when I was really writing and really getting focused. I was really upset by that; it was like a rape situation. I just lost it. I just split in two . . . My mind just . . . I couldn't think straight and I certainly couldn't have played any more.' Tommy hurriedly played a record.[26]

'I hate to get all sentimental but to write while you're travelling with no solitude is a lot harder than when you've got a bit of time to think about things,' Eddie tried to put it another way when he spoke to the *Melody Maker*, in August. 'And these words and passages were really hard to come by, much more work than usual. And they were gone, and some bastard had them. I felt totally raped, I lost my mind. Then I got home and found out that one of my friends, Stephanie from Seven Year Bitch, had died of a heroin overdose. And that . . . kind of put me in a tailspin.'[27]

7

The unofficial start of 'Lollapalooza II' – 'an annual touring carnival of all-round-youth culture,'[28] according to the mastermind behind the event, former Jane's Addiction leader, Perry Farrell – had taken place at the newly opened Terminator club in Los Angeles, at the end of July. Pearl Jam, Soundgarden and the Red Hot Chili Peppers all arrived at the club at midnight, just in time to catch sets by Flame and Life Sex & Death. The night ended with various members taking it in turn to help themselves to the available equipment and pumping out whatever weird noise came into their over-addled minds. The following morning, they set off by car and by plane for San Francisco, where the two-month tour began, working its way up the west coast as far as Vancouver, and then back down again.

In 1992, American 'youth culture' equalled 'Seattle' and the 'Lollapalooza II' bill reflected that fact. So alongside rap stars like Ice-T and Ice Cube, you got Pearl Jam and Soundgarden. Topping the bill were the Red Hot Chili Peppers. Floating around in there too were Ministry, and from the UK, the Jesus and Mary Chain and Lush, as well as a host of lesser-known local artists on a second stage located to one side of the booths that circled the main stage wagon-train style. Farrell's new band, Porno For Pyros, had made a surprise appearance on the second stage at the opening pair of shows in San Francisco. 'It's so big, it's really interesting. Twenty thousand people coming to the show, it makes a dent in the city,' Eddie told Tommy Vance. 'It actually changes the cities as you roll into them. You talk to young people and get them interested in voting, get them involved. It's a good monster.'

Although Farrell organized the concert with a consciously left-wing sensibility, he also went out of his way to invite the National Rifle Association and various Pro-Life anti-abortionist groups to set up booths in tandem with the nipple-piercers, Pro-Choice booths, tarot-readers and voter-registration booths that travelled as part of the carnival. At one point, Farrell had entertained the idea of having Timothy Leary along to try and construct his idea of a tent you could walk into and immediately start hallucinating, but the old mescaline gobbler had declined the offer.

The whole tour, said Stone, had been 'such a high point . . . the spirit of the thing was, we can be jerks to each other or we can be nice to each other. Al Jourgensen and all of Ministry were great . . . We even kind of semi-bonded with the guys from Jesus and Mary Chain, which was kind of funny because they're very introverted. By the end of it, we had their guitar player, Jim Reid, coming out and doing "Sonic Reducer" with us!'[29] 'The cool thing about it is that it's not just music,' said Eddie. 'There are other kinds of art offered, many of which are in different forms; whether it be tattooing, painting, exposing people to different issues or hanging a twenty-pound brick from your nipple . . . If people are coming to a show with an open mind, and they see something they connect with – whether it's a booth about animal rights, or a censorship law or whatever – it's important for them to get involved. But the great thing about it is that Lolla doesn't preach anything. Everything is off to the side, there for anyone who wants to take a peek – it's not being forced down anyone's throats.'[30] 'I think it was the alternative culture coming together for a non-alternative audience to check out. I don't think the audience we're getting is an alternative audience,'[31] said Soundgarden's Chris Cornell. 'I don't believe in preaching,' said Jeff Ament when it was all over. 'If we put our name to something, it's more a form of exorcism than preaching . . . But there's a lot of shit about; if you're bored get busy.'[32]

Eddie was, as usual, more forthright in his own opinions. If the music didn't address real 'issues', things you could 'see on TV every night',[33] then it was fake, unreal and uninteresting. Talking about the riots that had taken place in Los Angeles that summer in the wake of the Not Guilty verdict reached in the trial of the policemen that a video camera had recorded beating Rodney King, Eddie was philosophical: 'What happened in LA wasn't just because of Rodney King. It was something that's been brewing for a long time, and finally it just exploded. If people had been dealing with these issues and the obvious social problems all along, the rioting might not have happened . . .'[34] On his support for the Pro-Choice lobby, Eddie, who had talked the whole thing through with his girlfriend Beth a thousand times, was just as unequivocal. 'The thing is, these people don't understand that in these modern times, there are too many people here on the boat, and they're trying to tell us to put more people on the boat. The boat is already capsizing, and these people tell me they're concerned with life? Well, so am I! It should be a woman's choice what she does with her body and how she plans her future . . .'[35]

When 'Lollapalooza II' reached Houston, in August, Doug Pinnick of local heroes King's X got up and sang with Pearl Jam. 'I hung with them one evening and they asked me if I wanted to sing "Rockin' In The Free World". So I went out on stage with Chris Cornell and Al Jourgensen. We had a lot of fun,' he recalls. Jeff had confided that after Andy Wood died he had spent a lot of time listening to the 1989 King's X album, *Gretchen Goes To Nebraska*. 'He said he was having a "down time" in his life and that that record really helped him, sort of gave him hope.' Eddie, Doug found to be a little more distant. But then, as

Doug points out, he had just sold his first million records so the stars were still clouding his vision. 'We've talked a couple of times. He's a very, very, very nice guy,' says Doug. 'In the beginning, when I first met him, this was all new to him, he wasn't quite sure if he could even do this or not. He was like, I don't know if I can take on this. Then all of sudden it went, like the band just kind of exploded. Then, the next time I saw him you could tell that it was wearing him down.'

8

The two-month Lolla shows finally drew to a close with a three-day stint at the outdoor, seventeen thousand capacity Irvine Meadows, in Southern California ... three hot days and nights that blended into one, highlighted by a rare performance from the Temple Of The Dog conglomerate (Chris and Eddie had only sung those songs on the same stage together twice before) of 'Reach Down' and 'Hunger Strike'. Then the entire cast of both Soundgarden and Pearl Jam stood toe-to-toe and thumped out killing-floor versions of both 'Sonic Reducer' and 'Rockin' In The Free World'.

The impromptu Temple Of The Dog get-together was well timed. Only released the previous year, the *Temple Of The Dog* album was relaunched wholesale by A&M in the late summer of 1992, hoisted into record-store racks with a large *Including members of Soundgarden and Pearl Jam* sticker plastered across its face like a whore's dishevelled make-up. 'We weren't planning on re-releasing the record. It was like, fuck, this thing sold seventy thousand records. But there was an audience out there for it, so we put it out again,'[36] Chris Cornell told *Kerrang!* with an elaborate shrug. But there was even a spin-off single, 'Hunger Strike', complete with hurriedly assembled video footage which was slipped on to immediate blitz-rotation on MTV. Where just twelve months before it had sold fewer than a hundred thousand copies worldwide, the album now sold a million, skyrocketing into the US Top 10 within a month of its re-release. Which was the cue for Polygram to finally make a return on the half-million dollars or so they had sunk into Andrew Wood's endless dream with the release of

Mother Love Bone, a twin-CD package – the first disc containing the *Shine* EP and *Apple* album combined; the second a two-track single that never was comprising the original black fingernail version of 'Capricorn Sister' and a previously unreleased pout into the Love Rock mirror called 'Lady Godiva Blues'. Wrapped in a sleeve lavishly laden with pictures and memorabilia, when *Mother Love Bone* was released in August 1992 it immediately jumped into the *Billboard* charts at No. 77. The same week, *Temple Of The Dog* stood at No. 19, *Ten* was at No. 4, having narrowly been kept from the No. 1 spot by Billy Ray Cyrus, saving at least one achievement for later, and the *Singles* soundtrack was hangin' tough at No.14. Still in the Top 10 was Nirvana's *Nevermind*, and about to join them was the next Alice In Chains album, *Dirt*, released in September and destined to sell more than three million copies, despite the fact that five of the songs on the album ('Junkhead', 'Dirt', 'God Smack', 'Hate To Feel' and 'Angry Chair') were about heroin.

Back home in the Virtuous City, where five years before there had been hardly anywhere for new bands to air their original material before their peers, now new clubs were springing up with an alarming regularity. Most prominent was the bohemian enclave atmosphere with overstuffed chairs of RKCNDY; the dark labyrinth of the Off Ramp club; the former big-band ballroom vibe of The Backstage club; Ballard Firehouse (a remodelled vintage firehouse); and the New Melody Tavern, the new acoustic-folk headquarters. All were different; all had one thing in common: they encouraged local bands that played original music, of which Seattle suddenly seemed to have literally thousands.

In June 1992, six months after they almost went broke, Bruce Pavitt and Jonathan Poneman received the Joel Webber Award For Excellence In Music And Business, given out at the New Music Seminar, in New York, the largest music business convention in the US. Proud as they were of the recognition, they were scathing of the way they felt the major labels had left their corporate bootprints all over their right-on little town. By then, Nirvana and Soundgarden were long gone from the label. Even Mudhoney, who had steadfastly refused offers to switch to a major label, finally succumbed to a pitch from Reprise (distributed by Warner Brothers) and signed to the label in March 1992. Their début major-label album, *Piece Of Cake*, was released six months later. Seattle was becoming like LA North, Pavitt and Poneman argued. Stone Gossard took the opposite point of view. There was no secret as to why the music of the Northwest was becoming so prevalent, he said, and it had little to do with geography. 'People used to try to write good songs to get on the radio, but they didn't really think in terms of having fun with their instruments or taking chances. Recently, a lot of people have decided that fun is the only thing that really matters.' It was 'more of a Nineties thing than a Seattle thing'.[37]

The third single from *Ten* arrived in the middle of this retrospective activity and proved to be their biggest hit yet, making mincemeat of the US Top 10 throughout the rest of 1992. The mind-bending story of one lost boy's failure to come to terms with the unfeeling world he found himself in, 'Jeremy' proved, paradoxically, to be Pearl Jam's passport into the equally unfeeling world of big-time pop stardom.

However, when Mark Eitzel from the group American Music Club told Jeff that he liked their 'hit', but that 'the video sucked. It ruined my vision of the song,' it confirmed Eddie's worst fears. Success equalled compromise: they should have just performed the song straight to camera or not at all. There would be one further video shot from *Ten* – 'Ocean', a return to the grainy black and white performance vibe of the 'Alive' video, inter-cut, rather too literally, with the band surfing in Hawaii – but no further singles. Epic had felt that 'Black' was not only a plausible follow-up to the enormous success of 'Jeremy', but that it might be the track to take the band to No. 1 in both singles and albums charts in the US. But Eddie would not hear of it. His pride dented by the continuing jibes from Kurt Cobain and his cronies on the UK music press, stung by the jealousy and criticism that surrounded the furore about 'Jeremy', Eddie was determined to prove them all wrong, even if it was to the detriment of the band's short-term career; Eddie would make Pearl Jam credible even if it meant stopping them having any more hits. He even took to phoning up radio stations he'd been told had been playing 'Black' a lot on their day-time programmes, demanding to know if Epic had suggested the station play that track in order to drum up the demand from the audience for it to be released as a single.

9

The *Singles* soundtrack album had sailed up the charts before the film was even released. When the movie premièred in Hollywood, in September, it was afforded a gala night out at the famous Mann's Chinese Theater. In attendance were the entire cast, led by a side-burned and unshaven Matt Dillon, Bridget Fonda in her most heart-stoppingly 'distressed' dress and a decidedly self-conscious looking posse from Pearl Jam and Soundgarden. Afterwards, The Cult's Ian Astbury admitted that he hated the film but added that his wife loved it. Red Hot Chili Peppers' singer Anthony Kiedis, who was there with his parents, said: 'It made me sad I didn't have a girlfriend.'[38]

At the plush party at the Park Plaza hotel that followed the screening, director Crowe's wife, Ann Wilson, got up with her sister Nancy and they re-enacted their role on the soundtrack as The Lovemongers, dueting and playing acoustic guitars. It wasn't long before they were joined by Stone and Jeff, and Jerry Cantrell of Alice In Chains. There were some tense moments when Eddie sauntered into the party carrying two cases of Meisterbeer and accompanied Mickey Rourke-style by a large entourage of surfer buds, biker pals and general San Diego-style misfits from his Bad Radio days. But in general, everybody was happy just to slap each other on the back and congratulate themselves on their fabulous luck. When Pearl Jam clambered on to the corner stage at a little after 1.00 a.m., Eddie appeared to be so drunk he was barely able to stand up, mumbling about fucking this and fucking that and forgetting the words, well fuck you and fuck me. He also sang at least two of the four-song set with his flies undone and made several aborted attempts to climb back into the crowd, except it was one of those rare occasions where the audience would actually have preferred it if he hadn't come amongst them quite so often, thank yew.

The band lovingly dedicated The Who's 'Baba O'Reily' to Crowe, 'Because he has good taste in music', and threw in 'Sonic Reducer' and 'Sate Of Love And Trust' and 'Rockin' In The Free World' just for bad measure, joined on a stonking version of the latter by Jerry Cantrell and Chris Cornell. As they launched into the first chorus, Ministry's Al Jourgensen, the Darth Vader of the Seattle scene who had fled the city and vowed never to return, pushed his way through the crowd with a bottle of red wine in each hand and Soundgarden's Kim Thayil and Ben Shepherd in tow. Total mayhem ensued with Jourgensen and Cornell rolling around laughing and shouting on the floor . . . By the end of the song the drum kit had been demolished, the stage soaked in beer and wine and the mike-stands left for dust.

When *Singles* opened in Seattle in September, the local music community wondered what it would do to the already intense spotlight of national media attention focused there. Bill Reid, DJ at KNDD-FM, predicted that it would 'do for the Northwest what *Saturday Night Fever* did for disco. I think it's going to be a turning point in making the scene a mainstream scene.'[39] Mark Arm, who had not gone to the Hollywood opening, queued to see the movie in Seattle and afterwards declared that he thought 'a good exploitation film is healthy. I went down to Cameron Crowe's office to see if we could put one song on the soundtrack, and I got a call a couple of months after that to be an extra in the film. I'm in the background in one scene at a coffeehouse, which is really funny, because I don't even drink coffee.'[40] He denied that there was any truth in the rumour that Mudhoney had received $10,000 for a song that only cost $200 to record. 'The truth of the rumour is that they gave us $20,000 and it only cost $167 to record it.'[41] Audiences at all the early showings in Seattle cheered the scenes depicting familiar local spots like Pike Place Market, the Space Needle, Gas Works Park, the OK Hotel and the Virginia Inn. A special treat for locals included a club scene where Alice In Chains were shown performing live; it was filmed at the Under The Rail club, a new place that wasn't even open yet.

On September 10th, MTV aired a one-hour special on *Singles* taped around the Hollywood première. Suddenly everybody knew all about the Space Needle and the coffee shops, the micro-breweries and the clear-skinned girls. Steve Freeborn, owner of the OK Hotel (the Java Stop in the movie), had never sold so much mocha in his life. 'So much has happened the last eight or nine months here that we already have people snapping pictures of the place,' he gleefully told the *Seattle Times*. 'Tourists coming in all the time . . . "Is this where the Seattle scene is?"'[42]

10

The release of *Singles* coincided with the discovery and risible subsequent championing of 'grunge' by the extremely trend-sensitive world of fashion. Nobody knows who was the first person to use the term, but suddenly it was the turn of grunge as fashion statement to make the headlines. And not just in the mousy music press. Seconds after 'grunge' was codified – aggressively mix 'n' match postmodernism, quintessentially anti-Eighties – the *New York Times* Style section had begun hyping it as a way of life. *Vogue*, the designer-fashion bible, ran a December 1992 'Grunge & Glory' cover special, discussing the latest trend that had 'broken out of the clubs, garages, and thrift shops of Seattle'. All the models were photographed in decidedly up-market settings but wearing a range of 'designer' Doc Marten boots and the inevitable flannel-print shirt, tail flapping in the breeze like a giant price tag, which of course all of the items came with. The 'flannel' was really silk and the seemingly *de rigueur* nose-rings were gold and diamond-studded. Ralph Lauren, Calvin Klein, Anna Sui and many others were happy to stick them with price tags in the $480–$1,400 range. Consequently, you couldn't give away a pair of new DMs to anyone from the Northwest by the end of 1992. The pendulum had swung towards Redback workboots; symbolically, Seattle was already undergoing its own backlash.

You could see their point. Over the decades, 'thrifting' had become a verb in Seattle. 'It wasn't like somebody said, "Let's all dress like lumberjacks and start Seattle chic!"' Jonathan Poneman told the *New York Times*. 'This stuff is cheap, it's durable and it's kind of timeless. It also runs against the grain of the whole flashy aesthetic that existed in the Eighties.'[43] Fashion designer Marc Jacobs proclaimed himself the 'guru of grunge' and his latest collection for Perry Ellis contained new items for the ladies like the artfully 'dissed' zip-up sweatshirt for £195, or mould-coloured jackets with apparently uneven sleeves and lapels for £495. Frederic Fekkai, the famous New York hair stylist, claimed that all the young models who regularly visited his Manhattan boutique were begging him to make their carefully conditioned locks more ratty looking.

Things were clearly getting out of hand long before designer

Christian Francis Roth dressed for his latest show in a wool cap, appearing on the catwalk at the end of the parade strumming an unplugged electric guitar. You didn't have to live in Seattle to wish people would stop going on about the place. And besides, who doesn't have a check shirt and a pair of falling-to-bits jeans in their wardrobe? 'Some of us are consciously awkward wearing the clothes we've always worn,' reflected *Rocket* staffer Grant Alden, who has lived in Seattle all his life. 'I try not to think about it, but occasionally, I'm caught in spots where I look at myself and am suddenly aware that I'm wearing jeans and Doc Martens and a flannel shirt and I'm from Seattle and oops.'[44]

Of course, the designers justified their ludicrous prices, as they always do, by arguing that their creations bore only a cosmetic resemblance to their original thrift-store templates. While a $200 Donna Karan shirt may have resembled one bought from a thrift store for a couple of dollars, there were those who would ask the quality question and others who would simply prefer not to wear secondhand clothing, and are wealthy enough not to have to, even if they want to look as though they have. 'Grunge is street fashion that just happens to be labelled grunge right now,' explained Donna Karan to those that still needed it explained to them. 'It's an independent state of mind, the individual interpretation of style and fashion . . . almost a state of un-design.'[45] James Truman, editor-in-chief of *Details,* took the opposing, equally supercilious point of view. 'To me, the thing about grunge is it's not fashion. It's un-fashion. Punk was anti-fashion. It made a statement. Grunge is about not making a statement, which is why it's crazy for it to become a fashion statement.'[46]

Not everybody liked to read so much into it, though. 'There's something creepy about taking the whole sort of Salvation Army sort of aesthetic and marketing it with a designer name,'[47] said Kim Thayil. *Kerrang!* editor Geoff Barton was more prosaic. 'I think it's something people have latched on to, regardless. You know, it's from this place, Seattle, in America, and it's called grunge and that's an interesting name. If it hadn't been for grunge what *else* would they have written about? And grunge *per se* was never just a musical thing to your general newspaper-buying punter. It covered everything; it was a fashion, it was an attitude; it was a look . . . it was even a movie. No wonder the bands seem to be as confused as the rest of us as to what this "grunge" thing really is.'

11

Pearl Jam finally got their free concert in Seattle, not at the Gas Works Park, as they had originally planned, but at Magnusson Park, on Sunday, September 20th, 1992. When local radio stations KISW-FM, KXRX-FM and KNDD-FM simultaneously announced the location for the ticket giveaway at Seattle Center, it unleashed a mad rush that flooded the Center grounds with thousands of fans within minutes. Traffic on the main Interstate 5 road drew to a standstill and all other roads leading to the Center were jammed solid. None of which, naturally, daunted the determined. By noon all fourteen thousand packets, each containing two tickets, a map of the site and instructions on when and how to get to and from the site (no cars were allowed), had been taken.

That Sunday morning, miraculously, nearly twenty-nine thousand people rode the bus, bicycled or walked to the gig, waylaying fears that the neighbourhood would be turned into a giant parking lot. The concert began at 11.00 a.m. sharp with smoky acoustic sets by Peter Droge and Lazy Susan, followed by an in-yer-face midday appearance from hardier-than-the-rest LA rappers Cypress Hill, something more mellow from silver-throated local singer-songwriter Shawn Smith, and something inbetweeny from Tacoma-based junk rockers Seaweed. Jim Rose of the majestically masochistic Jim Rose Circus MCed, and prior to the main event writer–philosopher Robert Anton Wilson got up and said a few words, though what about nobody seemed able to remember afterwards.

Finally, at 2.00 p.m., to huge roars of approval, Pearl Jam themselves took the stage. It was all over by 4.00 p.m. In between times, Eddie's penchant for climbing things reached new levels of athleticism, hurling his mike up high over his head so that the lead caught up in the overhead stage scaffolding. Without missing a beat, he shinnied up a support pole, swung hand-over-hand to the tangled mike and finished the song while hanging there, dangling his legs, the crowd craning their disbelieving necks for a better look. Then he slid down the wire and went on with the show. It was an incredible moment in what had been up till then, truth to tell, a less than incredible performance. Whether it was the nerves or just the exhaustion brought on by almost a year's planning, from drunken idea to cold-light-of-day inception, it wasn't until Eddie did his Indian charmer routine with his mike that the set moved out of the realms of the workaday into something truly memorable.

The most satisfying aspect of the concert, from Eddie's point of view, was that it also worked as an effective young-voter registration-drive. The goal was to spur registration among eighteen- to twenty-four-year-olds. According to the non-profit group Rock The Vote, almost three thousand young people signed up to vote for the first time in their lives that day. 'If you don't vote, you can't complain about the outcome,' Eddie lectured his fans. 'I'm going to be voting. But that's because I've stayed up on these issues and I kind of know what's up. It's not about whether I give a fuck who's going to be president because the president's just a puppet; everybody's gotta understand that. It's more like voting on the local issues and things like that. That's how you're going to make a difference for your own personal lives . . .'[48]

At the end of the show, Eddie flashed the crowd one of his rare on-stage smiles. 'I can't believe we did it,' he cried emotionally. 'You did it! We're like a fucking rash on Seattle they thought they'd never catch!' Best of all, the crowd had behaved impeccably. Seattle police reported just two on-site arrests, one for allegedly assaulting a security guard and another for allegedly hitting a police horse. 'It's nice to see twenty thousand kids get together and get along,' said Seattle police officer Felix Solis, who said he had enjoyed what had amounted for him and his troops to 'a day off'.[49]

The reverberations were lasting. 'That free show they did really cemented Pearl Jam's relationship with local people,' reckons *Rocket* editor Charles R. Cross. 'The fact that they put on this free show which must have cost them around $100,000 of their money to do [and] the fact that they followed through and did this thing really helped their PR within the community tremendously. For a group to want to do a free show to give something back to the fans really was a very classy thing. Everything about the way that band has operated locally has been very classy and they gained points for that.'

12

As 1992 spiralled dizzily to its close, Pearl Jam enjoyed a brief hiatus from the road. The hardest part about touring at that speed and altitude, they all discovered, was stopping touring. 'When I come home my girlfriend looks at me as if I was a stranger for the first four days,' Eddie complained. 'I sit in the corner with a book and a paper and scrawl on it, or I keep walking through the room. This sounds funny now, but it's not good when it happens. That's another reason why I don't want to be a part of that lifestyle.'[50]

'When the success started coming, with all the attention that went along with it and everybody wanting a piece of us, it really took its toll on us individually,' said Dave Abbruzzese. 'I didn't start being aware of how I felt and come to grips with the whole thing until we got off tour and went back home.'[51] Dave didn't even bother going back to Texas, but elected to stay in Seattle. 'I felt like I needed to be alone. Over a year's time had passed, and my whole life was completely different. My relationship had taken a permanent sabbatical, and I had pretty much cut myself off from a lot of people who still mean a lot to me.'[52]

An eight-page election special in the November issue of *Spin* included contributions from Krist Novoselic, Mark Arm and Eddie Vedder, who contributed a brief article on abortion. 'This is not just a women's issue,' he wrote. 'It's human rights. If it were a man's body and it was his destiny we were deciding there would be no issue.' The same month, *Rolling Stone* celebrated the magazine's twenty-fifth anniversary with their very own MTV special. Featured prominently alongside Nirvana were Pearl Jam, Soundgarden and Cameron Crowe, as well as Aerosmith, Bono, David Byrne, Eric Clapton, Peter Gabriel, Guns N' Roses, Ice-T, Mick Jagger, Elton John, k.d. lang, Jay Leno, Metallica, Paul McCartney, Luke Perry, Iggy Pop, Jason Priestly, the Red Hot Chili Peppers, Keith Richards, Sting, Hunter Thompson and Bruce Willis. This was a different class of company the band was keeping now. With *Ten* nudging the five-million mark in America alone, Pearl Jam had started to become bigger than Guns N' Roses, more popular than Nirvana even – both of whom they outsold in 1992. Officially the No. 1 hard rock album of the year in *Billboard*, by the end of 1992, *Ten* had already been listed as one of the Top 10 Albums of the Nineties in both *Spin* and *Rolling Stone*.

Even Eddie had to admit it would be unfair to expect life to get any sweeter. But, in the event, things somehow conspired to do just that when Eddie was asked by the maestro personally if he would care to take part in the Columbia Records 30th Anniversary salute to Bob Dylan at Madison Square Garden that November. It was what they call in the trade a glittering occasion, as mega-star after mega-star trotted out to sing one or two personally chosen songs from the Great Man's immense and daunting back catalogue ... Neil Young, Eric Clapton, George Harrison, Robbie Robertson, Sinead O'Connor, Tom Petty, Jeff Lynne ... Eddie took Mike. Theirs were amongst the youngest faces on the stage and yet their version of 'Masters of War' was brimming with elegiac older-head power, Eddie's tortured vocals soaring effortlessly over Mike's mournful Gibson Hummingbird.

While Eddie and Mike were taking bows at Madison Square Garden, Jeff Ament was talking groupies with the feisty new teen magazine, *Screamer*. 'There's this kind of macho thing, especially with rock music, that if someone had an alternative sexual lifestyle, it wouldn't be mentioned. Like the Freddie Mercury situation. He waited until the day before he died to announce he had AIDS.' Jeff claimed that he had taken an AIDS test regularly 'for the last five years ... It's a pretty intense thing. But I don't do it just to find out about AIDS. I do it for other things. I think you can have sexuality without actually being involved in the physicality of it. Many times, I think not having sex is more sexual than having it, especially if it's casual. If I feel the need to have a physical release I can masturbate. On a one-time only basis I would much rather masturbate than have casual sex.'[53]

13

The very last night of 1992, the year that *Ten* toppled the Top 10 and Pearl Jam began their ascendancy towards 'biggest-selling rock band on the planet' status, they celebrated in typically hair-over-the-eyes style by opening the show for another band entirely. The ticket-board for that night's show at Times Square's modest Academy Theater, in New York, announced that the headliners, Keith Richards and his solo band the X-Pensive Winos, would be on stage by 11.30 p.m. But at 9.30 p.m. . . .

No introduction of course . . . just a tune-up here and there and the sound of sustained feedback beginning to build to pain threshold . . . into 'Wash' . . . Stone, his long brown hair cropped close to the skull and bleached blond, chopping out riffs like wood for the fire of Dave and Jeff's elemental funk . . . Eddie mumbling the lyrics, face hidden beneath an incongruous ski-cap . . . whipped off for only a few moments all night, halfway through 'Alive' . . . Mike's amp covered in miniature basketball figures, his guitar a blue flame to Eddie's hydro-genous mental gas . . . incense sticks burning around the stage . . . 'Is this camera on?' Eddie asks the shadows . . . only the mumbled, drunken reply of the crowd . . . 'This is going to Times Square, right?' . . . the video cameras are transmitting the show to a mother-sized TV screen in Times Square, directly adjacent to a Marky Mark billboard . . . 'I wanna give Marky Mark the fuckin' finger,' Eddie scowls, pacing back and forth, arm raised in salute . . . the crowd a ball ready to be . . . bounced . . . 'Sonic Reducer' delivered deadpan snotty . . . a bottle of booze in Eddie's hand . . . 'Even Flow' and 'Why Go' passing in a blur of Stone's Eastern riffs and Eddie's Western ethics . . . a new number, 'Brother', haunting, jagged, wordless in its intensity . . . then 'Alive' . . . biggest cheers of the night . . . immediately segued into another new one, 'Drop The Leash' . . . crowd eager, eating it up, already pretending they know the words . . . closing with a subdued 'Porch' . . . no 'Jeremy', no 'Black', no '. . . Free World' . . . just Sean Lennon standing at the front of the guest balcony, looking startled as Stone nonchalantly tinkers out the chords to his dead dad's utopian crowd-pleaser, 'I've Got A Feeling' . . . around the corner, midnight strikes and the huddled masses in Times Square ignore the pimps and the pushers and blow their car horns, toot their noise-makers and act like the year . . . the world . . . really was still . . . new.

14

Back in 1988, King's X was a rare bird indeed. Nothing like the arena-friendly Van Halen school of put-your-hands-in-the-air rock. King's X was a heavy rock band that wrote rock songs about real things. As such, and in every way, they were ahead of their time. Drummer Jerry Gaskill was virtually the first person in a rock band to sport a goatee since 1971; Ty Tabor was the first guitarist to wear his glasses on stage since Elvis Costello threw away his contacts. And, of course, vocalist Doug Pinnick was the first black man to convincingly front a white rock band since the great James Marshall Hendrix his sweet self strode the magic boards. And yet, talk to their accountants and they will tell you that, for all the critical back-slapping, the biggest-selling King's X album to date was their third, *Faith, Hope, Love*, released in 1990, which sold a little over two hundred and fifty thousand worldwide. Not to put too fine a point on it, someone like Axl Rose or Jon Bon Jovi wouldn't get out of bed for those kind of figures. Add another zero and you still wouldn't be even near the same ball park as a Pearl Jam or a Soundgarden or Nirvana. So I asked Doug one night: 'Why them and not you?' What was it, did he think, looking at things from the inside, that made Pearl Jam successful when King's X – one of Jeff Ament's all-time favourite bands and one of the most innovative new age metal bands of the modern era – were not? Doug shook his dudelocked head and smiled. 'I think it was everything . . . the right time, the right place. They just had all the right things going for them . . . Nowadays, a band just can't go out there and put a record out and have it sell. It has to be all those other aspects, the whole thing has to line up. They had the right place and the right time and rightfully, they deserve the attention they have got.' Was that it then? A question of luck? Mother Love Bone's bad luck was Pearl Jam's good fortune? 'Sure, why not?' said Doug, nonplussed. 'Hey, don't knock luck . . . without luck you can't even get started. But you have to remember, sometimes you make your *own* luck. That's important, too.'

CHAPTER FIVE

THE LEASH

'... *the record-breaking début week of Pearl Jam's* Vs. *and the staying power of Nirvana's* In Utero *strongly suggest that the two bands most linked to the 'Seattle Sound' have transcended any such scene and are well on their way to careers that will continue long after grunge is a memory.'*

– Billboard – November 6, 1993

'I'll stare at the sun
till I go blind
I won't change direction
I won't change my mind . . .
But what difference
does it make?'

– 'Indifference' from *Vs.*, words by Eddie Vedder

1

In January 1993, the *Los Angeles Times* asked twenty-five movers and shakers in the American music industry which acts they would sign tomorrow if every chart-topping group in the country were suddenly a 'free agent'. Top of the list, unsurprisingly for the times, was U2, closely followed by REM, and then, in third spot and still just one album old, came Pearl Jam. Though not as critically fêted as U2 or

REM, or even fellow-travellers Nirvana, Pearl Jam was the name that cropped up on almost everybody's list. Five million sales of their first album notwithstanding, the reasons for their vast popularity, the *Times* article deduced, were less musical and more to do with the band's 'charismatic lead singer'. 'Whatever happens to Pearl Jam, this guy is going to be an immense star,' said one judge.

Indeed, what had undoubtedly begun as a vehicle for Stone Gossard and Jeff Ament to continue their careers without Andrew Wood had been transformed, by Eddie Vedder, into something else again. His glorious voice had brought new depth and resonance to the music Stone and Jeff dreamed of creating but it was Eddie's vocal commitment to children's charities, his whole antipornography Pro-Choice animal-activist environmental-terrorist stance that had transformed Pearl Jam into something more than just the latest 'rock and roll band with an attitude' to stink up the charts. By 1993, to millions of young people all over the world, Pearl Jam had become an outlook, a way of thinking, of seeing; a way of life that had little to do with 'grunge' and more to do with growing up in a modern world where sex is death and TV talks back.

You never knew what to expect. The last story to come out of 1992 was that Stone had completed a solo album called *Shame*. Set for release by Epic on March 30th, 1993, *Shame* was far from being a solo album by anybody. True, Stone played guitar on the album, and it was Stone's name that had sold the idea to Epic, but the *Shame* album was the work of four individual minds jamming spontaneously in a studio, letting the music take its own shape without undue nudging from any of them. Comprised of Stone, vocalist and keyboardist Shawn Smith, drummer Regan Hagar and bassist Jeremy Toback, *Shame* had been the working title for the project. Had it not been for the fact that the title *Shame* is held under copyright in America by an obscure LA musician, they would have called their makeshift band Shame. According to copyright law, it was all right to call the album *Shame*, but not the band, so instead they called themselves Brad – after the guy that owned *Shame*.

Shawn had been introduced to Stone by Regan Hagar back in the shameless Mother Love Bone days, and now played and sang with Regan in another local Seattle outfit called Bliss. Regan and Stone had been introduced to Los Angeles bassist Jeremy Toback through a mutual friend just prior to when recording began in November 1992.

Described surprisingly accurately in a brief Epic press release as 'part avant-rock, part old-school funk, part mood music, part accident', *Shame* was written and recorded in Seattle at Avast Recording. Mixing was overseen at Electric Ladyland, in New York, by producer Brendan O'Brien, who was already booked to record the next Pearl Jam album. 'We spent a total of seventeen days writing and recording with *Shame*,' Stone told *Rolling Stone* without bothering to conceal his pride. 'Everyone went into a total zombie state. It turned out pretty cool, very diverse. We screwed around with drum loops and lots of keyboards. The group compositions are, like, jams we arranged as we went along . . .'[1]

There would be no live dates, but they did shoot a video for '20th Century', one of the 'drum-loop' things, which Epic released as a single in April. 'It's a kind of funky-pop record, a whole different kind of vibe from what you've heard from me before,' said Stone. 'I've been pushing myself to develop more of a soloing style, and I was just thinking that there's a kind of "hats-off-to-Neil-Young tribute" quality to them.'[2] The chief player in the Brad line-up, though, was clearly Shawn Smith. With a voice that echoes Stevie Wonder, Prince and Otis Redding all at the same time, and a feather-light touch on the keyboards that was almost hymnal, it was Smith's presence that turned the *Shame* album from being merely an orgy of blissed-out funk-atronix into something far more focused, more stirring and profound.

The idea for *Shame* was born when Stone happened to overhear something Shawn was tootling around with on the keyboards one day. 'I was playing the organ parts that became the first song on the record ("Buttercup"), and it came togather so quickly that we decided to book studio time,' Smith recalled. 'That was the only song that we wrote before we went into the studio. We wrote the stuff in five days, recorded it in eight and then mixed it. It happened very quickly.'[3] Many believed that Brad's refusal to do any interviews at the time of *Shame*'s almost ridiculously low-key release was a direct result of pressure from the Pearl Jam camp. 'Oh, it was more of a management decision to let the thing come out on its own,' said Shawn, dismissing the idea as puffed-up nonsense. 'We really believed in it, and we didn't want the blitz – we just hoped it would roll on its own.'[4]

But was Stone expressing dissatisfaction with the way Pearl Jam were going musically, perhaps? *RAW* editor Jon Hotten thinks not. 'I think Stone writes so much, it's inevitable he's going to lean in different directions once in a while. And of course he's found another great singer in Shawn Smith.' Nevertheless, you can't help but wonder why. Stone: 'Probably a number of reasons, the biggest one being that playing music is always fun, so why not do a record with people I've been friends with for a really long time? I waste many hours of the day not doing anything but practising, anyway.'[5] He had come home from a two-week vacation in Hawaii at the end of the 'Lollapalooza II' tour tanned and rested, he said, and 'just excited about making music with my friends . . . I can play music all day and not be bored with it. And that's the way we made the record, just going into the studio and jamming every day. It's very spontaneous, which is part of the reason I'm really pleased with it.'[6] Being in a band could get 'political', said Stone. 'With this, we just said, "Let's do it!" The whole point of this record is to completely put yourself out on a limb . . . You don't know what's gonna happen, you don't know if you're gonna get along. We really didn't know if this guy Jeremy's gonna be able to play bass! There was a strange, almost uneasy freedom about it – like being not afraid to suck!'[7]

Stone said the approach he adopted for the Brad sessions had already started to infiltrate the early spirit of the new Pearl Jam material . . . 'I hope it gets fucked up. I hope there's one song on there that's just *way out* there, that's not typical at all. Either really, really clever, or full-blown disco, or something just to make sure we're not taking ourselves too seriously.'[8]

2

The first week of January 1993, *Ten* climbed defiantly back up the US album charts from No. 11 to No. 6: it had now spent thirteen months in the Top 10, more time than any other rock album during the same period, and both Pearl Jam and Nirvana landed in the Best Rock Song category of the Grammies: Nirvana for 'Teen Spirit' and Pearl Jam for 'Jeremy'. The second week of January found Eddie in Los Angeles for the eighth annual Rock and Roll Hall of Fame induction ceremony at the Century Plaza Hotel, where the blessedly un-tuxed singer had been invited to take the rostrum and effect the induction of The Doors into the fold. He then gave an extraordinarily fitting performance as a Jim Morrison stand-in as he took to the stage with the three surviving Doors members for surprisingly shit-kicking versions of 'Roadhouse Blues', 'Break On Through' and 'Light My Fire'. At the end, Ray Manzarek gave the keyboards a final flourish and invited the crowd 'to keep the fire alive, keep it together'.

Eddie had initially turned down the offer of a jam with the ageing legends of American rock, then changed his mind at the last minute and was driven down from Seattle with Beth, listening to Doors tapes all the way. 'They just needed somebody to be in the band ... We played just one night. It was no big deal,' he said afterwards, half modestly, half seriously not giving a fuck. 'They called me and asked me what songs I wanted to do, and I said, "I don't care, it's your band. I'll just show up and sing." My voice just got to the right register, it just fits right in, that's why they chose me. But I didn't take it too seriously and I tried not to think of Morrison. When we actually did it that night it was a little bit spiritual, but before and after it was nothing.'9

The third week of January, Pearl Jam won two awards at the twentieth American Music Awards, just pipping Arrested Development, in a widely divergent field, to the award for Best New Pop/Rock Artist, and clearly out-sprinting the rest of the field for Best New Artist in the Heavy Metal/Hard Rock category. The same week, MTV repeated their ... *Unplugged* session for the third time. And at the end of January, Polygram released *Mother Love Bone: The Love Bone Earth Affair*, a thirty-five-minute music-video compilation featuring the only taped performances available of the tragically short-lived band. The whole rocking world, it seemed, wanted to dip their spoons in the lucky jar marked Pearl Jam and the aftertaste was seemingly endless. When *Rolling Stone*'s annual music awards issue, based on polls of readers and critics, hit the news-stands in February, it revealed that readers had voted Pearl Jam Best New American Band, and the No. 2 choice for Artist of the Year (beaten only by U2); *Ten* was runner-up for Best Album of the Year (after *Achtung Baby!*); they were second for Best Band (next to U2); but Eddie won Best New Male Singer and was runner-up as Best Male Singer (after Bono) and the Sexiest Male Artist (second to Bono again); the band was No. 5 in the balloting for the Best Heavy Metal Band (after Metallica, Guns N' Roses, Alice In

Chains and Soundgarden); and readers picked Pearl Jam's 'Jeremy' as Best Video of the Year.

Elsewhere in the same small town, Sub Pop, recently pulled from the brink of bankruptcy by the apparently fathomless retroactive interest in former Sub Pop artists like Nirvana, Soundgarden, Mudhoney and Green River (Green River's two Sub Pop records had always been in print), were now doing so well Pavitt and Poneman were opening a small Boston office. Over at *The Rocket*, circulation had shot up 30 per cent in the last six months alone. 'It's all a big mystery to us,' admitted staffer Jeff Gilbert. 'It caught everybody by surprise . . . although we're not above exploiting it.'

3

The release of *Shame* coincided with Pearl Jam's arrival at The Site recording studios in California to begin the serious business of coming up with a credible follow-up to *Ten*. Sessions took place on and off between March and May (they had also logged a couple of days at Seattle's Potatohead Studio and at a pre-production suite in Atlanta). The initial week of recording had yielded new titles like 'Rats', 'Blood', 'Go' and a venomous low-bellied version of their previously unrecorded stage favourite 'Drop The Leash', now shortened to just 'Leash'. Then the band hit a wall. Or rather, Eddie did. Still missing the nine months' worth of lyrics, journal entries and odd bric-à-brac of the road lost in Stockholm to prompt his dark thoughts, and intensely disliking the drastically sugared tones of the plush Site facilities, Eddie disappeared into nearby San Francisco, often sleeping in his truck to toughen up his resolve. He'd even picked up a nasty case of poison ivy while hiking in the hills. 'Eddie is a very intense fellow,' said Kevin Scott, one of the three engineers who recorded *Vs.*, in a vain attempt to scoop an understatement of the year prize. 'He's always thinking some sort of deep thought, and he felt that the studio was a little too nice to really write some of these heavy lyrics that he'd been thinking about.'[10]

Nevertheless, when Eddie returned, good as his word, the songs began to flow . . . next came 'Glorified G' – the 'G' standing for gun. '"It's stupid," opined Jeff. "You hear so many stories about people having a gun in their house and then being shot by a robber with their own gun." "I was standing in a shop recently and there were these five guys talking about guns, and one of them told the story about himself sitting in a rocking chair with his gun and accidentally shooting himself in the foot," said Eddie. "Everybody was laughing, including him. These guys are idiots." Jeff shook his head. "And this goes back to the whole lack of creativity nowadays. A gun is an uncreative thing. There was this one guy being caught by his wife with another woman, and his wife got into the kitchen, poured oil on his face and set him on fire, and I thought, well at least she didn't shoot him. That was creative."'[11]

The band was intent on going with their instincts when it came to compiling material for the new album, letting the drummer write the first track of the album on guitar, and having Stone spend hours alone in a rehearsal room, playing drums, so that he would be able to transfer certain grooves to his flexituned Les Paul. The process was considerably aided by the – in the words of one of his many satisfied clients – 'intensely relaxed' approach of producer Brendan O'Brien. Having worked on both the Black Crowes' albums, the Red Hot Chili Peppers' *BloodSugarSexMagik*, début albums from the Stone Temple Pilots and Jackyl, plus releases by Aerosmith, Danzig, Raging Slab, King's X and the Four Horsemen, and as amiable a personage as his Southern drawl is long, O'Brien was *the* name producer to throw your hat into the ring with in 1993. A guitarist in his own right, it is O'Brien's rude axe that can be heard biting lumps out of Mick Jagger's 'Wandering Spirit'. A native of Atlanta, Georgia, O'Brien had started out playing in the mid-Eighties with the Georgia Satellites before turning his attention full time to the other side of the console. 'It gives me a sort of instant communication with the guitar players I work with . . . Sometimes a word or just a gesture is all it takes to communicate an idea that it might take another producer all day to explain.'[12]

O'Brien liked to work quickly, and as far as possible, tracks were recorded at one go, with the band playing together as-live; overdubs were kept strictly to a minimum. 'I put them all out into the same room with the drums, with the amps all lined up like on stage and monitor speakers in front of them.'[13] The songs kept coming . . . Eddie wrote the whole of 'rearviewmirror' on his own – a bloodshot descendant of The Who's 'I Can See For Miles' – and also played guitar on that and a folksy lament he had written 'almost without thinking' called 'Elderly Woman Behind The Counter In A Small Town'. 'It's kind of about a lady, and she's getting on in years, and she's stuck in this small town. Small towns fascinate me. You either struggle like hell to get out, or some people want to stay, 'cause then they're big fish in a small pond, and then others just kind of get stuck there,' he explained. 'So here she is working in this little place, and then an old flame comes in, and . . . at first she doesn't even remember who he is, and then she realizes who it is. She's just too embarrassed to say hello . . . Stone heard me warming up with the guitar and the Vocal Master one morning, and he came down and said, "That was a fucking really cool song," and it wasn't a song, it was just me kind of warming up, and making up some of those words. [But] I went up and recorded it on acoustic guitar.'[14]

Another track, 'W.M.A.' (White Male American), about racial harassment by the police force, was again based on a real-life incident Eddie had observed. 'Our practice place's in a pretty hard-core part of Seattle . . . There's always cops hanging around and a lot of weird shit going on, like people smoking crack right in the alley near where we practise,' Jeff took up the story. 'So that day Eddie went out to the grocery store or something, and I think he saw some pretty intense stuff going down concerning these street people. And when he came back in we happened to be jamming on what later became "W.M.A.".'[15] Then there was 'Blood', in which Eddie appeared to take the media to task for pumping up his name so much he thought it was going to explode and the real person – the 'blood' underneath – was going to get buried in the fall-out . . . *'paint Ed up'*, he groans. *'Turn Ed into one of his enemies . . .'*

Driven by lusty acoustic guitars, the instrumentation and theme of which made it eerily reminiscent of REM's 'Wrong Child', came 'Daughter'. 'There was a time when they thought that children with learning difficulties were stubborn and selfish. It's only recently been recognized for what it is,' said Eddie.[16] One of the album's dramatic highlights was an epic narrative ballad about the betrayal of a political fugitive, called 'Dissident'. 'The tragedy of the song is that this woman takes in the person, but she can't handle the responsibility,' explained Eddie. 'She turns him in. Then she has to live with the guilt and the realization that she's betrayed the one thing that gave her life some meaning.'[17]

The anti-parent anthem 'Leash' was written about the same girl, Heather, that Eddie had penned 'Why Go' for, who had been sent away to a home by her parents for smoking pot. 'Now Heather finally gets out, but the mom's still doing the same thing, and threatening her with putting her back in the hospital. I mean, this girl was fifteen or sixteen years old, she couldn't be on the phone after eight at night . . . she couldn't go out . . . It was after talking to her again one day that I wrote the song in the car. Drop the leash, you know? Get out of my fuckin' face . . .'[18] And then there was 'Indifference' – the transcendental highlight of the album – questioning the notion of attempting to do something worthwhile in an increasingly worthless world, Eddie delivering his most literally impassioned vocal of the set, gradually building to a mood of heroic defiance in the face of loneliness and fear . . .

'When we first went into the studio, there wasn't any talk of following up a successful record. We just wanted to make songs that represented us. We didn't want to make Pearl Jam *Eleven*,' said Dave Abbruzzese. 'We took the approach of recording one song at a time, setting up the room and our gear, getting everything down right, and putting it away before moving on to the next song . . . it kept it fresh for everybody. A lot of bands miss out on that. On "Go" . . . You know, it's not the easiest thing in a band like this for the drummer to strap on a guitar and say, "Hey, I've got some songs I want to show you." With "Go", I just happened to pick up the guitar at the right moment. Stone asked what I was playing and started playing it, then Jeff started playing it, and Eddie started singing with it, and it turned into a song.'[19]

4

With the still untitled album finished, the band prepared themselves to go back out on the road. At the end of June, after a small unannounced warm-up gig in Jeff's home town of Missoula, Montana, Pearl Jam set out for a thirteen-date trek around some of the biggest and smallest stages they had ever seen in Europe. They began with a clutch of dates opening the show for Neil Young in Oslo, Norway (June 27th), Stockholm, Sweden (28th) and Helsinki, Finland (30th), then hooked up as Special Guests on the latest leg of U2's two-year-old 'Zoo TV' world tour, joining the only rock and roll band in the world still officially bigger than them for four huge outdoor stadium shows in Italy: two nights each in Verona (July 2nd and 3rd) and Rome (6th and 7th). For the week they spent on the road with U2, Eddie took to wearing a T-shirt with a different message gaffer-taped to the front every day. On stage in Rome, the gaffered message read 'Paul Is Dead': a hardly concealed reference to U2 singer Bono, whose real Christian name is Paul. The set closed with Eddie donning a grotesque fly mask and dancing around dementedly as though he were caught in a giant web while Bono looked on expressionless from the wings . . .

Three days later, they rejoined Neil Young's tour as it arrived for a large outdoor show of its own, in Dublin, Ireland, on July 10th. Whether it was because their songs were better known, or because the convivial local people and rain-strafed streets reminded them of home, nobody could say for sure, but the show, held in the grounds of the magnificent two-hundred-year-old Slane Castle, was by far the most enjoyable performance they had given since the 'Lollapalooza II' tour almost a year before. The Dublin audience was almost as entertaining as the acts they had come to enjoy: joyous, energetic, fuelled by draught Guinness, cheap hash and a hunger for the good times to begin. Van Morrison, a one-off addition to the bill, performed first and was greeted like the beloved black sheep he undoubtedly revels in believing he is. As he left the stage, though, the rapture quickly subsided as the mainstay of the audience, in anticipation of Pearl Jam, surged to the front of the stage. When the band appeared twenty minutes later, the strain of the on-rushing crowd buckled some of the crash-barriers and the security teams were needed to yank semi-conscious members out of the crowd and ferry them on stretchers to the first-aid tent. Eddie strolled on wearing a gorilla mask, then pulled it off and hurled it into the sky as the band, grinning from amp to amp, plunged heads-down into 'Why Go', Eddie's girlfriend Beth standing off in the wings, catching it all on Super-8, what must have looked like the whole of Dublin jumping up and down and waving into her lens . . .

The following day, July 11th, hangovers worn like fancy hats at the gates of hell, the party moved to London, setting up shop on a cold Sunday afternoon in Finsbury Park where Neil Young and Pearl Jam were joined on the bill by James, Teenage Fanclub and 4 Non-Blondes. However, the reception Pearl Jam received upon their return to England was decidedly frosty, at least as far as the professional fans – the critics – were concerned. What hadn't helped was the fact that so far they had refused practically all requests for interviews. This was as much a paid vacation as it was a mini-tour, the band had insisted to their record company promotions department chiefs. 'That's the problem you run into,' Jeff reluctantly conceded when it was all over. 'Last year there were times on this tour when we did six or eight hours of press on our days off. And it was just this whirlwind, when you did have a little bit of time and you just wanted to go out in the city. You were in a numb state. And that left a bad taste in our mouths.' 'It becomes such a big production,' Eddie shrugged. 'You can't talk to him unless you talk to him and talk to him . . . And then you think, Wait a second, this is just a guy I remember having a good time with last time I was here, so I just want to talk to him. Sometimes a radio station comes up and asks you to get on the air for a second. You agree. And then three other radio stations complain. It's a huge ordeal, because of companies and money and politics. Then they say: "How could you have done that without asking us?"'[20]

All the same, the knives were out, certainly as far as the *Melody Maker*'s resident grungespert Everett True was concerned. Reviewing the show in Finsbury Park that day, he wrote that people 'who are into Pearl Jam as a live experience, as a viable credible alternative, as something exciting and different and cool, are those who have absolutely no fucking idea of what heights or depths either (*i*) metal or (*ii*) grunge can aspire to'. Going on to describe Eddie memorably as 'that sensitive, overblown, preening, gibbering pretence of a poet' he finished with a final poisoned flourish: 'Pearl Jam exists, like bad Hog Roast dinners exist,' he sniffed, '. . . like Jon Bon Jovi exists, like Bono's wankometer exists, like curtains, like tablecloths, like video consoles exist. They affect nothing.'[21] The *NME* was equally prejudiced in its summing up of the Finsbury Park performance: 'Pearl Jam are nothing more than a marketing man's idea of Nirvana, a bulging duffle-bag of dreary metal riffs where the words Emperor, New and Clothes sit comfortably side by side. I think Shakespeare put it best when he coined the phrase "much ado about shite".'[22]

In truth, it had not been a great performance – an hour or so of highlights from *Ten* and one or two unfamiliar ditties from the still unreleased new album that frankly failed to catch fire for anyone, least of all the band themselves – Eddie muttering a stilted apology at the end of the set, complaining how uncomfortable he felt at vast open-air shows where 'I can't see your faces', and hoping he would see them all more clearly at the band's two headline shows at London's Brixton Academy theatre later that same week. Perhaps they were still drunk from the day before. Indeed, Eddie, who had what looked like 'Fuck it all' written on the back of his jacket, appeared to be out of it on something, repeating his line from the band's first appearance at Finsbury Park with The Cult a year before, about 'Even Flow' being dedicated to Dee from L7's irregular periods. The only truly inspired moment was at the end of their set when the band threw carrots into the crowd, 'so that you can see Neil better in the dark', as Eddie told them earnestly.

But if Finsbury Park had been a disappointment, the first Brixton Academy show, on Tuesday, July 13th, more than made up for it. The stage lit with what appeared to be a blood-red backdrop of glowing candles, Jeff's miniature basketball team and Stone's now-obligatory farmyard animal (a large cow for these dates) perched on top of their respective amps, Mike arrived on stage carrying a vase of flowers, followed by Eddie holding aloft a mask on a stick flanked by four candles. Before you could really take in what was going on, the others had slipped from the shadows and the tense beginnings of 'Release' began to seep from the stage into the wide-open faces below . . . Then the expected explosion into 'Why Go?'. 'It isn't cool to like Pearl Jam any more,' said Eddie, as the number juddered to its climax, as if anticipating the reviews they were about to get for their tired appearance at Finsbury Park two days before.

Up front the crush was so heavy the band had to stop during 'Even Flow', and ask the kids to take three steps back. Eddie himself seemed in high good humour, stumbling around a little like Joe Cocker, tugging at his T-shirt until the neck stretched down to his navel and colliding with the drum kit. Not that it affected his singing voice, that extraordinary instrument which gave the band its essential character. At times the guitars threatened to overwhelm the vocals, but this was Pearl jamming, not playing safe . . . pristine sound was never on the menu. When someone threw tampons on to the stage,

Eddie leaned over, picked one up and stuffed it into his mouth; the timing strangely appropriate as the band launched into 'Blood', one of nine new songs that were effectively a preview of the forthcoming second album. A ferocious 'Animal' followed, chased by a steamin' 'rearviewmirror', Eddie picking up a guitar and punching it until it made the right noise, a loud cry.

'Alive' and a serenely weird 'Black' unfurled . . . Stone running in circles like a rat on a wheel, his newly shorn head making him look even younger, Jeff toiling over his bass like a mother hen crooning over her eggs . . . A soul-shaking 'Porch' ended the set. When they returned after five minutes of roof-lifting by the enraptured crowd, Eddie threw out his arms and begged the audience for requests. 'Leash' was the answer. 'State Of Love And Trust' and 'Garden' glided by, the salty smell of riffs cooking in their own fat mingling with the smell of dope, followed by a typically spiky 'Sonic Reducer' . . . before one last heady farewell, 'Indifference'; tenderly calm, almost unnervingly quiet after the mayhem that had preceded it, Eddie's voice radiating like the world's last echo. As the *Melody Maker*'s editor Allan Jones conceded, 'you could spend the rest of your life going to gigs and not witness anything as good as this'.[23]

Two more gigs, small headlining club dates at the tiny Ahoy club in Rotterdam (cancelled from the previous summer's tour) on July 16th and 17th, and the band were ready to return home for a short break before rejoining the Neil Young tour once more for outdoor dates in Calgary, Canada (August 12th); Ottawa (17th); Toronto (18th); and Montreal (19th), with the added attraction this time of also having Soundgarden on the bill. A kind of mini-Northwestern version of 'Lollapalooza'. Strictly for lumberjack-haters.

5

At the beginning of September, with the new album, now tentatively titled *Five Against One*, about to be released, Pearl Jam broke with the road in order to appear at the tenth annual MTV Awards, held at Universal Studios on Thursday, September 2nd. Despite scooping four awards, the band was hardly mentioned in any of the newspaper reports in the UK. Instead, Madonna made all the headlines with her Marlene Dietrich act – tuxedo, top hat, tails and no trousers – warbling 'Bye Bye Baby' while straddling three lingerie-clad beauties in a set apparently designed to resemble a brothel . . . 'Get the picture?' she teased the shrieking audience, as she petted and slapped one of the shapely dancers' buttocks. Janet Jackson, who had the joyless task of following Madonna on to the stage, did her best to match the tempo in a skimpy breast-thrusting two-piece, fondling her male dancers and writhing with intent, but after Madonna's bravura tongue-in-ear performance it all looked rather tame and somewhat forced. As an MTV executive was overheard to sigh, 'You certainly get your money's worth when Madonna is on the bill.'

Pearl Jam won Best Video for 'Jeremy'; Best Group Video for 'Jeremy'; Best Hard Rock Video for 'Jeremy'; and Best Video Director, again for 'Jeremy'. 'If it weren't for music, I would have shot myself,' Eddie told the goggle-eyed audience from the podium. He and the band declined to play the song live on the grounds that they had already done so at the previous year's awards ceremony. Instead, they gave a rousing, white-knuckled version of 'Animal' from the forthcoming album, and were then joined on stage by Neil Young for a hair-tugging version of 'Rockin' In The Free World', at the end of which Mike McCready smashed his guitar and Eddie dismantled first his microphone then whatever else came to hand.

Actress Sharon Stone (in a red £5,000 Valentino dress) presented the Best Video Direction award. Elsewhere on the bill, Alice In Chains won Best Video From A Film for 'Would?' from *Singles*; Nirvana's controversial 'In Bloom' video, for which the band dressed up in drag, won the Best Alternative Video category – somewhat ironically, in view of the fact that the band had been obliged to shoot an alternative, frock-free version of the clip due to their record company's fear that the video would not be screened on MTV; k. d. lang won Best Female Video for her hit 'Constant Craving'; Lenny Kravitz won Best Male Video for 'Are You Gonna Go My Way?' (which he performed live, joined on stage by veteran former Led Zeppelin bassist John Paul Jones); and Arrested Development picked up the prize for Best Rap Video with 'People Everyday'. While the Stone Temple Pilots, who had spent the previous twelve months living down accusations of being a poor man's Pearl Jam, ironically beat

Pearl Jam to the Best New Artist In A Video trophy with their 'Plush' video.

'In Los Angeles, "fake" really becomes a problem,' Eddie commented wryly. 'People were asking me at that MTV thing, "What's wrong with you? Are you drunk? Is something wrong?" They were all acting the same, like rock stars, and if you don't act like a star or you don't look like a star, they think something's wrong.'[24] Eddie didn't even have cable installed at his apartment, so he never watched MTV anyway, he shrugged. 'I really should have said, "Uh, thanks but you know, I don't have MTV, so I don't know what this means."' It was difficult for him to work himself up to perform for a video because 'I just don't put any weight into those things at all . . . being nominated [for an MTV award] is such a weird thing . . . I'm just like, "I don't know, whatever, you know, thanks." When other bands are nominated for awards, I'm rooting for them. It's really weird. I don't understand it when it's our band.'[25]

One prize not surprisingly discarded from the 1993 ceremony was the Michael Jackson Video Vanguard Award. MTV naturally denied that the decision had anything to do with the growing scandal Jackson became embroiled in over his alleged sexual assault of a thirteen-year-old boy: vice-president of programming at MTV, Doug Herzog, describing the timing of the move as merely 'a coincidence'. (Janet had been whisked to and from Universal in a smoke-screened limousine and had refused to comment on her brother or anything else to the reporters present. She even refused to pose for pictures.)

Other guests that night included actress Demi Moore, singer Sinead O'Connor arm-in-arm with Peter Gabriel (who won Best Special Effects for 'Steam'), Sting (plus wife Trudie Styler), U2 (whose guitarist The Edge gave a stunning solo performance of 'Numb'), supermodel Cindy Crawford (arm-in-arm with Lenny Kravitz) and tennis star Monica Seles (making a rare public appearance after the knife attack on her at the Italian Open six months earlier). Event organizers boasted of over a hundred million viewers. After a three-hour show, more than five thousand people enjoyed the half-million-dollar party. MTV had constructed a high-tech 'video garden' replete with a £1 million simulator where guests could become an active part of any of the videos being aired for the rest of the night. Guests had to pass through *three* security checks before being allowed entry.

But if the biggest horse-laugh of the night was prompted by REM's

Michael Stipe testing his microphone by repeating the word 'fuck' into it live several times quite clearly in whatever language you happened to be sniggering in, the weirdest sight of the night was Kurt Cobain, wife Courtney and their recently born baby, Frances, dancing slowly arm-in-arm with one Eddie Vedder ... Had they healed the rift, then? Was Kurt Cobain about to start announcing suddenly that no, wait, maybe he'd been a bit hasty and that, shucks, well, Pearl Jam wasn't such a wicked bunch of creeps after all? 'I didn't talk about it to anybody except for my little brother the next day, when we went surfing. But that's all been taken care of,' was Eddie's only comment afterwards, but looking at them huddled together swaying in time to the music at the MTV Awards it was clear something had gone down ... had changed. 'It was a sacred moment and I just kind of feel weird talking about it,' said Eddie, lowering his eyes. 'We slow-danced; everything was fine. It was actually an apology.'[26]

On September 4th, they returned once more to the Neil Young tour for three final outdoor shows: in Vancouver; The Gorge, in Grant County (5th); and finishing up in Portland Meadows, Oregon, on Monday, September 6th. Their appearance at The Gorge was their first gig close enough to home not to have to book any hotel rooms since the free festival in Magnusson Park twelve months before. Playing for ninety minutes, the band previewed a number of songs from the recently completed album, Eddie ad-libbing madly in the places where he hadn't learned all the words yet. The highlight, though, was an extended, thunderous rendition of 'Alive' that raged as the light in the sky slowly died ... For the encore, Mudhoney's Mark Arm turned into Green River's Mark Arm for the night and got up and sang 'Sonic Reducer' with the band. Halfway through the show, however, hundreds of locked-out, ticketless fans tore down two metal fences with their bare hands, then ran and slid down a twenty-five-foot drop and hurled themselves past guards in an effort to rush the stage. Over a hundred people were treated for minor injuries during the show, according to Dr David Hugelmeyer, the chief medical officer in attendance in the first aid centre backstage. Several people also suffered broken bones, he added. Five people were taken to hospital.

6

Back home, even as the Tom Hanks–Meg Ryan romance picture *Sleepless In Seattle* opened to rave reviews in movie houses all over the Northwest, Seattle was starting to buck against what it had long ago stopped seeing as a naïve fascination for the city by outsiders and had begun to look on as simple invasion of privacy. By 1993, the *Seattle Times* was regularly reporting on the growing number of people moving back to the city . . . not an entirely meritorious trend for those who had never been away. In August 1993, Seattle celebrated Stay Away From Seattle Day; an event not without precedent in the city's colourful history. For example, on his trips to New York in the Forties, Stewart Holbrook, then the Northwest's most talked about writer, deliberately played up the floods and rain endemic to the region beyond the bounds of credibility, and a notorious former governor of Oregon was best remembered for always saying that people should only visit the state, never stay.

But what was happening now, in the Nineties, was beyond the realms of reason, the city's elders argued. It was one thing attracting young families looking for a better life; quite another to play host to a steady stream of Kurt Cobain and Eddie Vedder clones pouring their weird proclivities into town and expecting to be tolerated. It seemed like every half-arsed band that ever set out on the rocky road to fame and/or disaster via New York or LA suddenly decided to cash in their chips and return to the golden-egg laying nest they had misguidedly abandoned so long ago. Even bands with no visible connection what-soever to the Northwest were now claiming some sort of ancestral musical attachment to the place and were arriving in droves, doubtless believing the sidewalks to be paved in flannel-shirted babes and stacked high with already written out record contracts.

Or something. Commendably selective or needlessly picky, depending on how long you'd actually lived in Seattle, one thing long-time local residents all seemed to share was their fierce independence of mind. On September 10th, three weeks before the album was due to be released, Kelly Curtis informed Epic that the band had decided to flex their own fierce independence of mind and ditch the *Five Against One* title – too combative, too many wrong vibrations –

and now wanted to call the album simply *Pearl Jam*. Epic's chief executives held their collective breath, clung to their balance sheets that showed the *Ten* album now nudging worldwide sales of seven million and reluctantly agreed to the last-minute alteration, even though it represented a logistical nightmare from their point of view. Two weeks later, the band changed the title again. They didn't offer an explanation, they just insisted it had to be changed. By that time the artwork had been shot and printed and the new eleventh-hour alteration meant that the initial quantities of the album eventually arrived in the stores with no title at all on the sleeve.

Pearl Jam advised an open-mouthed Epic that they wanted their first single from the new album, 'Go', to protest at the state of the UK singles chart, pointing out that as they thought the chart did not accurately reflect the public's interest and fondness for guitar-led pop music, they had no desire to appear in it. It seemed like an unnecessarily churlish statement to make, considering the lavish attention foisted on them by other sections of the world's media, not least MTV and the music press, but they still went ahead and instructed Epic to take various steps to ensure that 'Go' was immediately pronounced ineligible for a placing in the UK Top 40 upon its release. Issued in 12-inch vinyl and CD only, backed with a new song, 'Alone', and an acoustic version of another album track, 'Elderly Woman Behind The Counter In A Small Town', copies of the single were also accompanied by a shrink-wrapped cassette featuring 'Animal', recorded live at the MTV Awards. The gift was only made available with British copies of the single, its very presence guaranteeing that the record would be instantly banned from the chart. To further make their point, they even stickered their own package with the words: NOT ELIGIBLE FOR THE CHART THAT COUNTS. The advertising campaign in both trade and consumer-press emphasized the message still further, containing the single's chart shop bar-code – another means of ensuring that the record was disqualified from the chart. They even had T-shirts made up which included the bar-code in big letters on the front.

Either somebody somewhere was taking themselves far too seriously, or the band had developed a seriously warped sense of humour while they were out there on the road with Papa Young, Booker T and the boys . . . either way, this so-called 'anti-chart campaign' was beginning to make the band's whims seem ludicrous. Not least to the uncomplicated fans who would have been delighted to see their favourite band with a single in the national Top 10 with a few TV appearances thrown in for good measure. But no. Not yet, anyway . . .

7

By coincidence, the second Pearl Jam album, now officially titled *Vs.*, had originally been timed to come out the same week as the next Nirvana album, their own follow-up to their first mega-success, entitled *In Utero*. When Pearl Jam discovered what was about to happen they insisted that Epic forestall the release by a couple of weeks. As *Seattle Post-Intelligencer* music columnist Gene Stout points out, 'They would want to avoid the press comparing the two side by side, like a "Battle of the Seattle bands".' The inference was that they weren't at all confident what the result of such a comparison would be. Released finally, worldwide, on October 11th, 1993, *Vs.* immediately entered the charts at No. 1 in Norway, Sweden, Holland, Israel, Australia, New Zealand, Canada and the US. It was only kept off the top notch in the British album charts by the new collection of hits from then current UK weeny-bop faves Take That.

Initially released in America for a seven-day period on vinyl only – a limited edition of thirty thousand which sold out immediately – the real frenzy began when *Vs.* became available in all formats the following week. *Billboard* reported that the album had achieved the largest first-week sales figure since the *Billboard* Top 200 began using Soundscan data, in May 1991. Although Nirvana's *In Utero*, released a fortnight before, had also débuted at No. 1, its first-week sales of more than 180,000 paled by comparison. Indeed, *Vs.* trounced the previous first-week record of 770,000 set by Guns N' Roses with their album, *Use Your Illusion II*, in 1991. The follow-up to *Ten* racked up over-the-counter sales of 950,378 in its first week of release, bouncing *Bat Out Of Hell II* off the No. 1 spot and out-selling every other album in the US Top 10 that week combined. 'This is not a record done with a lot of pre-release air-play, video or hype,' said Mike Shallett, chief operating officer of Soundscan. 'These are real hard-core fans out this week.'[27]

Vs., Shallett predicted, would become the biggest selling album in Northwest rock history. In addition, *Ten* was still glued to the US Top 30 two years after it was released, still selling in excess of forty thousand copies a week in America alone. In Britain, where *Ten* had eventually gone gold twice over (two hundred thousand plus sales), Epic began promoting *Vs.* with a series of playback nights at specially selected rock clubs around the country. The band did not appear at any of these launch nights but DJs spun tracks from the album and gave copies away. But in all the excitement to get their hands on a copy of the new album, the one thing very few of the initial stories that surrounded the furore of the new release covered was the music.

'Anyone who's expecting, like, *Ten – The Sequel* will maybe think that it's kinda weird and out there, and maybe even completely fucked up and doesn't work at all. [But] this isn't the kind of band that works to a formula,' said Stone. 'That would kill us. All we were concerned with was making a record that we were proud of, and I'm real proud of this one.'[28] As Jon Hotten put it, reviewing the album in *RAW*: 'There are no anthems here, no "Alive", no "Jeremy", no "Black", no "Porch". This album is about groove and vibe . . . No one will notice, but the real stars are probably Dave Abbruzzese and Jeff Ament, whose fluid, tight-but-loose rhythms are the spine of "*Vs.*".' Without the immediacy of those anthems, *Vs.* was a far less obvious, minor-key release than *Ten*, Hotten concluded, adding: 'Of course, Eddie Vedder's pain can match anyone's. "*Why do you want to hurt me?*" he pleads via "Animal"; "*Get out of my fuckin' face!*" he spits during "Leash". However, Vedder, unlike his more introverted contemporaries, is an inspirational writer when he turns his angst outward . . . "*Got a gun,*" he hollers on "Glorified G", "*but that's OK, man, 'cos I love God.*" And later, "*Never shot a living thing, but I always keep it loaded . . .*"'[29]

Not everybody was so entranced, of course. Gazing down from its lofty perch, the *Independent* newspaper declared that Eddie's singing was 'the same tortured, quavery rumble of portent as before, while the music is merely doggedly competent – with the notable exception of "Indifference", whose quiet, organ-fuelled moodiness and subtle guitar play is left stranded at the end of the album, as if the group are embarrassed by its gentleness'.[30] The truth was, in pure rock terms, as second albums go, *Vs.* was always more *Straight Shooter* than *Led Zeppelin II*. Meaning that unlike the latter, which was an album so precipitously greater than its predecessor that it established a new degree of critical and commercial success for its makers, *Vs.* had more in common with the second Bad Company album: stuffed with crowd-pleasers and, though the band would not thank you for saying so, very much the sort of follow-up their mainstream fans would have been hoping to hear – familiar but new, exciting but focused, ener-gized but ... different? Never in a million B-sides. 'It is not a signifi-cant advance on what they've done before, no,' agrees *Record Collector* editor Peter Doggett. 'But then who is there who does anything different from one album to the next? In the Nineties, you create the sound then you reproduce it. I loved the Black Crowes' albums because the guy has such a great voice. But the second one isn't that different. It's the first one with a bit more Gothic feel.'

'I think that Brendan the producer did a much better job on the second record. The sound quality and the energy level, to me, was much better. It makes *Ten* sound like a demo,' says Doug Pinnick, sticking up for the musicians. 'It's not *Ten II*, that's what I like about it. It's still Pearl Jam, it still sounds like them but they have progressed into new areas of songwriting to me. I think it's a really good record but I played it several times before it really grabbed me. That's sort of good, the first album did that too, but then you get it.'

8

But while the critics debated and the cash registers continued to ching, the band themselves remained determinedly aloof from proceedings. Still hugely sensitive to the accusations of hype that had dogged them from the moment Kurt Cobain had randomly thrown their name into the shit-pot and handed the spoon to his groupies on the rock press, the members of Pearl Jam were deeply reluctant to be seen over-indulging the media to promote *Vs.* Yet to even shoot a promo video for either 'Go' or 'Daughter' (scheduled as the second single), MTV had been reduced to programming the clip of their live performance of 'Animal' from the awards show in September. A specially commissioned cover story for *Rolling Stone* written by their neighbour Cameron Crowe was the only major interview the band had given in over a year. American national radio host Howerd Stern, complaining about Eddie's sudden reluctance to speak to anybody with a microphone in their hand, said: 'I remember when this guy was just a fresh face . . . He was all bubbly, like, "Hi, I'm Eddie." Now he can barely speak a word of English.' As if by magic, Eddie proceeded to appear on Stern's radio phone-in show, *Rockline*, the night before *Vs.* was released, giving out his home phone number and encouraging listeners to call him themselves and put the questions they wanted answered to him personally. Needless to say, you couldn't get through to Eddie's number for weeks afterwards. Those that were fortunate enough to find the lines free and got through were treated to a-cappella songs which he made up on the spot, he told friends, such as 'Don't Pick Up That Fork', 'Bread Basket', 'College Boy With A Dildo Toy', 'Flipper and Lou', 'Chimney God' and 'Bored Education' . . .

They even refused to speak to the reporter from *Time* magazine, who splashed Eddie's mug across its cover at the end of October, as *Vs.* hung like a dart from the bullseye of the Top 10. Rumour had it that *Time* had originally wanted to publish a 'Pearl Jam *vs.* Nirvana' story – prompting Eddie to quip that he would agree to a joint cover with Nirvana only if the picture showed him kissing Kurt Cobain on the mouth, an offer the magazine's besuited editors failed to see the funny side of and declined. Nevertheless, they still managed to work in the implication in the story that the title of Pearl Jam's album was a nudge-nudge reference to the rivalry between Pearl Jam and Nirvana.

The official 'Vs.' world tour began at the Warfield Theater in San Francisco at the end of October; with rotatable support slots from the likes of Mudhoney, Rollins Band, Butthole Surfers and Urge Overkill. At their own request, the band would be headlining at unseated venues only, with a maximum capacity of eight thousand. Unofficially, the 'Vs.' tour kicked off with a hush-hush gig in Seattle at the tiny Off Ramp club. Billed as a performance by Green Apple Quick Step (another band managed by Kelly Curtis), when word got out locally that afternoon, a large crowd gathered at the doorway, hoping to be let in while fire-department personnel stood and counted heads. Admission was just one dollar per person. So fierce was competition for tickets that when Chris Cornell showed up late, at first even he couldn't get in (he only got in after Pearl Jam's tour manager, Eric Johnson, persuaded the fire department officials that Chris was an integral part of the show).

Pearl Jam shuffled on stage at about 11.00 p.m., Eddie wearing a Charles Bukowski mask and mumbling about his arsehole being sore from wiping it with the cover of *Time* ... The band performed without a spotlight, giving them a gaunt, shadow-laden look as they crab-walked around the small under-prepared stage. As the show went on, Eddie quipped, 'Hey, who's been calling my house?' – a reference to his having given out his private phone number on Howerd Stern's *Rockline* ... The changes in the band were obvious to those that knew them best. Eddie no longer thrashed wildly about the stage, looking for something to climb on to, preferring to stay steady in one spot with a bottle of wine in his hand ... less spontaneous perhaps, more professional ... still charming, still magical, but for different reasons now.

9

But still they proved elusive to the world's press. By the start of the 'Vs.' world tour proper in the autumn of 1993, they had even introduced contracts for journalists and photographers to sign, empowering the band with story and picture approval, before they were allowed anywhere within the same breathing space as the band members. Ross Halfin, one of the most acclaimed rock photographers of the last ten years, who has spent years working with the likes of Led Zeppelin, Guns N' Roses, Def Leppard and Metallica, was one of the few influential media personalities that flat out refused to sign any of the Pearl Jam photo-approval contracts.

Halfin had first met Pearl Jam when he had been assigned to shoot them for the cover of an American magazine around the time of the 'Jeremy' video shoot in Germany, and again backstage at The Cult gig in Finsbury Park a few days later. 'I had the bloody flu that day, so I was really ill but they were really nice,' he recalls now. 'And I gave Eddie Vedder some Who tapes – I found out he was a really big Who fan, so we'd got quite a lot in common to talk about. Then that was it. Said goodbye, and I went home with the flu, never heard from 'em again until this thing about the contracts came up . . .'

When *Vs.* had been released, Ross had been besieged by calls from client magazines all over the world screaming for up-to-date snaps to run with their *Vs.* stories. No problem, said Ross, only to his surprise when he contacted the Epic Records press office about arranging a photo session he was told he had been banned from shooting Pearl Jam. 'It wasn't just that they wouldn't shoot with anyone unless they'd signed the contract, they particularly wouldn't shoot with me, they said, ' Halfin recalled, his face still registering the shock weeks later. It seems the band had taken exception to some of the pictures they had done with Ross in Europe being used in an American one-off publication issued by the publishers of the popular *RIP* magazine, billed with the admittedly cringe-inducing title of a 'Grunge Special'. 'The magazine was nothing to do with me, they had bought the shots and were using them as they saw fit,' Ross says. 'But because of this, you know, *heinous* crime, I was the reason why they wouldn't do pictures with photographers and I was banned. You know, totally banned out the window!'

RIP editor Lonn M. Friend had tried to rectify things but the band remained 'adamantly against it', says Ross. 'I was just this evil person . . . which was a shame. I thought I got on with them really well, but there you go.' Then when, at the end of October 1993, Ross was on the road with Henry Rollins, shooting him for the cover of his next album, the Rollins band happened to be opening for Pearl Jam on that leg of their newly begun tour. 'So I got backstage and Henry ran into Eddie Vedder and they were talking. Henry pointed out I was in his dressing-room, then Eddie came in the room, and I went to shake his hand and he gave me a big hug and I was really, really surprised,' Ross recalls. 'And he was holding a video of The Who from the Cow Palace, in San Francisco, '73. He goes, "Hey, look what I've got," and we started talking Who stuff, and we didn't mention photographs at all. So we went and watched this video together, you know, and we were, like, buzzing, and at the end of it, as we were walking along the hallway, Eddie stopped me and said, "Hey, if you wanna take some pictures of me later, I'd be more than happy to."' Ross was at that time compiling shoots for his next book and suggested they do something specially for that, to which Eddie readily agreed.

'So the next day the tour arrived in San Jose, and I'm doing some pictures of Henry, and this girl called Julie Framer, a press officer, asked to speak to Ross Halfin. I said, "That's me." She said, "I'm the photo police." I said, "What are they?" And she said, "My job is, I hear you are doing a picture of Eddie Vedder and if you are doing a picture of Eddie Vedder you have to sign this contract," and offered me a contract. I said, "I'm not signing anything, you can take my word for it that it won't be used, you know, apart from in my book." And she went, "That's not good enough!" She said again, "You *have* to sign this." I said, "Wait a minute, I have a choice and my choice is I will not sign this." And she stormed off.

'So it all gets a bit aggravating. I heard she was bad-mouthing me inside the production office to other photographers, what an asshole I am, etc. So I went and got hold of Eric the tour manager and explained that the reason I refused to sign the contract was because I'd never signed a contract in my life. I said if that means Eddie doesn't want to shoot with me, that was entirely up to him. But, you know, I had never signed anything like that in my life and I wasn't going to start now, I've been doing this too long.' Eric had denied that it was anything personal, just that the 'Grunge Special' had really upset them and they didn't know who to trust any more. 'I said, "Look, Eric, I am a photographer, I sell my pictures. If someone puts the words Grunge Special on top of them I cannot help that. That is not my doing. If they don't like that they should take it up with the magazine, not me. It's not published by Ross Halfin Productions! So he said fine, he took my point and was very nice about it. Then they went on stage and I left with Henry.'

The next day when the tour set down in Berkeley for a show that night at the famous Greek Theater, Eddie was waiting for Ross as he arrived at the venue with the Rollins crew. 'It was an early show that day and so I'd gone to the store on my own and got him a couple of Who bootlegs he wanted. And he was totally friendly. He said they'd played "Baba O'Reilly" the night before because I was there and did I hear it? I said no, I'd left. And we were just chatting about fame and he was saying that he finds it hard to deal with things. I told him to enjoy it rather than, you know, get all depressed about it. Then he played me a DAT he'd made of a Pete Townshend solo concert from the "Naked Eye" era and it was really good.

'So we were getting on great, and at the end of it I said, "Look, about this picture for my book, if you don't want to do it, I really understand. But if you do it, it would be really great if you wrote something about Pete Townshend and did a picture to go with it." And I said, "I'm not going to sign the contract but if you really want to, I'll write something to you, personally, you know, saying that this will only be used in my book." He looked at me and said, "Your word is good enough for me," and shook my hand, and we did pictures before the show and pictures after the show. And they played "Baba O'Reilly" that night again, and Jeff Ament said, "This is for a special friend of ours," and as they came off the stage Ament looked at me and goes, "That was for you." He was laughing as he said it. And then Eddie came and did the shots with me. And that was the last I've seen or heard.'

Despite the hoops he was eventually forced to jump through to prove his worth to Eddie and the rest of the band, Ross obviously still holds the Pearl Jam singer in personal high regard. 'Yeah, I do. I think that he means really well, he puts a lot of thought into what he says before he answers you, and he's a Who fan, which also means he's got a lot going for him ... The only thing I really don't like is all this *Angst*. It's a bit, you know, unnecessary, really.'

Ross had hit the nail on the head. For all his exemplary song-writing ideas – the lyrics on *Vs.* dealt with child abuse, dyslexia, racism and the US gun laws, and that was just side one – his endless grumbling about the trappings of success were beginning to sound suspiciously like special pleading: tedious at best, manipulative and arrogant at worst. Undoubtedly, the *Angst*-ridden teens of the world related to Eddie's immense dissatisfaction with his even more immense success, his distrust of his grossly inflated circumstances. But at the end of the day, how tough could it really be making millions of dollars a year for singing songs you yourself wrote and loved and believed in more than anything else in life? So the world's media wants to talk to you and take your picture, so the kids all want to tell you their problems, that wasn't pressure, that was the sound of life noisily stacking the chips up in your favour. As Jon Hotten says, 'Pressure is spending the night hungry and cold on the side of a hill in Bosnia, pressure is finding out you've got AIDS.' There was substance to the man – as *Melody Maker* editor Allan Jones observed with his usual insight, 'Vedder's lyrics address an agenda of social woes that would be merely right-on if they didn't so powerfully transcend social commentary and fill us with a profound sense of desolation, a real feeling for the helpless and oppressed' – but not maturity.[31]

That would come later, hopefully. In the mean time, sensing the mounting criticism, Eddie announced that his approach to the media had undergone another twist and that, as of now, he was carrying around a list of all the people who had requested an interview with him since the release of *Vs.* and would call them up at random in the near future. Rock journos all over the world suddenly thought about holding their breaths then changed their minds just as quickly and went back to what they were doing . . .

10

And the play banded on . . . The performances on the first leg of the *Vs.* tour reached their apotheosis at the end of November, as the tour began its swing through Texas. Their insistence on playing smallish venues had led them to the smallish stage of the students' hall at the Stephen F. Austin University, in Nacodoches, Texas . . . Starting the show with their current US single, 'Daughter' (a picture of Kelly Curtis's own new-born baby daughter had been used on the posters), a seated, upright-bass playing Ament and a stationary Vedder recreated the song's slow build like potters spinning the wheel, the clay clinging to the thoughts of all those present. During the intro to 'Jeremy', Eddie turned to the crowd and asked: 'I know my life's been really fucked up of late. How 'bout yours?' 'Alive' closed the show and nearly closed Dave Abbruzzese along with it, the drummer having passed out as he left the stage. The band were forced to resort to a series of largely unfamiliar acoustic numbers as an initial encore. Then the appropriately named Blackie Onassis, drummer for openers Urge Overkill, arrived on stage in time for a full tilt an' slant at 'Rockin' In The Free World' . . .

On December 7th, 8th and 9th, Pearl Jam returned to Seattle, the well from which they still drew their deepest inspiration, for three nights at the Seattle Arena. To coincide with the shows, the band offered to allow one show each to be broadcast live by each of the three major Seattle-based radio stations. 'But in return they're making each station come up with a promotion on anti-hate,' explained Kate Ellison, music director of the biggest station, KXRX. 'I think they're just very aware of the community.'

And yet, in spite of their anti-hate campaigns and all the wonderful things that were happening for them career-wise, 1993 ended on a series of discordantly down notes for Pearl Jam. First off, Eddie was arrested in New Orleans after a fight in a public bar. The incident occurred several hours after another sell-out show, when Eddie was out drinking with members of support band Urge Overkill and Jack McDowall, a pitcher for the Chicago Whitesox (Urge Overkill's local baseball team). Eye-witnesses later reported that while drinking in the French Quarter, Eddie had become involved in a loud beery argument with another patron – a local New Orleans bod by the name of James Gorman – which resulted in Eddie spitting in Gorman's face after he had been abusive about Pearl Jam's music. A fight between the two broke out, with Eddie allegedly knocking Gorman unconscious. Eddie, who suffered cuts to his lip and head, was the only person the police arrested following the incident, and now faced a possible ninety-day prison sentence and/or a $500 fine. He was freed, pending further enquiry, on $600 bail.

The Christmas 1993 issue of the *Melody Maker* ran a story in the news pages saying that the band had that week denied rumours that they were to split up and confirmed that they would definitely be touring Britain and Europe again in April or May of the new year. The 'split' rumours escalated in Seattle, when Pearl Jam pulled out of a planned MTV special which was supposed to feature them, Nirvana and Soundgarden. There was certainly no sign of Eddie Vedder, who was officially suffering from a 'shot voice', although other members of Pearl Jam did turn up to join Cypress Hill on stage. MTV organizers were reportedly furious. A hastily drafted in spokesman for the band, reading from a prepared statement, was reported thus: 'Eddie was, truthfully, under the weather, and the band had to pull out of another couple of gigs, too. They are going to have to reschedule those.'

'They've always said they will come back to the UK in April or May of next year,' he went on to add for the benefit of the glowering English press. 'They will do that and they will play a proper tour.' Oh no they wouldn't . . .

CROWN

'I need honesty, I need truth, and I need hope – I need it! That's what music means to me . . . I'm probably concerned with too many issues, animal rights, multiple sclerosis, environmental issues and homelessness in America, so I'll have to focus myself, but there's going to be a revolution, you know, and Perry Farrell will be at the front of it and I'll be right there next to him!'[1]

– Eddie Vedder

'Pearl Jam, the Northwest's most prestigious rock group, wasn't nominated for any Grammies yesterday, but only because the hugely popular band's atest album, Vs., was released after the Grammy deadline. But wait until next year – Pearl Jam undoubtedly will be nominated in multiple categories . . .'[2]

– Seattle Times

'You ever heard the story
of Mister Faded Glory
Say he who rides the pony
must someday fall . . .'

– 'Crown Of Thorns', words by Andrew Wood

1

Predictably, Pearl Jam never did make those spring UK shows. Instead, they did what any other right-thinking American band would have done in the circumstances of their enormous success: put the British and European legs of their world tour back indefinitely and went for broke out on the dollar-long American road. 'Commercial lightning rarely strikes twice in the same place in this business,' as one record company exec puts it. 'With U2 off the road, right now Pearl Jam are the biggest fucking band in America – they would be crazy to turn their backs on the kind of business they're being offered in the US to go to England where nobody ever makes any money anyway and the critics all hate them.' But then, their whole performance had taken on a far more professional hue than in times of old. The band no longer condoned stage-diving, for safety reasons, and even Eddie's rafters-scaling antics seemed to be a distant memory. The only thing he swung from these days was the wine bottle that seemed to be glued to his hand throughout every performance.

And they had gradually lost their antipathy toward playing arenas. 'We can play anywhere we want, it's not the venue that is the death of bands,' Jeff Ament reasoned. 'I mean, there's bands that know how to play those [places]. I used to go see Van Halen, and that's a band that knew how to . . . it felt like an intimate club. Or, like, Bruce Springsteen can go out and play for five hours in a giant coliseum and really translate to that medium. It's not so much the venue, it's that arena rock approach that's been copied to the point where it's such a cliché. It's that whole, "Is anybody out there?" attitude.'[3]

At the time of writing this epilogue, six months after its release, *Vs.* has already sold over four million copies in America and another couple of million elsewhere in the world; in all likelihood it will be the biggest-selling rock album in the world this year. Good songs, good melodies, good voice, good guitars, five good-looking guys brimming with good intentions . . . it still doesn't explain the reason why Pearl Jam remain so special to the people that are buying all those records. But then if you could just nail it down like that in a few sentences neither the band nor their fans would probably want to read them anyway. They all have their own stories to tell. Perhaps, at the end of the day, that it is the real key to the astonishing success of the band: their uncanny ability to draw the listener into the emotional centre of their musical web, Eddie's unfinished lyrics and Stone's trancelike guitar riffs allowing their listener to fill in the gaps for themselves, to make the mental leap from merely listening to actually believing that what Eddie is singing about is part of their own innermost thoughts.

More than their politically correct attitudes and their oft-stated determination not to let fame go to their beds with them when they took the stage garb off and went to sleep at night, perhaps the really appealing thing about Pearl Jam's music, and the real reason why *Ten* will always be a better and more popular album than its manicured follow-up, is that quivering state-of-the-heart vulnerability that is the pearl within the tough, grisly, grungy shell of their experience, their street-smarts, their inferiority complex and their fear. Here, at heart, are a bunch of emotional softies – essentially good people who believe that life doesn't necessarily have to turn out bad *all* the time, and that even though it does mostly, bottom line, there is a tomorrow and there is, please God, a better way. Just like most of us, in fact. Scared shitless and acting smart to conceal their own confusion, most of all in songs like 'Alive', 'Jeremy' and 'Indifference', they remind us of ourselves.

'I was talking to Jeff Ament about this,' says Gene Stout of the *Seattle Post-Intelligencer*. 'It's a little silly but there are times that you wonder if Andy Wood has provided some guidance from beyond. I did not expect Pearl Jam to become as big as they have become [and] I think [they] are a little freaked out about the level of fame they've reached. I think they would like to cool things down so that the media will look somewhere else for the next big story. But that's not going to happen ... all musicians and all entertainers go through this to a certain extent. They, essentially, strike a deal with the devil. They grab it, then they get it and then they want to renegotiate on it. I think that it just overwhelms people and I think, just being human, that's how Pearl Jam are reacting to it ... they may be apprehensive about adjusting to yet another level of fame, but I think they are probably going to get used to it.'

Meantime, Seattle has had its own problems adjusting to its new-found fame. It may have been the place to be in the late Eighties, but now, after a 21 per cent population increase in less than a decade, Seattle-ites have woken up with a shock to find their ever-increasing suburbs cutting into surrounding forests, and smog hovering over rush-hour traffic. The locals say the one thing they dread more than anything is to discover that Seattle has become just another long-distance suburb of California.

As Alice In Chains leader Jerry Cantrell said, 'It's our home town, you know? I'm very proud of it. I'm proud of the people from that city, I'm very proud of the musicians and I'm definitely proud of all the music that's been created. How could I feel anything else?'[4] But according to Soundgarden bassist Ben Shepherd: 'Seattle used to be a really cool friendly place. When you walked down the street everybody, whoever they were, would ask how you were doin'. Nowadays nobody does that, except the weirdos, it's become really hostile.'[5] 'In a place like Athens or Seattle, when there's a scene happening, everyone puts out a record, gets signed, then everyone goes out on the road and the scene dies,'[6] shrugged Bob Mould, former leader of Husker Du, the band that led its own popular regional US scene in the Eighties, in Minneapolis. 'Seattle is kind of a weird place to play, right now,' admitted Shawn Smith. 'Everyone and their grandma goes to everything, or nobody goes to anything. It's not very stimulating. It's definitely been ruined, to a certain extent.'[7]

'When you start talking about strategy, what's the next big thing and can you duplicate your success, that is poison!' Jonathan Poneman shook his head. 'That is the thing that's going to sink you.'[8] In 1994, with the Screaming Trees (whose double single on Sub Pop was an interim step between labels (Epic)), L7 (Slash/Warner Brothers) and Tad (BMG) also now lost to the fat wallets of the major labels, Sub Pop are already involved in bringing on the next generation of Northwest acts such as The Afghan Whigs, Seaweed and Love Battery. But it is the always in demand back catalogue of their roster alumni – Green River, Soundgarden, Mudhoney and Nirvana – that still pays most of their bills.

These days, Sub Pop's operation continues to spread outward beyond the Northwest region. As Bruce Pavitt said, 'We've really grown beyond being a local and regional label and become more of a national label. About a third of our acts are from the Northwest right now.'[9] And, of course, there's always the attitude, still intact six years and who knows how many free lunches later. The sleeve notes for *We're Only In It For The Money*, a recent overseas compilation of Sub Pop bands, has Poneman and Pavitt expounding hilariously on the meaning of it all with typically snub-nosed aplomb. 'If anybody tells you that they play rock music for any other reason than to make millions and millions of dollars ... they're lying,' writes Poneman, adding, 'But while you're buying the implied importance of rock music, I'm buying houses, cars, villas on the Costa del Sol! That's rock 'n' roll!!'

If only Eddie Vedder – who claimed that he didn't want to be a rock star, then performed all the tasks one performs in order to become a rock star – could take things so lightly. 'I used to think, before any of this, that I could change part of the world. I never expected to be in the public eye, ever, but even without that option I thought I could change things. People don't understand; they forget how good it feels when you do something for someone – and the feeling is great, it's incredible! People are just shocked when you give them something; they're always looking over their shoulders, and you can't blame them.'[10]

'You have to grow together,' said Stone stoically. 'Where you run into problems is when one person finally takes over and turns it into their thing. And it's never as good after that as when it was this magnificent rickety bicycle which was some of this person's thing there, including some weird nuts and bolts that maybe a few people in the band hated at the time, but two weeks later wound up loving.'[11] Green River has become a minor legend, he said, 'probably because no one can remember who was in it'.[12] 'I think the band itself helps ground Eddie, and all of us,' offers Mike. 'Eddie always says the music is the key thing to him, not awards and all that baggage,' offers Jeff. Stone talks of people leaving the guy alone when he needs it, 'so he might actually, you know, keep singing and writing for a while'.[13]

'I don't want to be Bono,' insists Eddie. 'He sang about issues in songs and suddenly people were turning to him for answers. And he was like, "Oh fuck, I just want to drink Heineken, you know?" So then he had to go out of his way to say, "Look, here I am drinking Heineken and smoking cigarettes and being decadent ..."' But, he says, 'I can't really kick back and sing about how life is good and everything is good while all I see is tragedy around me, to the point where I could easily let it catch me in a downward spiral and suck me under ... I'm meeting these people first hand, and I'm reading these letters from people who somehow relate to our songs in some tragic manner. I walk up on stage with a whole lot of baggage, and you gotta sing it as hard as you can, just to get it out. I'm not just singing for myself any more.'[14]

Commenting on the practice, now largely abandoned, of replying to all his fans' 'problem' letters personally, which he used to do religiously until the trickle became a deluge, Eddie said, 'A fucked-up person who's had bad things happen can relate to me because he sees someone else who's fucked-up. But . . . they don't understand that, at the bottom level, we're both fucked-up. And when ever you do have answers, it's at three thirty in the morning, and you're alone – and you can't find a pencil and paper.'[15] But Eddie still works hard with manager Kelly Curtis at keeping ticket prices down and policing the powerful promotions machine of Epic Records. But therein lies the grand contradiction. The artists Eddie most admires are the very ones who have turned their backs on the machinery of big-time rock that he, whether he is prepared to admit it or not, has *de facto* embraced. To his credit, Eddie appears to realize that he will never be like Henry Rollins, or Ian MacFaye of Fugazi. But that doesn't mean he thinks he shouldn't have been, somewhere, in some parallel universe of his mind, perhaps, who knew any more.

'It's just not normal,' Eddie frowned. 'You're talking about people who have lived their lives from pay-cheque to pay-cheque; who are going from not knowing where the next thing's coming from to having security. Are they gonna kick back and start relaxing? Is that going to change the music? Of course it will. At the same time, there's people telling you, "Well, you better make sure you sign your own cheques, and you better make sure that you count that money daily, because it's yours and it'll be gone." The thing is, money's not my trip – it never has been – and I don't want it to become my trip.'[16] Eddie has compared his own position to that of Neil Young, another artist known for his intractability in matters relating to the making of music. 'Neil gets obsessed with his work, and when he does, everyone says, "OK, he's going to be building a bridge out of matchsticks for the next six months, leave him alone." That's great. I'd love to see what would happen if I were left alone for six months to make music instead of having to find the time to do it. Isn't it silly? That's the biggest shock of this whole scene: I thought your job was to make music, then you'd be able to write songs during the day, take a piano lesson at four o'clock, come home and work on the four-track, make your girlfriend dinner and go out and see a show. But somehow that hasn't worked out. But I'm going to try to make that time, and who ends up alienated, I don't know.'[17]

That Eddie is 'the emotional leader' of Pearl Jam is beyond question, but he still needs the band just as badly as they need him. For now, anyway. Too long in the tooth for the usual all-for-one, one-for-all band mentality, Pearl Jam are caught between humouring their singer's more indulgent eccentricities and respecting his unquestionably high ideals. In many respects, Eddie remains the quintessential outsider, even within his own group. 'Eddie's not really close to anybody in the group,' says one acquaintance. 'His best friend in Seattle is probably Matt Chamberlain from the New Bohemians.' 'Everyone says, "You've got to expect it, because you put yourself out there." So maybe I won't put myself out there. I like my privacy too much to deal with that.'[18] Always the subject seems to return to whether he will quit one day or not. 'I'll quit the whole thing altogether, it doesn't matter,' he threatened everyone when *Ten* was first soaring up the world's charts. 'Right now there's enough people, if I made tapes out of my house and sold them for a buck apiece, I could keep my house, could keep my rent paid. I could get music out there, be real and could still be in control of the artwork. All the important things would still be there. I never had this lifelong dream to be a rock star. It's a problem being bothered by infatuated kids. It's lost on me. You picked the wrong guy to give all this stuff to; I'm into playing music and that's it.'[19]

The last time Doug Pinnick saw his friend Jeff Ament was when he invited Doug up to sing with the band before Christmas 1993, when Pearl Jam played at the Moody Coliseum, in Dallas. The last time Doug saw Eddie, 'he was giving me every indication that this is really hard. You know, "Eddie Vedder the God of Rock 'n' Roll". Right now, it's very hard for him to deal with that because he just doesn't feel a part of all that. It's sort of taken the fun out of what he loves to do, you know? But I think he'll work it out. That's what I love about them. They're such purists at heart, they just want to make music. I probably would have felt that way too if King's X had just started and that had happened . . . Eddie is such a charismatic person and I've been told that I'm a charismatic person, too, but I'm thinking, I ain't got nuttin' on him because look what he's doing. To me, it's the people that buy the music and that ultimately makes you who you are and right now everybody's buying Pearl Jam . . .'

Grunge as a serious fashion trend officially died in the spring of 1993 when a line of grungeian clothes by Perry Ellis, shown to the usual misplaced critical acclaim, failed to make an impression in the high street, and nationally, the cappuccino-based culture had become an easy target for the pundits to take the piss out of. Besides, Eddie long ago traded away the brown thrift-store jacket that Stone Gossard had given him when he first came to Seattle to rehearse and hadn't realized how cold it would be away from his beach hut in San Diego – the same jacket that was later remade and marketed by the fashion industry as a $1,500 piece of 'grunge wear'. 'Grunge as musical or fashion statement has definitely had its day now, I think,' says Peter Doggett. 'But as a historical monument it is still very potent. It was the first rock "craze" that actually was relevant to people like me who aren't in their teens any more, because it had such a long time to mature, ten years or so. And because it came from the same mixture of passion and excitement and anger that I got out of punk, that I got out of the Rolling Stones, that I got out of Jerry Lee Lewis.

'What bands like Nirvana and Pearl Jam and Soundgarden and the rest have managed to do is to almost reclaim working-class Seventies rock,' he continues. 'I'm not talking about Slade. I mean Zeppelin and Sabbath. They've almost managed to make an entire British and American rock tradition respectable again. You go through any vaguely intellectual rock history and you won't find Black Sabbath mentioned except in terms of lowest common denominator, prole fodder. Whereas right now they're seen as the incarnation of all secret teenage desires. But ultimately, I think it was a brief flowering. I think we're back to that position already where rock has retreated into trite mannerisms again as everybody jumps on the bandwagon. When you see the singer in INXS with a goatee you know the party's over . . .'

Jon Hotten sees things somewhat differently. 'I don't think people really perceive Pearl Jam as a heavy metal band, particularly. They could like Pearl Jam and still hate rock music. I don't think it's a huge sort of door-opening thing. I think the whole scene has broadened out, though. People who are committed to music and have heard everything on the periphery of metal from the Senseless Things and Red Kross on the one side, out to Pearl Jam and Nirvana on the other, they would probably see that. But I think just general punters who buy the albums the same way they'd pick up the new U2 album, it just wouldn't seem to them that they were buying a "heavy rock" album.

But these things go in circles often ... I think also because of the grunge thing, a lot of people have been put off Pearl Jam without having really listened to them. Kids are funny like that. Some of them would rather run a mile than have you think they're into *grunge*. Especially now that it's become a bit old. The music stands alone, same as it does with Nirvana, same as it does with Soundgarden and Alice In Chains. Eventually, it's like any scene. It's like the LA scene that produced Guns N' Roses and Mötley Crüe ... You can probably name, like, three bands that survived it and are still looked on with respect. The good bands survive and the rest just dies. The climate – the *Zeitgeist*, as it were – changes, doesn't it? People become aware of things. Right now, the youth of today are more *serious* than the youth of the Eighties. The youth of the Eighties were going through a fantastic boom time.'

Would Eddie ever recover his cool long enough to enjoy being in such a popular band or would he bail out sooner or later? 'What you have to remember about him is that he's obviously an intelligent guy and he will realize all those things eventually,' says Hotten, reading the tea leaves. 'He's just not realizing them at the moment. But I think he will. He's hanging out with guys like Neil Young, and Bob Dylan and all those guys. He's hanging out with the wise old heads of rock ... I'm sure they'll sort him out. He's just kicking against everything at the moment because he's a rebel, isn't he? I'm sure Pearl Jam will be around for a long time, but whether they'll stay within the arena they're in now ... I doubt that they will, I certainly hope they don't. Because I think they're the kind of band that can just grow as a band, and they'll go their own way, I hope. That's from a fan's point of view. It would be as easy for me to say it would be great if they just kept making an album every year that sounded just like *Ten*. Ultimately I hope just they do whatever they want to do, because I think it will be good, regardless.'

'First and foremost, Pearl Jam really do have good songs. Whether you're Mötley Crüe or Right Said Fred, the longevity of your career will be determined by the structured appeal of your songwriting,' says Geoff Barton, managing editor of *Kerrang!*. 'I think Pearl Jam have got that above and beyond. I think with Nirvana, they can hit a burst of good songwriting but it's almost anathema to them. "Oh God, I've written a new song, it might be a hit, throw it in the bin!" "Smells Like Teen Spirit" was the exception, rather than the rule, with them. I don't think that is an issue with Pearl Jam.'

What happens, though, if in their hunt for privacy they lost touch with the street-level reality that had informed all their best songs? Eddie didn't foresee a problem. 'You'll never cut yourself off from someone who says that a song like "Jeremy" meant a lot to him, especially when that person has been in a wheelchair for three years after a car accident. That kind of thing really gets to you. You don't cut yourself off from that kind of input. The only thing that takes away from that is when people start grabbing you and taking pictures and wanting autographs . . . When people say things like, "Oh, I love you sooo much,' it makes me want to turn around and punch them. But I can't do that, so I just look at them like, "Do you realize how ridiculous you're being?" It just bothers me when people come up to me and start treating me like I'm different. I'm not. My name is Eddie, and I'm a human being. What's your name?'[20]

Stone Gossard is typically less emotional about the question. Whether success will eventually change the band for the better or the worse, change them it already has and Stone recognizes this. 'But I'm sure as long as the band sticks together, as long as we won't let anything come between our friendship, we will be safe from most of the dangers of success.'[21] 'We want to make sure that we keep our feet on the ground,' says Jeff Ament. 'We don't want success to change us, it's something that we think about but we'll do everything we can to keep our feet on the ground. We feel pretty overwhelmed by our success because when it was happening we were unaware of it because we were on tour for so long. All that happened was that we began to notice that the gigs were getting bigger and bigger.' 'Having gone through Mother Love Bone and Green River has been a totally intense learning experience as far as dealing with people and starting to grow up has been concerned,' said Stone. 'After being in a band you start seeing things differently. It's like in a long guy–girl relationship, the only way you can make it work is by learning to communicate and tolerate each other. With this band we're all very different, but music holds us together. It's the glue and I think we'll be around for a long time.'[22]

As for Eddie, for all his grumbling and hair tugging, music, he insists, is still the one thing that comes through when all else lets him down or disappoints him. 'There's always something new or something old that I'll feel like hearing while we're on the road and I'll go out and buy it. The best thing is to go to truck stops and buy the cassettes that sit next to the popsicle and chewing-gum stands. You think of buying *The Best Of Conway Twitty* but you pick up the tape of *Love Gun* by Kiss instead. We'll put that album on in the bus at three in the morning and the whole band will be rocking to it . . .'²³

Certainly, this was not a band that was going to burn itself out on drugs. 'We have, of course, all had our experiences with drugs,' says Jeff. 'Among our friends and our environment here in Seattle, drugs [can be] a problem. But I'm convinced that the band, all of us, by now have learned to handle drugs and be able to do without them. Our music and our band are just too important.' 'We've all had our experiences of drugs and we've all found out their dangers. We know what we can tolerate and we're trying to keep it under control,' says Stone. 'Remember that we've seen friends die through drugs.'

As to the short-term future for Pearl Jam, their true place in the rockular scheme of things has yet to be fully determined. If they were to split up tomorrow and never release another record, they would be remembered as the band that never quite lived up to its full potential. Mostly through Eddie's own personal neurosis – you just know that deep down he suspects that everything his harshest critics have ever said of him is at least partly true – right now Pearl Jam are still struggling to bridge the credibility gap that exists outside the slack-jawed acceptance they have become used to in America.

Musically, though, at heart they are all musos, and if and when Eddie starts to feel as relaxed as he did the morning he first wrote and sang 'Alive' and 'Once' and 'Footsteps' to himself, crooning over Stone's brittle riffs like a mother preparing a bottle for the baby, they are capable of making some of the most potent rock music this side of Led Zeppelin and Eddie's beloved Who. If and when.

On the other hand, maybe the boy who never seems to stop crying wolf really will be eaten by the beast of the music business and Pearl Jam will go the way of Green River and Mother Love Bone. More what ifs for Jeff Ament and Stone Gossard to ponder. But that seems unlikely. Even Eddie Vedder would surely admit that if there is one thing harder to deal with than success it is failure, and right now in 1994 things for Pearl Jam and their immediate musical relatives are simply looking too good.

There will probably never be a *Temple Of The Dog II* album, no matter how much their respective record companies might rub their hands together salaciously at the very thought; however, it is not inconceivable that Eddie and Chris Cornell will work together again some day, and although vocalist Shawn Smith and drummer Regan Hagar are involved now in their own Epic-signed band, Satchel, there will almost certainly be a second Brad album at some stage. There have already been various one-offs like Stone's distortion-friendly 'Real Thing', a track cut with rappers Cypress Hill for the *Judgement Night* soundtrack (Immortal/Epic Soundtrax), and a finger-bleeding version of Jimi Hendrix's 'Hey Baby/Land Of The New Rising Sun', reteaming Mike McCready with the Temple gang on the 1993 Reprise LP *Stone Free: A Tribute To Jimi Hendrix*.

Dave Abbruzzese, who has now relocated to a country town outside Tacoma, Washington, in order to be closer to the band, says there's still a lot he'd love to do besides playing drums in Pearl Jam. 'I'd love to play on some rap and hip-hop stuff because I just love to play that kind of funk drumming. I'd also like to eventually make a record with some of my old friends and just make music, maybe play guitar on something and produce other bands some day … But I don't really think about it. There's no place I'd rather be right now than making music with Pearl Jam. There are so many avenues for us to explore, and we get tastes of that every time we jam. Maybe the greatest thing about this band is that the jamming aspect never takes a back seat. That's why I love the word "jam" in the band's name. I can never see the music just stopping for us.'[24]

And what about Jeff – would he ever consider packing it all in for art? 'When I'm older!' he laughs. 'I do all our record covers, T-shirts and all that and sometimes it is infuriating when you're on the road and you want to paint or sketch, because you don't get the opportunity. Someday I'll have the time and motivation to discover thinks like photography properly – I'm still learning. One day when I'm sick of all this, I'll pack my bags and live in the countryside and paint all day!'[25]

Evaluating the band in the cold bleachy light of another rainy Seattle day, *The Rocket*'s editor Charles R. Cross sums it up well enough. 'Pearl Jam is more derivative and Nirvana's more innovative. Whereas the innovative group breaks the ground, in general, in America, the group that is more derivative is more successful. If you were to ask me and I were to guess I would say that twenty years from now it will be Nirvana records that will be remembered more over time, whereas Pearl Jam will have a much longer and more successful career. You look at the Sex Pistols and say how many copies did 'Never Mind The Bollocks' sell? Nothing, but in terms of influence, it was and still is massive . . . With Pearl Jam, so many more people think they are the future whereas Nirvana's long-term future nobody feels very solid on [because of] the personalities in that band.'*

In Pearl Jam's favour is their intrinsic 'decency', says Cross. 'Pearl Jam became a national band and then worked very hard to create their local roots. They could have been real assholes, and they are not. What that means long term . . . These guys have only been stars for two years. Three years from now will they be nice guys? Will Eddie Vedder turn into Jim Morrison? That's a good question. So far, they're showing class and maybe they will in the long term. But put out consistently quality records and be commercially successful – that's hard to do most of the time.'

2

Next to 'What if Jimi Hendrix hadn't died?' or 'What if Jim Morrison hadn't died?', 'What if Andrew Wood had not died?' might seem like small beer. What would have happened next, in all likelihood, is that Mother Love Bone would have gone out on tour in 1990 and provided a perfectly amenable antidote to some of the two-year-old withdrawal symptoms America's frustrated Guns N' Roses fans were then undergoing. 'I'm not sure that you can answer that question in one answer because I think you'd have two answers. One answer for Vedder and one for the rest of the band. They're two very different things,' points out Peter Doggett. 'The rest of the band do have the community background: their immediate peers might not necessarily agree with what they've done and where they're coming from but they did at least come from one common tradition. Whereas Vedder, the

---

* A prophetic piece of speculation, as Kurt Cobain was to take his own life just a few weeks later, effectively ending Nirvana's career.

outsider, seems to have taken on not so much of the cross of Seattle as the entire universe on his shoulders.'

Does that mean that if Andy Wood had lived there might have been no 'grunge', either? Not necessarily. Grunge as fashion statement was always more the domain of Nirvana and Mudhoney and the nasty boys at Sub Pop than it was the buttoned-up utility garb of an Eddie Vedder or a jet-booted, sequin-skinned Andy Wood. Nevertheless, it is not difficult to imagine Andy swiftly reinventing himself, yet again, for the post-*Nevermind* masses, though Andy's DMs would probably have to have been spray-painted gold, of course.

As for Eddie Vedder . . . who's to say he wouldn't still be out there in San Diego somewhere, pumping gas and surfing on nothing more tangible than his foggy sleep-deprived dreams. Of course, he would still have the voice, but not the music, the sense of place, the niche in history his name occupies with such solemnity now. 'My favourite band that came out of Seattle was Mother Love Bone, I fuckin' love Mother Love Bone,' says Skid Row bassist, Rachel Bolan. 'The lyrics and everything were very T. Rex-ish and the serious grooves they laid down . . . I don't know, it's just something about their music, it's just hypnotizing. I used to play the shit out of the CD.' Pearl Jam, he says, 'play good music but are way too fuckin' serious for me. I like to enjoy my music.'

So did Eddie Vedder . . . once. It was just the things he was prevailed upon to do to sell that music that had freaked him out. 'I'll probably not do interviews one day, because I don't want to end up convoluting the subject. Music is the thing. It won't be because of my attitude or anything. It's just that fifteen years ago, I found a beautiful way to express myself; I found a very powerful medium. Music is a way for people to come together and turn it on. It's there, and that's what I do . . . I don't want to be a star – it's not worth it, to have my picture taken and have my face everywhere. I could scare a lot of people with my face!' he joked at last.[27]

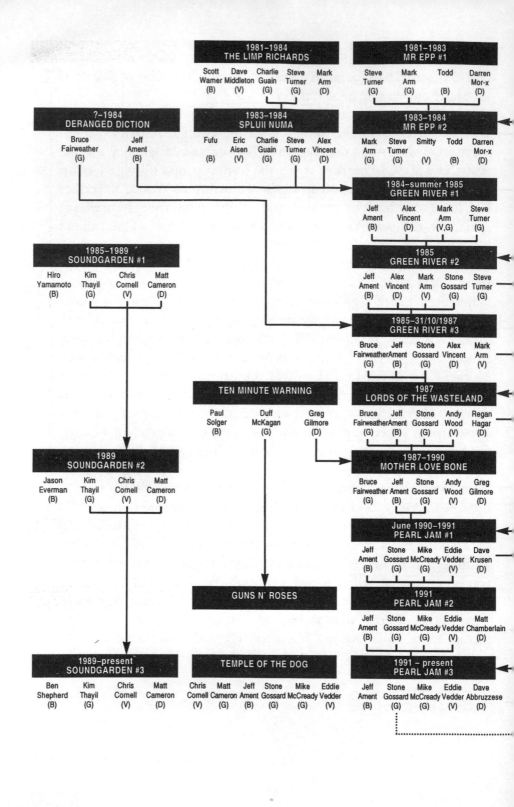

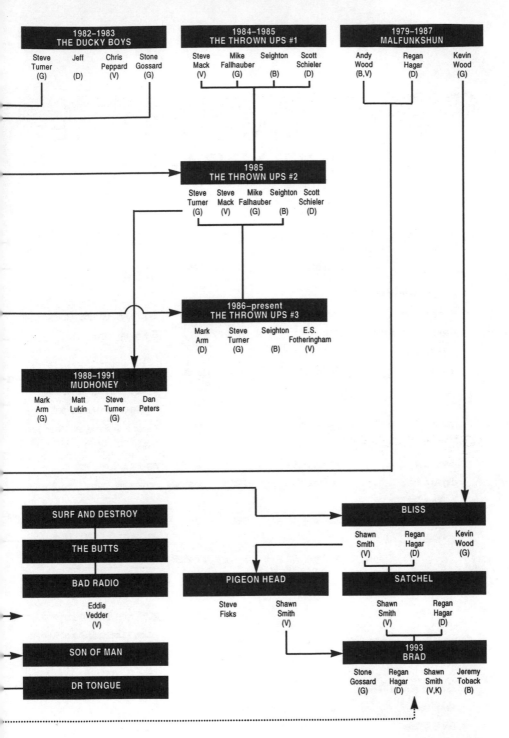

CHART OF THE SEATTLE SCENE

PEARL JAM COMPLETE DISCOGRAPHY

	CATALOGUE NUMBER	RELEASE DATE	FORMAT	SPECIAL FEATURES
Green River (US)				
Come on Down	Homestead HMS 031	9/85	12″ EP	Imported into UK 1985 and 1989
Together We'll Never/Ain't Nothin' To Do	ICP 01	11/86		Green vinyl, no p/s
Dry As A Bone	Sub Pop SP11		12″ EP	*Unwind/Baby Takes/This Town/PCC/ Ozzie.* First 2,000 with yellow inserts, second run with pink
Rehab Doll	Sub Pop SP15		12″ EP	8-track, inner sleeve, first 100 on green vinyl
Rehab Doll	Sub Pop SP15A		Cassette	Bonus cut, *Queen Bitch*
Dry As A Bone/ Rehab Doll	Sub Pop SP11A	7/88	Cassette	
Dry As A Bone/ Rehab Doll	Sub Pop SP11B	7/88	CD	
	Sub Pop SP25		3×12″ EP	With twenty-page booklet, 5,000 only; includes Green River
Sub Pop 200	Sup Pop 25A		CD	
Another Pyrrhic Victory	C/Z		LP	2,000 copies, 200 on orange vinyl; includes unissued Green River. Also on CD, *c.* 1990
Green River (UK)				
Rehab Doll	Glitterhouse GR 0031	2/89		
Dry As A Bone	Tupelo TUPLP 17/ RTDL 44117	3/91		

	CATALOGUE NUMBER	RELEASE DATE	FORMAT	SPECIAL FEATURES
Mother Love Bone (US)				
Shine	Stardog	89	EP	
Apple	Stardog	90	LP	
Mother Love Bone	Stardog/Mercury 314 512 884–2	92	2×CD	
Mother Love Bone (UK albums)				
Apple	Polydor 843 191 1	7/90		
	Polydor 843 191 2		CD	
Mother Love Bone	Polydor 514 177 2	92	2×CD	
Temple Of The Dog (UK singles)				
Hunger Strike/All Night Thing	A&M AM 0091	10/92	7″	Picture disc
Hunger Strike/All Night Thing	A&M AMMC 0091		Cassette	
Hunger Strike/Your Savior/ All Night Thing	A&M AMY 0091	10/92	12″	With free poster
	A&M AMCD 0091		digipack CD	
Temple Of The Dog (UK albums)				
Temple Of The Dog	A&M 395350 1	5/91	LP	
	A&M 395350 2		CD	
Pearl Jam (UK singles)				
Alive/Once	Epic 657572 7	2/92	7″	White vinyl
Alive/Once/Alive/Once	Epic 657572 4		Cassette	Flip-top
Alive/Once/Wash	Epic 657572 6		12″	In poster bag
Alive/Once/Wash	Epic 657572 5		CD	Picture disc
Even Flow (new version)/ Oceans	Epic 657857 7	4/92	7″	Competition pack
Even Flow (new version)/ Oceans/Even Flow (new version)	Epic 657857 4		Cassette	
Even Flow (new version)/ Dirty Frank/Oceans	Epic 657857 8		12″	White vinyl

	CATALOGUE NUMBER	RELEASE DATE	FORMAT	SPECIAL FEATURES
Even Flow (new version)/ Dirty Frank/Oceans	Epic 657857 2		CD	Picture dic
Jeremy/Alive (live)	Epic 658258 7	9/92	7"	White vinyl
Jeremy/Alive (live)	Epic 658258 4		Cassette	Special box
Jeremy/Alive (live)/ Footsteps (live)	Epic 658258 6		12"	Picture disc. *Footsteps* recorded live at Rockline, 11 May 1992
Jeremy/Yellow Ledbetter/ Alive (live)	Epic 658258 4		CD	Picture disc
Go/Elderly Woman Behind The Counter In A Small Town (non-album)/Alone	Epic 659795 2	12/93	CD	
Go/Elderly Woman Behind The Counter In A Small Town (non-album)/Alone	Epic 659795 6		12"	Plus free cassette containing live version of *Animal* from the MTV Awards show
Daughter/Blood	Epic 660020 2	12/93	CD	Contains extra track, *Yellow Ledbetter*
Daughter/Blood	Epic 660020 4		Cassette	
Daughter/Blood	Epic 660020 6		12"	Contains *Yellow Ledbetter*: poster sleeve of Jeff Ament and Eddie Vedder
Daughter/Blood	Epic 660020 7		7"	Red vinyl

Pearl Jam (UK albums)

	CATALOGUE NUMBER	RELEASE DATE	FORMAT	SPECIAL FEATURES
Ten	Epic 468884 1	2/92	LP	
Ten	Epic 468884 2		CD	
Ten	Epic 468884 0	3/92	Picture disc	
Singles	Epic 471438 4	7/92	LP	Film soundtrack with two Pearl Jam tracks and one by Mother Love Bone
Singles	Epic 471438 1		Cassette	
Singles	Epic 471438 2		CD	
Ten	Epic 468884 5	12/92	CD	Metallic-yellow digipack; three bonus tracks
Ten	Epic 468884 3		Mini-disc	
Vs.	Epic 474549 1	10/93	LP	
Vs.	Epic 474549 2		CD	
Vs.	Epic 474549 4		Cassette	
Vs.	Epic 474549 8		Mini-disc	

ADDITIONAL MATERIAL OF INTEREST

Fan club Christmas singles

Let Me Sleep, It's Christmastime/Ramblings 1991

Sonic Reducer/Ramblings Continues 1992

Brad

album: Shame (Epic Associated, May 1993: 473596 2 (CD), 4 (Cassette), 1 (LP))

7" single: 20th Century/Buttercup (deleted)

Other Releases:

Sweet Relief – A benefit for Victoria Williams (Chaos/Columbia, 1993) includes 'Crazy Mary' by Pearl Jam

Judgement Night – Music from the Motion Picture (Immortal/Epic, 1993) includes 'Real Thing' by Pearl Jam & Cypress Hill

In Defense Of Animals (Restless, 1993) includes 'Porch' by Pearl Jam

Guest Appearances:

Bad Religion by Recipe for Hate (Epitaph/Atlantic, 1993): Eddie Vedder lends guest vocals on 'American Jesus' and 'Watch It Die'

The 30th Anniversary Concert Celebration for Bob Dylan (Columbia, 1993): Eddie Vedder and Mike McCready perform Dylan's 'Masters Of War'

Course of Empire by Course of Empire (Carpe Diem/Zoo, 1991): Dave Abbruzzese plays drums on 'God's Jig'

Vs. sessions – songs recorded in the sessions that don't appear on the album – 'The Whipping', a pedal-to-the-floor rocker; 'Hard To Imagine', a ballad with the key lyric, 'Things were different then/All is different now/I tried to explain/ Somehow…'; and 'Alone', a mid-tempo funk rocker that has featured in the live Pearl Jam set, on and off, since the 'Lollapalooza II' tour in 1992.

NOTES AND SOURCES

As you can see from the listings below, I trawled through literally hundreds of cuttings and interviews in order to write this book. All of the interviews I have sampled quotes from were invaluable in increasing my understanding and grasp of the Pearl Jam story, and my heartfelt thanks and congratulations go to the individual authors for their fascinating contributions, both pro and con. In particular, though, I would like to express my enormous gratitude to the following articles, all of which were mini-masterpieces in their own right: Cameron Crowe's insightful October 1993 *Rolling Stone* cover story; Gillian Gaar's authoritative November 1992 feature in *Record Collector*; and Richard T. White's heart-moving April 1990 epistle in *The Rocket*. I would also like to bend a knee and thank the many voices echoed in this book that declined to have their names mentioned alongside their opinions and insider info . . . London, Los Angeles, New York, and Seattle . . . there are sticky fingers in all those towns and I hope they don't bitch too much about the result.

Any material not accounted for here is from interviews conducted by the author or his representatives.

CHAPTER ONE
The Virtuous City

1   Jay Cocks, *Time*, March 1992
2   Lester Bangs, *Creem*, December 1971
3   *Backlash*, June 1990
4   Xavier Russell, *Kerrang!*, 7–20 March 1985
5   *The Rocket*, June 1989
6   Alison Young, *The Rocket*, 1986

7   *Voice of Rock 'N' Roll*, Winter 1988

8–9   *Rolling Stone*, 16 April 1992

10   Dawn Anderson, *The Rocket*, December 1986

11–12   Steve Kelly, *Seattle Times*, 28 April 1993

13   Stoko, *Noise of the Nineties*, March 1992

14–16   Jodi Summers, *Hit Parader*, October 1993

17   *Raw*, 1992

18   Peter Doggett, *Record Collector*, March 1993

19   Jodi Summers, *as above*

20   *Guitar*, March 1993

21   *The Rocket*, February 1986

22   *Circus*, December 1993

23   Everett True, *Melody Maker*, March 1989

24   Paul Elliot, *Kerrang!*, June 1992

25   Gillian Gaar, *Record Collector*, November 1992

26   *Spin*, 1991/92

27   Gillian Gaar, *as above*

28   Grant Alden, *The Rocket*, August 1991

29–32   Gillian Gaar, *as above*

33   Grant Alden, *as above*

34–6   Gillian Gaar, *as above*

37   Jesse Nash, *Metal CD*, No. 9, 1993

38   *Circus*, *as above*

39   Roy Wilkinson, *Sounds*, March 1989

40   Everett True, *as above*

41   John Peel, *Observer*, 1988

CHAPTER TWO
Love Rock

1   Richard T. White, *The Rocket*, January 1989

2   Leone Pope, *Seattle Times*, 29 March 1990

3–8   Richard T. White, *The Rocket*, April 1990

9–10   Dawn Anderson, *The Rocket*, December 1986

11   Richard T. White, *as above*

12   Mark Arm, *Raw*, 1992

13   Corey Levitan, *Circus*, December 1993

14   Paul Elliot, *Kerrang!*, June 1992

15   Ralph Traitor, *Sounds*, 11 August 1990

16–20   Richard T. White, *The Rocket*, January 1989

21   From the sleeve notes to *Apple*, Polygram Records, 1990

22   Leone Pope, *as above*

23   Gillian Gaar, *Record Collector*, November 1992

24–5   Grant Alden, *The Rocket*, August 1991

26   As told by Cantrell to Daina Darzin: The Stud Brothers, *Melody Maker*, 27 February 1993

27   Everett True, *Melody Maker*, 24 June 1989

28   *Alternative Press*, August 1989

29   *Seconds*

30   *Seconds*, August 1989

31   Leone Pope, *as above*

32–4   Richard T. White, *The Rocket*, April 1990

35–6   Leone Pope, *as above*

37–8   Richard T. White, *as above*

39–40   Don Kaye, *Kerrang!*, 1992

41   DJ Justice, *Seattle Post-Intelligencer*, 1992

42–3   Jeff Gilbert, *The Rocket*, July 1992

44   Stoko, *Noise of the Nineties*, March 1992

45   Cameron Crowe, *Rolling Stone*, 10 January 1992

46   DJ Justice, *as above*

47   *Metal Hammer*, September 1990

48   DJ Justice, *as above*

49–50   Jeff Ament, *Kerrang!*, July 1992

51   Brad Balfour, *Creem*, October 1992

52   Stoko, *as above*

53   Gene Stout, *Seattle Post-Intelligencer*, 21 March 1990

54–5   Richard T. White, *as above*

56–7   Michael Browning, *RIP*, December 1990

58   *Metal Hammer*, *as above*

59   Jodi Summers, *Rock Power*, November 1992

CHAPTER THREE
Alive

1   Dave Di Martino, *Rolling Stone*, 20 September 1990

2   Gene Stout, *Seattle Post-Intelligencer*, 21 December 1990

3	Kim Neely, *Rolling Stone*, October 1991
4	Gene Stout, *as above*
5	Dave Di Martino, *as above*
6	David Browne, *New York Times*, November 1990
7	Gillian Gaar, *Record Collector*, November 1992
8–11	Grant Alden, *The Rocket*, August 1991
12	James Botondi, *Guitar Player*, January 1994
13	Paul Elliot, *Kerrang!*, June 1992
14	Liz Evans, *RAW*, February 1992
15–16	James Botondi, *as above*
17	Stoko, *Noise of the Nineties*, March 1992
18	Cathi Unsworth, *Melody Maker*, 25 January 1992
19	Gary Cee, *Circus*, 31 March 1993
20–22	Jeff Kitts, *Rock Power*, June 1992
23	Paul Elliot, *as above*
24	Andrew Mueller, *Melody Maker*, 22 February 1992
25	Mike Gitter, *Kerrang!*, February 1992
26	Kirk Blows, *RAW*, December 1991
27	Mike Gitter, *as above*
28	Jesse Nash, *Metal CD*, No. 9, 1993
29	Paul Elliot, *as above*
30	Kirk Blows, *as above*
31	Paul Elliot, *as above*
32	Jesse Nash, *as above*
33	Cathi Unsworth, *as above*
34	Brad Balfour, *Creem*, October 1992
35	Phil West, *Seattle Times*, 24 December 1990
36	Cathi Unsworth, *Melody Maker*, 20 July 1991
37	Mike Gitter, *as above*
38–9	A&M press release, April 1991
40	Liz Evans, *as above*
41	*Guitar*, March 1993
42	Kirk Blows, *as above*
43	Moe, *Hype*, 16 September 1992
44–7	*Seattle Times*, 13 September 1992
48	Gillian Gaar, *Hits*, 28 September 1992
49	Jonathan Bernstein, *Spin*, 1992
50–51	Gillian Gaar, *as above*
52	*Sky*, February 1993

53   Laura Lee Davies, *Time Out*, 1992

54   Phil West, *Seattle Times*, 17 September 1992

55   Steve Kelley, *Seattle Times*, 28 April 1993

56   Mike Gitter, *as above*

57   Steve Kelley, *as above*

58   Jennifer Clay, *RIP*, December 1991

59   Kirk Blows, *as above*

60   Kim Neely, *Rolling Stone*, October 1991

61–2   Matt Peiken, *Modern Drummer*, December 1993

63–4   Liz Evans, *as above*

65   Kim Neely, *as above*

66   Christopher John Farley, *Time Magazine*, 25 October 1993

67   *USA Today*, December 1991

68   *Sounds*, 9 June 1990

69–70   John Robb, *Sounds*, 21 October 1989

71   Chris Morris, *Q*, April 1992

72   *Guitar Player*,

73   Kirk Blows, *as above*

74   Cathi Unsworth, *Melody Maker*, 30 November 1991

75   Cathi Unsworth, *Melody Maker*, 7 December 1991

CHAPTER FOUR
Top Ten

1   *New Musical Express*, 3 October 1992

2   Brad Balfour, *Creem*, October 1992

3   Mike Gitter, *Kerrang!*, February 1993

4   Cathi Unsworth, *Melody Maker*, 25 January 1992

5   *Musician*, late 1991

6–7   Michael Azerrad, *Rolling Stone*, 16 April 1992

8   Barbara Ellen, *New Musical Express*, 3 February 1992

9   Steven Wells, *New Musical Express*, March 1992

10   *Melody Maker*, 7 March 1992

11   Ted Mico, *Melody Maker*, 14 March 1992

12   Allan Jones, *Melody Maker*, 22 February 1992

13   Cathi Unsworth, *as above*

14   Andrew Mueller, *Melody Maker*, February 1992

15   Paul Elliot, *Kerrang!*, June 1992

16   Mike Gitter, *Kerrang!*, February 1992

17   Liz Evans, *RAW*, 4 August 1993

18   Jeff Gilbert, *Sky*, April 1993

19   Charles Cross, *The Rocket*, June 1992

20   The Stud Brothers, *Melody Maker*, 20 June 1992

21–2   Mr Spencer, *Siren*, June 1992

23   Brad Balfour, *as above*

24   Steve Kelley, *Seattle Times*, 28 April 1993

25   *Melody Maker*, 11 July 1992

26   Broadcast on Radio One a fortnight after it was recorded in 1992

27   Andrew Mueller, *Melody Maker*, 1 August 1992

28   Glen Hirshberg, *Seattle Weekly*, 29 July 1992

29   Mike Gitter, *as above*

30   Jeff Kitts, *Livewire*, Summer 1992

31   Don Kaye, *Kerrang!*, 1992

32   Stoko, *Noise of the Nineties*, March 1992

33   Pippa Lang, *Metal Hammer*, August 1992

34   Jeff Kitts, *as above*

35   Liz Evans, *Kerrang!*, 23 October 1993

36   Don Kaye, *as above*

37   Jodi Powers, *Rock Power*, November 1992

38   Lisa Johnson, *RAW*, October 1992

39–42   Phil West, *Seattle Times*, 17 September 1992

43   Rick Marin, *New York Times*

44–6   Fannie Weinstein, 'Fashion', *Detroit News*,

47   Roger Tredre, *Independent on Sunday*, 31 January 1993

48   S. L. Duff, *RIP*, March 1992

49   Vanessa Ho, *Seattle Times*, 21 September 1992

50   Martina Wimmer, *Metal CD*, 1993

51–2   Matt Peiken, *Modern Drummer*, December 1993

53   Heidi Lynne, *Screamer*, November 1992

CHAPTER FIVE
The Leash

1   Mark Coleman, *Rolling Stone*, 2 April 1993

2   *Guitar*, March 1993

3–4   Paul Rees, *RAW*, 7 July 1993

5–8   Mike Gitter, *Kerrang!*, February 1993
9   Martina Wimmer, *Metal CD*, 1993
10   Corey Levitan, *Circus*, December 1993
11   Martina Wimmer, *as above*
12–13   Alan di Perna, *Guitar World*, November 1993
14   Jim Greer, *Spin*, November or December 1993
15   *Guitar World*, February 1994
16   Liz Evans, *Kerrang!*, 23 October 1993
17   *Melody Maker*, 10 February 1993
18   Jim Greer, *as above*
19   Matt Peiken, *Modern Drummer*, December 1993
20   Martina Wimmer, *as above*
21   Everett True, *Melody Maker*, 17 July 1993
22   Terry Staunton, *New Musical Express*, 24 July 1993
23   Allan Jones, *Melody Maker*, 24 July 1993
24   Liz Evans, *Kerrang!* (pull-out), September 1993
25   Jim Greer, *as above*
26   Matt Snow, *Q*, October/November 1993
27   Gene Stout, *Seattle Post-Intelligencer*, 29 October 1993
28   *Melody Maker*, 10 February 1993
29   John Hotten, *RAW*, 1993
30   Andy Gill, *Independent*, 14 October 1993
31   Allan Jones, *as above*

EPILOGUE
Crown

1   Liz Evans, *RAW*, February 1992
2   Patrick MacDonald, *Seattle Times*, January 1994
3   Mr Spencer, *Siren*, June 1992
4–5   Lisa Johnson, *RAW*, August 1992
6   *Seattle Times*, January 1993
7   Paul Rees, *RAW*, 7 July 1993
8   Dawn Anderson and J. R. Higgins, *Backlash*, June 1990
9   Gillian Gaar, *Record Collector*, November 1992
10   Liz Evans, *Kerrang!*, 23 October 1993
11   *Guitar World*, February 1994
12   Cathi Unsworth, *Melody Maker*, 7 December 1991

13   *Guitar World, as above*
14   Jeff Gilbert, *Sky*, April 1993
15   Matt Snow, *Q*, October 1993
16   S. L. Duff, *RIP*, March 1992
17–18   Matt Snow, *as above*
19   Martina Wimmer, *Metal CD*, March 1993
20–21   Jeff Kitts, *Livewire*, Summer 1992
22   Liz Evans, *RAW, as above*
23   Jeff Kitts, *Rock Power*, June 1992
24   Matt Peiken, *Modern Drummer*, December 1993
25   Stoko, *Noise of the Nineties*, March 1992
26–7   Liz Evans, *Kerrang!, as above*

CHAPTER X

IMMORTALITY

IF THE Seattle scene had taken off in earnest with the leering, ironic challenge of Kurt Cobain's best-known line from Nirvana's best-known hit, 'Smells Like Teen Spirit' – 'Here we are now/Entertain us ... ' – it surely ended the afternoon of April 7, 1994, when the singer balanced a six–pound Remington Model 11, 20-gauge shotgun between his knees, carefully placed the end of the double-barrel into his mouth, closed his eyes and pulled the trigger.

Beside him, Cobain had arranged a few personal effects – the plaid hunter's cap with ridiculous ear-flaps he used to wear sometimes to disguise himself when he went out in public, his driver's license, credit cards and the old cigar-box he used to keep his hypodermic syringes in – all the outward signs of his public identity, the face he had made famous to the world. It was as if he wanted the world to know that he really didn't need it after all. That he simply refused to do an encore. Why? Because Kurt Cobain, like his music, was the sort of person about whom anything you said could be countered with its opposite and both statements would probably be true. There seemed to be not a single issue in Kurt's short and tragic life that he wasn't agonisingly ambivalent about. For him, the talent to write, play guitar on and sing some of the most affecting rock anthems for a generation was both a blessing and a curse. The most famous rock star in the world, he recoiled in horror at the attention he received wherever he went.

Marriage to Courtney Love was always of the love-hate variety, too. "They were totally in love. You couldn't separate them," recalled photographer Michael Levine at the time of his photo–shoot with the couple for their joint front cover of Sassy in 1992. 'I'm married/Buried!' Kurt would scream on his very next album, released a year later. Kurt was, by common consent, an attentive, loving father, yet even that simple pleasure was somehow sullied for him by a deep foreboding over his daughter's almost preternatural physical resemblance to him. Frances Bean has her father's alien blue eyes. And finally, of course, as we now know, Kurt was unable to decide even on the fundamental question of life itself: should he stay or should he go? Did he dig in and take it or fuck the whole deal off? Given the unrelentingly bleak demeanour that endured throughout Cobain's last days - Courtney fleeing to Los Angeles, Krist Novoselic's aborted attempt to get Kurt into rehab - the fact that in the end he settled for the latter option should have come as no surprise at all to those who knew him best. Instead, his suicide cracked them like a mirror, reflections of their own monstrous fame hurled back at them through a million un-put-backable shards, seven years bad luck guaranteed ...

The morning after Kurt's mutilated body was discovered, the Seattle Times ran a full-colour, page-one photo of the scene – "as dirty a stinking drug box as I've ever seen," according to one of the police officers present – zooming its tabloid eyes in one last time on the motif baggy jeans and dirty trainers, one tatty pyjama-sleeve ending in a porcelain-white clenched fist.

All journalists are ambulance-chasers, in the sense that there's no news like bad news, but the unmitigated glee with which the world's media fell upon the suicide of the Nirvana leader had more than a little to do with told-you-so sanctimony. Proof positive that the path to oblivion is crowded with loser musician types, that there was something rotten buried at the bottom of the grunge-garden after all. But then, witnessing the distressing haste with which Nirvana's contemporaries jumped aboard the nowhere-train (Soundgarden refusing to speak to anybody and trashing all their dressing rooms on their UK tour; Pearl Jam cancelling all immediate plans to tour amid floods of 'Eddie's next' innuendoes), who knows, maybe they had a point. Maybe Seattle really was the city that was born to die; grunge the music that didn't know how to grow up and simply refused to back down – until it ended up cancelling itself out.

No doubt the reasons for the overriding depression that beset him could be traced back to the emotional upheavals of his childhood. Kurt's parents broke up when he was eight and the battle for custody was ugly. On the wall of his bedroom he wrote the words: 'I hate Mom, I hate Dad, Dad hates Mom, Mom hates Dad, it simply makes you want to be sad', and drew a picture with a big question mark over it. "I used to try to make my head explode by holding my breath, thinking if I blew up my head, they'd be sorry," Kurt once confessed, prophetically. But the punk ethos that he followed – that to get to the top you have to aim for the bottom, rigidly rejecting the fake, the dishonest, the greedy and the hypocritical – was just as compellingly imbued in the musical outlook of the other key shakers and movers on the Seattle circuit. So what happens when you become popular? When friends used to tell Kurt how much they liked his paintings (always more than just a hobby) he would immediately rip them up and start again. But it simply wasn't possible to tear up all nine million existing copies of 'Nevermind', so what then? Are you still legitimate? Is your work still any good – or have you sold out?

Typically, Kurt didn't hang around long enough to find out. Now it looks like Eddie Vedder will have to do it for him. "After I reached my teens, I decided I didn't want to hang out with anyone," Kurt once said. "I couldn't handle the stupidity ... " Who can? Since his death, nobody is pretending that Seattle is a cool town anymore. According to friends, Courtney won't even go near the place these days. "She's afraid," Henry Rollins confided shortly after Kurt's death. "Seattle is Heroin City these days, and Courtney's afraid that if she even goes near the place she'll be sucked into it, too." The OD of Hole bassist Kristen Pfaff – found dead in the bathtub, in June 1994, with the needle still stuck in her arm – was seen as another warning. Kristen had planned to leave Seattle for the same reasons as Courtney. She just hadn't moved fast enough. Even official end-of-year police statistics appeared to back this grisly theory up. Heroin-related deaths in Seattle were up 60 per cent in 1993 on what they were just 12 months before.

Senior staff at Geffen Records in America, who have both Nirvana and Hole on their label, were said to have become so inured to the idea of their artists "dropping like flies", a joke press release began circulating around their LA headquarters, in the summer of 1994, that read, in part: Geffen Records regret to announce the death of (insert name) of (insert band) who died on (insert date) ... When Courtney caught sight of it by accident one day, she told the Geffen execs they were "sick." It seems the only people left who still think the Seattle scene exists are bone-headed perps like the whacko who showed up at Courtney's house in Los Angeles in a red Porsche with the word 'nirvana' spray–painted across its hood. At first, he told a questioning security guard that he merely wanted to give Courtney the car. When the grim–faced guard tried to send him on his way, he began yelling, "I don't care if I die tonight! I want to see Courtney!" Bizarrely, the parents of the loony (later identified as one Robert Sceeles, 25, from Alaska) had already phoned Geffen and told them to warn Courtney that their son had just informed them he was on his way to become the next singer in Nirvana and that he was going to marry Courtney. An anti-harassment suit has since been served on Sceeles while the police wait to see what he might try next.

And the beep beep of the cash register just goes on and on. The suicide of Kurt Cobain had brought the opportunist out in everybody. Before the year was out, Geffen would make an album out of Nirvana's neo-legendary MTV Unplugged session (including unbroadcast outtakes); overnight Soundgarden became the most famous hermits in the world, playing the biggest and best known arenas, selling squillions of CDs, records, tapes, videos, t-shirts, baseball caps turned backwards, you name it – and hating every minute of it, such was the trauma unleashed by Kurt's death. And it was not just the big boys cashing in. In London and New York, Paris and Tokyo, there were already an abundance of 'Eddie's Next' and 'Courtney Killed Kurt'-type t-shirts being manufactured and sold while the Kurt-obits were still being written. Nothing sells better than death, it seems. But the killer, must-have t-shirt to end them all was the one originally only available in the Washington area with extracts of Kurt's suicide note printed on it, including several paragraphs not read out by Courtney at Kurt's anodyne public memorial in Seattle. Only the medical examiner, Courtney, and Kurt's family had a copy, so how the makers of the shirts – Grunge Enterprises, would you believe? – obtained a copy remains a mystery. An official from Gold Mountain, Nirvana's management office, described it as "the sickest, lowest and most pitiful thing I've ever heard of."

As for the ghost of Kurt Cobain, he had begun speaking privately of a life without Nirvana for almost a year before his death, threatening to quit, by one insider's estimation, "at least 10 times."

The same restless energy and inability to merely follow trends that had driven Nirvana to the tremulous peak of its artistic and commercial success in the space of just two albums, was what was now urging him on to do something new. Soft, then loud, then soft again – that was how Kurt sarcastically described the typical Nirvana song to friends. Indeed, Kurt's first choice title for the 'In Utero' album was 'Verse Chorus Verse'. Nirvana had become boring, he said; too formulaic. Worse, the other band members were far too "normal" – at least in Kurt's eyes. When Nirvana kicked 1994 off with a show at the Seattle Center, Kurt introduced 'Smells Like Teen Spirit' by saying, "We have to play this next song – it's in our contract. ... This is the song that ruined our lives and ruined Seattle and ruined your lives, too."

The European tour which followed was a disaster. Kurt was convinced Courtney was having an affair with her former boyfriend, Smashing Pumpkins singer Billy Corgan, something Courtney continues to deny, though she will admit that Corgan had begun calling her on the phone regularly again. Whatever the truth of the situation, there's no doubting that in Kurt's mind the threat of betrayal had bared its teeth yet again. That and the fact that both he and Courtney were increasingly worried by the threat of having baby Frances Bean taken away from them and placed into care if they didn't clean up their act were more than enough to pull the final rug from beneath Kurt's already scurrying feet. When, on the night of March 3, while staying in Rome "resting" following the cancellation of Nirvana dates in Germany, Kurt sent the bellboy to a local pharmacy to fill a prescription of the powerful tranquilliser, Rohypnol (related to Valium) and also asked for two bottles of champagne, there was nothing careless or accidental about his actions. Kurt planned to take his own life. Viciously down-played at the time as the over-indulgence of someone merely trying to secure a good night's sleep, the truth is Kurt, an experienced drug user, had swallowed more than 50 pills that night, plus most of the champagne. A suicide note, the first of two he would eventually write, was found nearby. When a bewildered and clearly unhappy Kurt was revived 48 hours later at Rome's The American Hospital, his only thought was to get even. "I believe firmly in revenge," Kurt once said. He may have screwed up that first attempt at killing himself, but that didn't mean he thought he had in any way been saved. It merely underlined his determination to do the job properly next time. The fact that when he pulled the trigger on his own life he also managed to take Nirvana, probably Hole, and possibly even Pearl Jam with him, would not have mattered to him. Indeed, the thought that he might have single-handedly burst the grunge boil with one last follow-that anti-everything blast of hate might even have been an incentive to do 'the unthinkable'.

Kurt's favourite pet was his turtle, which he said he could relate to because of its "basic 'fuck you' attitude – 'I'm stuck in the tank, I'm miserable, I hate you, and I'm not going to perform for you'." Ultimately, reading the cards as best you can, the sudden suicide of Kurt Cobain and the slow subsequent death of the Seattle scene had perhaps been on the agenda from the very beginning. Kurt confessed as much, didn't he, in the opening line from 'In Utero': 'Teenage angst has served me well/Now I'm bored and old ... '

Life, death, re-birth - Kurt had an almost obsessional interest in what might be deemed 'foetal imagery'. The covers of both Nevermind and In Utero abound in visions of babies in strange surroundings; of innocence hurtling towards corruption. The naked dolls he used to collect and dissect and the absurd frocks he used to dress up in sometimes on-stage and in photo-sessions, testified to Kurt's conviction that, for him at least, the innocence behind who he really was and what his music was really all about had long been expunged from the equation. This was not the beginning of anything, just possibly the end of everything.

On the cover of the Nirvana rarities album, 'Incesticide', is a painting by Kurt depicting a crying baby reaching out for a shadowy parent whose back is turned and whose expression is cold and blank. You notice that the baby's head is cracked open like an egg. It could be a depiction of the Seattle scene at the end of 1994. In despair and with the top of its head missing...

KURT COBAIN'S suicide had been national news in the US for about eight hours when Pearl Jam took the stage that night at the Patriot Center in Fairfax, Virginia. Eddie had wanted to call off the show. He later told MTV that if it had been solely up to him, Pearl Jam would have scrapped all the remaining dates of their US tour, which had been in swing for just a month, but that the rest of the band were against it. Once the current dates were over, though, he said, "I might not ... we as a band might not play again for a very long time ... I can't go out and play if I don't feel real, I just can't do it." The first anybody outside the band and Pearl Jam road crew saw of Eddie the day Cobain's death was announced was when he made his way slowly up onto the stage to watch openers Mudhoney that night. Walking with the stooped shoulders of a much older man, hair hanging down over his face to shield him from prying eyes, Eddie picked his way through the backstage detritus of cables and scaffolding, to a chair at the side of the stage, where he leaned his head forlornly against the speakers and closed his eyes. He looked broken, distant, his thoughts clearly elsewhere.

"I think you all know what's on our minds tonight," Eddie told the crowd as the band took the stage an hour later. "I don't think any of us would be in this room here tonight without Kurt Cobain ... " Despite the too-often media-fuelled rivalry between the two most well-known Seattle-based bands, it seems Eddie was genuinely distressed by Kurt's terrible end. For Eddie, the shock of Kurt's death appeared to have changed everything. You could see it in his eyes on stage in New York during the final show of the tour three weeks later when, during a furiously overwrought version of 'Daughter', he broke off into a few spontaneous verses of 'Tonight's The Night', the title track of the album Neil Young recorded in the mid-Seventies after the sudden deaths (both from a heroin overdose) of his guitarist, Danny Whitten and roadie, Bruce Berry, both of whom had been close friends of the singer. "Sometimes it can be very easy to go up there, because playing music's a very emotional thing," Jeff Ament told MTV. "But then sometimes ... I don't know. It makes you wonder if this is all worth dying for." Echoes of Andrew Wood's own unnecessary death reverberated, as always, throughout everything, good or bad. "Always kept it loaded!" Eddie screamed the 'Glorified G' lyric on stage in New York, the new twist in the line left hanging in the air like an unexploded bomb. But then every song they played now had taken on a new meaning suddenly ... 'Daughter', 'Why Go', 'Once', 'Jeremy' ... "If you ever feel like saying 'I'm getting the fuck outta here', just remember – living is the best revenge," Eddie told the crowd. The encore that night began with a new number the band had begun to feature in the set which had also undergone a dramatic alteration in emotional focus since Kurt's death: 'Not For You'. 'Small my table,' Eddie intoned solemnly, 'Seats just two/Got too crowded/Can't make room/Where did they come from/Stormed my room/And you dare say/This belongs to you/This is not for you ... '

There had been a party for the band after that final New York show. Singles star Matt Dillon was there; cult film director Jim Jarmusch, Sonic Youth's Thurston Moore and Gene Simmons of Kiss all attended. But Eddie Vedder did not. He spent most of the time locked behind closed doors in deep conversation with his new buddy, Henry Rollins, whose band had opened for Pearl Jam on several dates on the early leg of the tour. "He's just someone who wants to do the right thing but doesn't know what the right is any more," Rollins said later. Meanwhile, Kelly Curtis confirmed that Cobain's death "threw everyone for a loop" and that the band would be cancelling all touring plans for the foreseeable future. Kurt's tragic demise apart, there was a new foe for the .band to concern itself with beginning to loom menacingly on the horizon. The band had decided to take on Ticketmaster, one of the largest ticket agencys in America, disputing the agencys right to charge what Curtis and the band saw as exorbitant 'cover charges' for tickets, sometimes as much as an extra 20 per cent, or anything from three to six dollars per ticket – thereby adding as much as a third again to their face value.

"The band just wants to explore doing things in a different way," said Curtis. "If that means not playing some markets or scouting out open fields, that's fine." Pearl Jam would rather play in an open field, he said, than further accede to the unreasonable demands of promoters. "Eddie Vedder knows what it feels like not to have enough money to buy a ticket or a T-shirt at his favourite band's show and he wants to turn this thing around," Curtis later told the Los Angeles Times. "We think the new policy is going to put a crack in the damn and other good bands will soon follow our lead."

To which end both Pearl Jam guitarist Stone Gossard and bassist Jeff Ament would swap their check shirts and Doc Martens for three-button suits and shiny black slip-ons later that summer while testifying before a Washington House Government Operations Sub-Committee, looking into 'anti-competitive processes in the ticket distribution business'. As Stone told the committee: "Our band, which is determined to keep ticket prices low, will always be in conflict with Ticketmaster." The touchstone of the debate centred around a memo filed by Pearl Jam with the Anti-Trust Division of the US Dept. of Justice, on May 6, 1994. The memo accused Ticketmaster of having "virtually an absolute monopoly on the distribution of tickets to concerts, charging exorbitant service fees on tickets and organising a group boycott against Pearl Jam." As a result, the band had repeatedly been thwarted in their attempts to mount a low-cost tour, they said. "It just doesn't seem fair to us the way a lot of this is done," Jeff told the hearing. Interestingly, Aerosmith manager, Tim Collins, also testified, asserting that when he approached Ticketmaster about lowering the surcharge for tickets for the band's Get A Grip US tour, officials at Ticketmaster actually recommended raising the service charge by one dollar, suggesting half the money go to Ticketmaster and half to the band. With the future of the billion-dollar-a-year US concert industry at stake, Ticketmaster continued to deny all charges, but clearly their supremacy was being challenged.

The rest of the summer of 1994 found Pearl Jam preparing their third album. If they had had enough of working on the road, they still remained enraptured by the possibilities of exploring a recording studio together. The genesis for much of the new material they were busy compiling went back to their disappointment with 'Vs.' 'Vs.' had been hastily conceived. Despite the smouldering candle-wax of 'Daughter' or the incandescently glowering 'Indifference', despite obvious hair-tuggers like 'Blood' or 'Rearviewmirror', and despite the band's oft-repeated claims that they were going for something "different", the truth is there was nothing on 'Vs.' that managed to take your mind prisoner in quite the same raw-handed manner as the ubiquitous anthems that studded 'Ten'. And though they were loath to admit as much in public, the band knew it. So when they set out on tour at the end of 1993 and, without warning, new songs began to take shape, almost of their own accord, during soundcheck and at rehearsals, the band decided to let matters take their own course and ride the lightning all the way to the nearest recording studio as soon as they next got some time off.

Most of the new material sprung from the highly developed on-stage jams that the band had begun regularly working up during that last tour. But to begin with there were two unfinished tracks left over from the 'Vs.' sessions – 'The Whipping' (later abbreviated to just 'Whippin''), and 'Hard To Imagine'. Their chance to do something concrete about it came as far back as November '93, during a short break from the tour when, without telling the record company, Pearl Jam entered U2 producer Daniel Lanois' recording studio in New Orleans and began laying down some of the rapidly emerging song-cycle onto tape. Then, after a break for Christmas, they discreetly set up temporary shop in Seattle's Heart-owned Bad Animals studio, where they could be found in January 1994, adding yet more material and ideas to their growing unreleased catalogue. It was never made clear if these were demos that the band were working on, or actual finished product. "They don't even think that way any more," claimed one insider. "They just look on it all as making music, released or unreleased." Whatever the initial intentions, the result was an impressive clutch of brand new titles, from which the band would spend the next three months liberally dipping into for new additions to their live set. When the cancellation of "all immediate touring plans" was announced, following Eddie's declaration that he could not see the future clearly any more in the wake of Kurt Cobain's lonely demise, and would certainly not be making an attempt to do so while still peering out at life through the goldfish bowl of the road, the rest of the band consoled themselves with the thought that at least here would be a perfect opportunity to finish off recording all the killer new material they had been compiling, and maybe even have a new Pearl Jam album out on the streets by the end of the year.

Maybe. Originally set for shock-release as early as September '94, and already christened 'Vitalogy', the third Pearl Jam album was originally to have contained 11 tracks. No singles would be issued either before or after its release. Then it was put back until October and there would now be 13 tracks; then it was back again to

November and 11 tracks. Word filtered out of Seattle that there was still some discussion going on over the final track listing; over the final mixes; over who made the coffee. They were also reconsidering their decision over whether or not to release a single from the album. The record company began to drum their fingers and hum loudly. The band said they would get back to them. Next, two finished tracks – 'Satan's Bed' and 'Corduroy' – were sent out on cassette to the heads of all departments at Epic and instructions were quietly given to start warming the record machine motor. Everybody waited for them to change their minds again. They didn't have to wait long.

In October 1994, Billboard magazine announced that 'Ten' had become the first rock album to sell more than eight–million copies in America since 'Appetite For Destruction' by Guns N' Roses five years before. No slouch either, 'Vs.' had so far sold roughly half that amount. That same month, Pearl Jam finally broke their long public silence when they undertook two 'unplugged' concerts in aid of the Neil Young-sponsored Bridge School charity at the 21,000-seater Shoreline Amphitheatre in Los Angeles, Eddie in retro denim baseball cap pulled down low over his curls. The band waived their objections to booking fee restrictions on the Bridge dates as "we were thinking of the money that would be raised," said Kelly Curtis. And their appearance helped raise over $750,000 for the Bridge's many causes – mainly helping children with severe physical and/or mental impairments. Eddie and the rest of the guys joined Young on stage for the final number of the night, 'Piece Of Crap', Young's dry-eyed ditty about how impossible it is to get your hands on anything of real value these days, be it in a local hardware store or in the music biz. It was a moment of tingling irony in a contemporary rock world where loyalties are still divided by both generational and stylistic ties. Like, at the end of the day, dude, it shouldn't matter whether the man from the magazine says your music is indie or pop, grunge or metal. But somehow it does. And you don't have to be Eddie Vedder or the ghost of Kurt Cobain to see it.

These were also the band's first live performances since drummer Dave Abbruzzese quit/was fired (depending on who you talk to) from the band. Former Red Hot Chili Peppers drummer Jack Irons sat in on the brushes, and has been playing with the band ever since. Any thoughts, though, that Irons might become a permanent member of the band were originally scotched by Eddie himself backstage after the Bridge dates when he admitted that if it was up to him, Irons would already be in the band, but that not all the others saw things the same way. Typically, Eddie wasn't about to let the matter rest there, however, and by Christmas '94, Irons was accepted as a full-time member of the band. Meanwhile, a still stunned Dave Abbruzzese told MTV that Stone had fired him over breakfast one morning, mumbling something about "different philosophies" and reasons that he didn't "completely understand". As one insider, who wished to remain anonymous, put it to the author: "Eddie had never been that cool about Dave once he discovered that Dave actually enjoyed it when his records went to number one."

OFFICIALLY, THE curtain went up on 'Vitalogy', the new Pearl Jam album, at 6.00pm on Halloween, 1994. That was when radio stations around the US were told they could begin playing the new single, 'Spin The Black Circle'. Ironically, if the choice of single was meant to shock, it appears to have done just that in the US, to the extent that most radio stations subsequently dropped 'Spin The Black Circle' from their play-lists and replaced it with the flipside, the less musically fraught 'Tremor Christ'. As Cyndi Internet, editor of the longstanding US-based PJ fanzine Indifference commented, "It's kinda punk, isn't it?" Indeed, the shrill face-pulling vocals, the same slowly descending riff the Sex Pistols used to write most of their songs around – 'Spin The Black Circle' certainly wasn't the kind of rock-steady radio-chugger most people expected. It seems 'Vitalogy' really would be different.

Part tribute to the dragon-chasing memory of Kurt Cobain, part wise-cracking eulogy to their own quite different struggle to survive, listening to the wheezing accordion and marble-eyed vocals of 'Bugs' might give you the creeps but you couldn't complain that it wasn't different. Ditto the pulsing, Latino-flavoured instrumental, 'Aye Davanita'. Meanwhile, 'Not For You', 'Tremor Christ', 'Nothingman', 'Whipping', 'Corduroy', 'Better Man', and 'Immortality' are fit to stand shoulder-to-shoulder with the best of anything Pearl Jam have done before, including 'Jeremy' and 'Black'. Make no mistake, it may have taken a few plays the wrong side of midnight to sink in, but 'Vitalogy' is a classic addition to the Pearl Jam canon. That 'Hey, Foxymophandled Mama, That's Me' (at seven minutes-plus, a quite awesomely tedious piece of contrived weirdness, which closes the album) is the longest track on the album once again demonstrates the absurd lengths this band are prepared to go to in their belated attempts to net themselves the kind of credibility Nirvana could always count on. But that doesn't mean this isn't a great piece of work. Wilful as only the ego of one of the world's most popular singers can be; more contrived than a roomful of Stone Temple Pilots; if this really is, as Jon Hotten suggested in his review of the album in RAW, Eddie Vedder 'cutting off his nose to spite his face', it's a pity a few more of the mirror–gazers that front bands don't apply the scissors snoutwards. Let Vedder cut his whole head off, I say, if it means we avoid having to sit through another worthy mediocrity like 'Vs.'. You want answers? Try this one. 'Vitalogy': quack remedies for cracked times.

Though the word 'Vitalogy' is taken approximately to mean 'the study of life', the 14 tracks on the album are weighed down with casual references to suicide, drug addiction, and the perils of sudden, terrifying fame. In short, it is littered with references to Kurt. The opening track, 'Last Exit', even begins: 'Three days, maybe longer/When they find me here ... ' (Kurt's mutilated body is thought to have lain on the floor of his Seattle home for at least three days before it was discovered by a workman, who glimpsed the scene through an upstairs window). 'Three days, maybe longer/Let my spirit pass ... ' it continues, and it's impossible not to grasp the connection. And though 'Spin The Black Circle' is ostensibly about the good old days of shiny black vinyl, the "dropping the needle into the groove" metaphor is hammered home in this context with almost obscene precision: 'See this needle/See my hand/Drop, drop, dropping it down/Oh so gently ... '

Then there's 'Nothingman', with its mournful lines about 'Walks on his own/With thoughts he can't help thinking/Future's above/But in the past he's slow and sinking ... ' 'Immortality', the best track on an album apparently obsessed with the subject, is even more direct: 'Holier than thou/Surrendered/Executed anyhow ... ' goes one of the lines. 'Scrawl dissolved/Cigar box on the floor,' it concludes (a reference to the cigar box containing Kurt's syringes that was found next to his dead body, perhaps?). Even 'Pry, To' – 58 seconds of distorted electro–funk with Eddie enigmatically spelling out the word p-r-i-v-a-c-y over and over (and over) again – seems to refer back to the still unbelievable events of April '94. The very last words on the album, at the frazzled end of the most burn-out track, the macabre 'Hey, Mophandled Mama...' are: 'Did you ever think that you would actually kill yourself?/Yes, I believe I would ... '

The title, 'Vitalogy', was 'borrowed' from a book originally published in the 1890s – a relic from the American Wild West that also sometimes went by the name of 'Vitalogy' – written by Dr. E.H. Ruddick. Self–billed as 'An encyclopaedia of health adapted for the home, the layman and the family,' 'Vitalogy' was over a thousand pages long and advocated a turn-of-the-century American way of life, dispensing pages of advice on such things as how to get married, have children and stay healthy, with a definite moralistic tone behind it. So commonplace did the wisdom of the 'Vitalogy' became among frontiersmen, it quickly became transformed into an all-encompassing term used by travelling 'quack' doctors to extol the benefits of both the book and the rest of the medicines (often just coloured water) they were peddling throughout the West in those woebegone days. Eddie apparently discovered a dusty copy of the book on his travels and was so taken by it he arranged to have over 30 of the original pages reprinted in the booklet which accompanies the 'Vitalogy' album. As a result, all formats of 'Vitalogy' came with a booklet containing reproductions of several of its antique remedies, including a two-page spread on 'phrenology' (the science of 'bump-reading', where a person's mental faculties are presumed to be located in various parts of the skull and can be 'read' by feeling the bumps on the outside of the head), Eddie's dental records, and a letter from his aunt discussing his family's health problems (though no mention of any bumps). One page reproduced from the original book trumpets on about the dangers of young men dying from 'self-pollution'. While the gag is that the article refers to masturbation, there is an unmistakably dank echo of Kurt Cobain's own self-polluted demise in the observation.

But then nothing anyone did in 1994 was going to be received solely on its own merits after the dreadful events of April 7, least of all Eddie Vedder and Pearl Jam ...

1995 WAS supposed to be a better year. Really. In November '94, bored with sitting around the house, Stone Gossard announced the formation of his own record label, Loosegroove. In conjunction with local Seattle producer Dennis Herring and Satchel/Brad drummer Regan Hagar, the label was formed, said Herring, "because we felt we could offer something special to the bands." Distributed through the Sony-owned 550 Music, label-mate to Epic Records (also owned by Sony), who both Pearl Jam and Satchel/Brad are signed to, the idea, according to Herring, is to give the bands "full creative control with major distribution. The ultimate major/indie hybrid!" And a family-run one at that: Stone's sister, Shelley Gossard, was to be in charge of the day-to-day running of the Seattle–based label. Its first release came from Devilhead, a hard-edged funk metal band featuring Brian and Kevin Wood, brothers of deceased Mother Love Bone singer Andy Wood. Other acts on the fledgling label that would receive official Loosegroove releases throughout 1995 included Weapon Of Choice, Critters Buggin', and Prose & Concepts – all hardcore LA-based hip-hop acts. Also released was a compilation of material from the now-legendary Malfunkshun, the band that originally featured both Andy and Kevin Wood, as well as drummer Regan Hagar. And, pleasingly, a re-issue of Gossard and Hagar's much cherished Brad album, 'Shame', which of course also featured Satchel and sometime Pigeonhead vocalist, Shawn Smith. The label's signing policy is simply "based on our taste," says Herring. "That's the only requirement: that we can all get enthusiastic about it."

To launch the label in style, a special one-off concert was held at the Seattle Center, on November 5, which also doubled as a benefit for the Center's Peace Academy, a programme that teaches young people alternatives to violence. Devilhead, Prose & Concepts, Weapons Of Choice and Critters Buggin' all performed live.

Meantime, the man perhaps best-known as the other singer in Stone Gossard's life, the aforementioned Shawn Smith, was busy fighting a very different battle with the courts. The problem was the on-going plight of Regan Hagar. Arraigned on 'marijuana cultivation' charges, along with Thomas Harold O'Neill, co-owner of Seattle's premier live music venue, RCKNDY (Rock Candy), Smith and the rest of Satchel, whose debut album, 'EDC', was released in

September 1994, had been forced to shelve their touring plans until the full outcome of the drummer's sentence was known. "It's kind of scary," Smith told the authors. "Just getting convicted, it fucks up your rights. You can't vote, can't get credit ... It's just sick."

Charges were first filed in Seattle's King County Superior Court, in March 1993, when the deputy prosecutor alleged that O'Neill ran a series of 'marijuana farms' at several different residences he owned around Seattle, one of which was allegedly tended by Hagar. "Yeah, it's true," Smith admitted. "He was growing it ... He could go to jail for five to ten years!"

"It's amazing that there is a law against altering your consciousness," he added. "Alcohol is far more destructive." Hagar had been caught when the Seattle Light company noticed unusual amounts of electricity being used by Hagar's house. Most pot in Seattle is grown indoors using hydroponics. Power use is monitored for this reason. It seems the possibility - even with Pearl Jam temporarily out of action - of a Smith-Gossard follow-up to the astonishing Brad album had become even more remote. "Brad didn't exist prior to that nor after that," Smith decided philosophically. "It was just its own thing, and that makes it kinda special." But if Stone hadn't been in Pearl Jam, would Shawn and Regan have nixed Satchel and kept Brad going? "In a perfect world, if Stone wasn't in Pearl Jam – I'd have to say yes," Smith admitted.

Stone wasn't the only one to get itchy feet as 1994 dragged its weary feet towards '95. Mike McCready formed a 'one-off' line-up with an extremely pale and fragile-looking Layne Staley, erstwhile vocalist with fellow Seattleites Alice In Chains. The two had met while cohabiting the same drug-rehabilitation programme in Seattle some months before. Initially billing themselves jokily as The Drug Addicts & Alcoholics, and then the Gacey Bunch (after Jon Gacey, the US serial killer who liked to dress up as a clown before committing his atrocities on children), they eventually settled on the name Mad Season; their first album was released on Columbia Records in April 1995. A handful of small theatre dates also followed but both men denied rumours that they were to leave their respective bands and throw their all into Mad Season.

Why then was it always raining when Pearl Jam decided to come on? After profile-raising concert dates in the Spring of '95, in Australia and the Far East, Pearl Jam set out on their first US tour proper since Kurt's death in June 1995. And then, on the eve of the band's first official US date in over a year, at the Casper Events Center, in Wyoming, on June 16, unsettling reports began to filter through on the phone and fax, all said to emanate from an item in USA Today, which claimed that Pearl Jam had conceded defeat in their war with Ticketmaster. Manager Kelly Curtis scotched the rumours though by reasserting publicly that the band would definitely NOT be allowing the giant agency to handle their tours now or in the future - at least not while the 'handling charges' fiasco continued to prevail.

"I guess you've heard ... they are saying in the papers that we surrendered to Ticketmaster ... and that didn't happen," Eddie told the audience at the first show at the Casper Events Center. "And take my word, that's not going to happen!" Rousing stuff. According to the Los Angeles Times, however, Eddie's comments were in direct response to press reports in which Kelly Curtis is said to have admitted the group had "given up" trying to bypass the LA-based agency. Curtis further suggested, it was reported, that the band might work with Ticketmaster again if it was the only way to play the area.

When Eddie read the papers he "went crazy", say insiders. Curtis immediately issued a statement of his own, refuting the stories and claiming any quotes used were taken "out of context". "Eddie [was] furious after reading reports that we had changed our policy," he said. "Because that was not our intention at all, and we were all in agreement that it is not what we are going to do." Pearl Jam tour consultant Mike McGinley said he was exploring additional Ticketmaster venues for additional dates in the US this Autumn but that no itinerary was likely to take shape until much nearer the time.

A spokesperson for Ticketmaster, when told of Eddie's on-stage comments, remarked: "It seems like Eddie's frustration should be directed at his management since the band would not be able to play the San Diego Sports Arena shows without Ticketmaster's cooperation."

What Curtis could not deny, however, was the claim USA Today also made that some of the tickets for the tour, specifically the San Diego Sports Arena, where the band had been booked to appear at the end of June, had been sold by Ticketmaster controlled-agency outlets, under an agreement by which the agency would donate all profits from the disputed 'covering charges' to a charity of Pearl Jam's choice.

The truth, as always, was not nearly so clear-cut. Originally, with all ticket obligations being handled by the much smaller ETM agency and The Ten Club (the official Pearl Jam fan club), the band had agreed to perform two shows at the Del Mar Fairgrounds in San Diego, southern California. However, excessive ticket demand coupled with the leaking of a bizarre, 17-page report filed by the the San Diego Sheriff's Department, calling for the band to be banned from touring because, they said, Pearl Jam are "considered one of the least-safe acts currently touring" led to calls for the concerts to be switched to a regular rock arena. Eddie's "antics" were the cause of "riots", the report claimed, before adding, incredibly, that the band were planning on having a 4,000-person unregulated mosh-pit down the front of all their shows."

None of which was remotely true, of course, but the media smoke it caused locally persuaded Eddie and Pearl Jam that to reschedule the Del Mar Fairground shows for June 26-27 at the nearby San Diego Sports Arena - a venue, as it transpired, with a long-established 'exclusive' contract with Ticketmaster. But the band said they were content to play there as the fans would have bought all their tickets through ETM and/or The Ten Club first. What they didn't find out until too late was that Ticketmaster pocketed an 'undisclosed sum' from the venue itself for the privilege of allowing the venue to stage a non-TM event. Taking the 'high road', Ticketmaster announced that they intended to donate the fee to a charity.

But then there was always going to be trouble. Much as they did everything to disguise the fact, the organisers of Pearl Jam's ill-fated US '95 tour were walking around with worried expressions before the band had even arrived backstage at the first show in Casper. Though the Casper Wyoming Events Center was, for one night at least, the centre of the grunge universe, its red, Pizza Hut-style roof remained a symbol of the frustration and futility the folks of Casper mostly live under. Built in the early 1980s during an oil boom that pushed the local population to nearly 90000, the Center, situated on a hill overlooking the town, was designed to attract major touring talent. Which it did for a while, receiving regular visits from everyone from ZZ Top to Bob Hope and the Travelling Circus.

But the boom ended and the population is now approximately half what it once was. Ironically, the main reason why the venue was free for Pearl Jam to play there is because it doesn't do enough business these days to attract the full-time attention of Ticketmaster. Responding back-stage, after the show was over, to charges that he was becoming "obsessed" with this Ticketmaster business, Eddie assured everybody present that, despite the mounting evidence to the contrary, that wasn't the case at all.

"I understand how people might think that, but we're not obsessed with Ticketmaster," he declared to all and sundry. "Ticketmaster is just one tiny detail in a series of business details that we have to deal with. But we made a decision long ago about how we want to present our music, what we think is honourable and fair to our fans, and then we turned it over to our representatives to handle it for us. We don't sit around in a room all day and talk about it. We spend our time making music."

Eddie then went straight on air with local radio and began hosting his own version of the national underground radio show he broadcast from his own house in Seattle last winter, talking on the phone with fans and playing some if his favourite songs from the Foo Fighters album, plus some ancient Pete Townsend tracks. He was still there, talking to the invisible airwaves long after the rest of the band had fled the building.

The next stop, an open-air show before 12,000 people at the Wolf Mountain Amphitheatre in Salt Lake City, should have been better. But once again dark forces were gathering, this time from above. Two hours before the band was due to take to the stage, a freak torrential downpour erupted, sweeping the entire arena with freezing rain. The band had helicptered in from the airport, zig-zagging through forked lightning as the dark clouds collided with the tall Utah mountains. Then, moments before the show was due to commence, Eddie came on stage with an old-fashioned bullhorn (the power had already been switched off because of the danger of electrocution) and announced that the show would have to be cancelled because of the storm. Apologising to the soaked crowd, he vowed that he and Pearl Jam would return to Salt Lake where they would "play twice as long" to make up for it.

"Please come back next time!" he bellowed as the disappointed and soaked crowd made forlornly for the water-logged exits. "Thanks for coming out here. Please don't get sick. We're going to come back and play twice as long ... "

"It rained about two inches in an hour. Our PA is flooded and there's still one-inch of water all over the stage," Jeff Ament explained to friends and reporters backstage afterwards. If we'd switched the PA back on, we were worried it was gonna blow." An hour later, however, the rain had stopped and the sun came out. But by then everybody had gone home ...

Gig number three of the ominously 13-date tour was at the magnificent open-air Red Rocks arena in Denver; a natural amphitheatre set so high in the steep red mountains it actually overlooks Denver - the so-called Mile High City. Eddie arrived on stage peddling a mountain-bike, which he fell off as he reached the microphone. "This place f**king sucks!" he told the goggle-eyed audience, then grinned like an eagle. "That's obviously the farthest thing from the truth - just like us being in with Ticketmaster," he added, getting into his favourite on-tour topic straight away. "It's the farthest thing from the truth," he repeated himself. "Anyway, enough talk," he almost whispered. "Let's play some music ... " And they did. At last. Straight into 'Go', 'Last Exit', 'Spin The Black Circle', 'Animal' ...

Eddie stumbled with the words at one point in 'Alive'. "Sometimes it's weird to sing this song, it's just weird," he whispered to his mike. Was he referring to Kurt?

Then came the San Diego Sports Arena shows. Their next show after that was their last; a co-headliner with Neil Young & Crazy Horse before 55,000 fans at Golden Gate Park in San Francisco that somehow, in Eddie's mind at least, was doomed to go disastrously wrong. Five songs into the set Eddie simply put the mike down, took one last glance at the vast audience, then walked off the stage without another word. Moments later a roadie ran on to give Stone and the others the news: Eddie had "fallen ill" and would not be able to continue the show. In a panic, Neil Young strode back on stage to try and save the day and played an unprecedented 90 minutes with the band. Nevertheless, large sections of the crowd that watched Eddie walk calmly off the stage sensed that there was more than just physical illness behind his sudden decision to throw the show and loud boos and fuck-yous were heard throughout the remainder of the show, many of the disappointed 55,000 not even bothering to stay 'til the end.

Suddenly, all Pearl Jam's best plans had begun to look farcical; their 'commitment' to their fans called into question yet again. Whatever the official explanation given for Eddie's difficulties, behind closed doors it was clear that Eddie saw the San Diego Sports Arena situation as a defeat in his war with Ticketmaster; a war he appears determined to keep waging, no matter what the long-term cost to Pearl Jam's touring prospects might be. And all because Kurt went to his grave still dissing them. But at what cost to the patience and goodwill of the long-suffering Pearl Jams - deprived first of singles, then videos and now even live performances? Not to mention the effect all this was clearly having on the rest of the band.

And for what? Surely Pearl Jam couldn't be the only band in America that felt strongly about the absurd situation with Ticketmaster. Stone Temple Pilots manager, Steve Stewart, for one, is involved with the Consumers Against Unfair Ticketing coalition, a group currently exploring options to circumvent Ticketmaster's expensive 'service charges' and points out that on previous tours, the 'Pilots have played their part in the struggle by deliberately charging lower ticket prices for their shows and absorbing the agency's 'handling charges' themselves.

"I think it's admirable the way Pearl Jam have stuck their necks out," says STP singer Scott Weiland. "But I think it might have been a little bit more effective if there had been a coalition put together beforehand, because they're not the lone horses in their feelings about the whole ticket bullshit."

The only positive aspect that would emerge from Pearl Jam's lost summer was the release, at the end of June, of the Neil Young album, 'Mirrorball'. Recorded 'on-the-hoof' at two sessions in Seattle's Bad Animal Studios in January and February '95, with various members of Pearl Jam backing him, Young claimed that the band's playing on 'Mirrorball' "shows so much more wisdom than their years ... I think

Pearl Jam's older than I am." One track, 'Peace And Love', was co-written by Young with Eddie. While Young croons devilishly about the greed and hate in the world, Eddie murmurs almost convincingly about the importance of not giving up, of always putting something back into the environment you reap the spoils of. It's an achingly beautiful moment. However, it's the memory of Kurt Cobain that, as with 'Vitalogy', dominates the subject matter on tracks like 'Throw Your Hatred Down'.

When Kurt quoted a line from one of Young's more famous songs, 'Hey Hey My My (Out Of The Blue)' in his suicide note - 'It's better to burn out than to fade away', - Young was said to be so shaken friends claim his next album, 'Sleeps With Angels', released within weeks of Kurt's death, was partially re-written as some sort of emotional response to the shock Young felt at the extreme interpretation Kurt chose to give those careless lines, written in 1979 as little more than a hi-there to punk. Most of the songs on 'Mirrorball' concern the nature of heroism and its panda-eyed ugly sister, fame.

Like Kurt, Young admits he is "very extreme." And yet it can hardly have escaped Young's notice that Eddie and Pearl Jam were both Kurt's contemporaries and his media-nemesis. Kurt never disguised his distaste for Pearl Jam's music. Only now Kurt's gone but Eddie is still trying to fix it. It's plain that, to some degree anyway, Eddie hopes that hanging out with the self-proclaimed Don Grungeione of the no-wave will afford him some of the lost credibility he feels he is still somehow owed, maybe even give him a leg up.

What does Young think of it all, though? Pearl Jam were covering his 'Rocking The Free World' long before he'd even heard of 'em. "It wasn't just that they were good," he told one reporter recently. "I could relate to what I would do if I was playing with them. And I could see myself doing it."

Young had first coaxed them into a studio to do one song with him in the wake of the Bridge School shows, where they had jammed out a new riff together that Young had subsequently scribbled down some words to and was now calling 'Act Of Love'. Unsure how long he would be able to keep their attention, the track was recorded at high-speed, everybody pitching for the perfect first-take. Then, while everyone was still buzzing, Young immediately set to work laying down the foundations for another track, explaining that he never liked just going into the studio to do "one song". And then they did another ... and another ...

Arranging a second session a few weeks later was easy after that. He never asked which band members would actually be there at any given time, he just kept plugging away and hoped there would be enough to cover.

"I would look around and there would be Jeff or Mike, or sometimes Eddie ... I never kept score," the grizzled guitarist chuckled. "Me, is what I do. The rest I left for them to figure out for themselves." There's certainly no mistaking the distinctive Pearl Jam sound; guitars crackling with cold fire, the one-handed rhythms insistent as heavy rain.

"Neil felt there was some energy there," Stone Gossard would later recall, "and that it would be a good thing just to get into the studio and see what happened."

Some claimed Young had found himself the best backing band since Bob Dylan plugged in with The Band back in '65. Others pulled a face and feigned bafflement over his choice of recording bedfellows. For those of the latter opinion, salt was added to the wound by the announcement that Neil Young would be headlining a series of European festivals in August 1995 - including a moving appearance at that year's Reading Festival - and that his backing band for all the dates would not be Crazy Horse but ... Pearl Jam.

Outside, somewhere in Seattle, it was still raining.